Advances in Personal Relationships

Communicating Affection

Few behavioral processes are more central to the development and maintenance of intimate relationships than the communication of affection. Indeed, affectionate expressions often initiate and accelerate relational development. By contrast, their absence in established relationships frequently coincides with relational deterioration. This text explores the scientific research on affection exchange to emerge from the disciplines of communication, social psychology, family studies, psychophysiology, anthropology, and nursing. Specific foci include the individual and relational benefits (including health benefits) of affectionate behavior, as well as the significant risks often associated with expressing affection. A new, comprehensive theory of human affection exchange is offered, and its merits relative to existing theories are explored.

Kory Floyd is associate professor and director of graduate M.A. studies in the Hugh Downs School of Human Communication at Arizona State University. He holds a Ph.D. in communication from the University of Arizona (1998), an M.A. in speech communication from the University of Washington (1994), and a B.A. in English literature from Western Washington University (1991). He has authored or coauthored four other books and more than 60 journal articles and book chapters on topics related to affectionate communication, nonverbal behavior, and family relationships. In addition, he is currently editor of *Journal of Family Communication* and has been an associate editor of *Journal of Social and Personal Relationships*. He has earned a number of awards for his research, including the New Scholar of the Year award from the International Network on Personal Relationships.

Advances in Personal Relationships

Series Editors:

Harry T. Reis, *University of Rochester*

Mary Anne Fitzpatrick, *University of Wisconsin-Madison*

Anita L. Vangelisti, *University of Texas, Austin*

Although scholars from a variety of disciplines have written and conversed about the importance of personal relationships for decades, the emergence of personal relationships as a field of study is relatively recent. *Advances in Personal Relationships* represents the culmination of years of multidisciplinary and interdisciplinary work on personal relationships. Sponsored by the International Association for Relationship Research, the series offers readers cutting-edge research and theory in the field. Contributing authors are internationally known scholars from a variety of disciplines, including social psychology, clinical psychology, communication, history, sociology, gerontology, and family studies. Volumes include integrative reviews, conceptual pieces, summaries of research programs, and major theoretical works. *Advances in Personal Relationships* presents first-rate scholarship that is both provocative and theoretically grounded. The theoretical and empirical work described by authors will stimulate readers and advance the field by offering up new ideas and retooling old ones. The series will be of interest to upper division undergraduate students, graduate students, researchers, and practitioners.

Attribution, Communication Behavior, and Close Relationships
Valerie Manusov and John H. Harvey

Stability and Change in Relationships
Anita L. Vangelisti, Harry T. Reis, and Mary Anne Fitzpatrick

Understanding Marriage: Developments in the Study of Couple Interaction
Patricia Noller and Judith A. Feeney

Growing Together: Personal Relationships Across the Lifespan
Frieder R. Lang and Karen L. Fingerman

Communicating Social Support
Daena Goldsmith

Communicating Affection

Interpersonal Behavior and Social Context

KORY FLOYD
Arizona State University

CAMBRIDGE
UNIVERSITY PRESS

CAMBRIDGE
UNIVERSITY PRESS

32 Avenue of the Americas, New York NY 10013-2473, USA

Cambridge University Press is part of the University of Cambridge.

It furthers the University's mission by disseminating knowledge in the pursuit of education, learning and research at the highest international levels of excellence.

www.cambridge.org
Information on this title: www.cambridge.org/9780521731744

© Cambridge University Press 2006

First published 2006
First paperback edition 2008

A catalogue record for this publication is available from the British Library

Library of Congress Cataloguing in Publication data

Floyd, Kory.
Communicating affection : interpersonal behavior and social context /
Kory Floyd.– 1st ed.
p. cm. – (Advances in personal relationships)
Includes bibliographical references and indexes.
ISBN 0-521-83205-5 (hardcover)
1. Interpersonal relations. 2. Interpersonal communication. 3. Love.
I. Title. II. Advances in personal relationships (Cambridge, England)
HM1106.F56   2006
302.3′4–dc22   2005023097

ISBN 978-0-521-83205-2 Hardback
ISBN 978-0-521-73174-4 Paperback

This book is dedicated to my Master's degree advisor,
Mac Parks.
For turning me on to communication research,
for teaching me the value of a good idea,
and for being the kind of mentor that I myself strive to be,
I will always be most grateful.

Contents

List of Tables

List of Figures

Foreword

Talk not of wasted affection; affection never was wasted.
— Henry Wadsworth Longfellow

In virtually every typology of fundamental human needs, one finds mention of affection. Humans don't just *love* to be loved; we *need* to be loved. And, perhaps equally as important, we need to be *shown* that we are loved. This latter need, and the processes by which we meet it, are the focus of this text.

The communication of affection – the process of expressing our care, appreciation, value, and love for others – is so ingrained a part of the human social experience that it is fairly easy to overlook. We communicate affection to friends when they are feeling low, as a means of providing comfort and emotional support. We express affection to our children as a way of making them feel loved, cared for, and protected. We convey affection to potential romantic partners in order to signal our attraction, and to current romantic partners as a means of reinforcing the strength of our pair bonds. We can even behave affectionately toward people for whom we have no genuine feelings of affection, as a way to manipulate their behaviors, attitudes, or emotions. Affectionate communication is a ubiquitous aspect of human relational interaction – its presence can be the source of unparalleled joy; its absence can be the cause of pain and distress.

The question of why affectionate communication serves so many important functions in the human relational experience has been an intriguing one to me for more than a decade. In this text, I address a number of aspects of affectionate communication, including how affectionate messages are encoded and decoded, how we respond to them, what benefits they bring us, and what risks they expose us to. I have cast a wide net in this book by including research focusing on a number of populations and published in a number of disciplines. My aim in doing so is both to pull knowledge and insight from related areas of study and to spur new questions, new theories, and new empirical studies on the process of expressing affection.

My own research on affectionate communication began in 1995 with a diary study of platonic friends' affection behaviors over a 2-week period. Since that time, I have conducted multiple laboratory experiments, field experiments, and surveys focusing on how people express affection, how they respond to affectionate behaviors, how they evaluate the appropriateness of affection exchanges, and how these outcomes are influenced by characteristics of individuals, relationships, and situations. The sum of these efforts is a collective body of data involving more than 8,000 people, ranging in age from 12 to 96 years. They represent multiple ethnic backgrounds, socioeconomic ranks, relational experiences, and levels of education. Although my data come largely from Americans, I have sampled from every geographic area of the country. Obviously, no sample can capture all of the forms of human diversity that might affect the behaviors we seek to understand. This is why integrative reviews, such as the ones offered in this book, are important, as they draw on the strengths of multiple samples collected from a range of populations and with a variety of methods.

The profound joy of discovery I have enjoyed in the process of studying affectionate communication has been greatly enhanced with the help and input of several coauthors with whom I have had the privilege of working on this research over the years. Many sincere thanks to Judee Burgoon, Kristin Davis, Mark Di Corsia, Larry Erbert, Lisa Farinelli, Kelby Halone, Jon Hess, Colin Hesse, Jeff Judd, Angie La Valley, Lisa Miczo, Alan Mikkelson, Mac Parks, Mary Claire Morr Serewicz, George Ray, Jack Sargent, Melissa Tafoya, Kyle Tusing, Mike Voloudakis, Jason Wilson, Christina Yoshimura, and especially to my most frequent collaborator, Mark Morman. Each of these scholars and friends has made the process of learning about affectionate communication all the more rich and colorful.

1

An Introduction to Affectionate Communication

The choicest thing this world has for a man is affection.
— Josiah Gilbert Holland

Social scientists have long considered affection to be among the most fundamental of human needs (Rotter, Chance, & Phares, 1972; Schutz, 1958, 1966), and with good reason. The expression of affection is one of the primary communicative behaviors contributing to the formation (Owen, 1987), maintenance (Bell & Healey, 1992), and quality (Floyd & Morman, 1997, 1998, 2000a) of human relationships. It contributes to physical health (Komisaruk & Whipple, 1989), mental well-being (Downs & Javidi, 1990), and academic performance (Steward & Lupfer, 1987), and mitigates loneliness (Downs & Javidi, 1990) and depression (Oliver, Raftery, Reeb, & Delaney, 1993). Often, it is through one's expression of affection for another that a relationship is formed or transformed; indeed, relational partners often remember the first hug, the first kiss, or the first time the words "I love you" were spoken (see Owen, 1987). Affection is truly a central component of many social and personal relationships, from those that are casually close to those that are deeply intimate.

Despite the intuitive notion that affection is always a *positive* component of relational interaction, however, having affectionate feelings — and particularly communicating them — can in fact be fraught with risk. Consider the story of Jason and Lisa. They attend the same high school and have been dating each other for 3 months. In that time, they have enjoyed each other's company and confidences, and have both developed affectionate feelings for the other. For some time, Lisa has wanted to tell Jason that she loves him, but she has refrained from doing so because she worries that Jason might not reciprocate her expression. Jason, by contrast, has been able to sense Lisa's eagerness for them to express their feelings for each other verbally. He feels that he probably does love Lisa – or at least, that he is strongly attracted to her – and he would have said so already but he resents feeling pressured to say it. Finally, one evening while on a date, Jason takes Lisa's hand and says, "I love you." Even though she has been eagerly anticipating this moment for a long time, hearing Jason say the words aloud gives Lisa an uneasy feeling and questions begin flooding her mind. Does he really mean it? Is he saying it just because he wants to sleep with her? Is he saying it because he wants to make their relationship exclusive? Lisa doesn't feel ready for either sexual involvement or relational commitment, so she is caught somewhat off guard by Jason's expression and doesn't know what to say in response. Rather than feeling overwhelmed with joy, Lisa has a stress response. Sensing this, Jason begins to question whether he should have said anything in the first place. He wonders why his expression made Lisa flustered, and more important, why she didn't say she loves him back. He thinks that maybe she really doesn't love him; he feels embarrassed at having made the unreciprocated gesture and hurt at seeing Lisa's response. Jason and Lisa avoid each other for several days afterward, each uncertain as to what the other might be thinking or feeling. Their self-doubt and uncertainty cause each to consider terminating the relationship.

This example illustrates the true paradox of affection: Although expressing affection is often intended and usually perceived by others to be a positive communicative move, it can backfire for any number of reasons and produce negative outcomes, including mental and physical distress and even the dissolution of the relationship within which it occurred. These outcomes are often dictated not by the affectionate act itself but by the ways in which people negotiate their competing needs: their needs to give affection and not to give it, and their needs to receive affection and not to receive it. Both Lisa and Jason felt affection for each other and wanted that to be verbalized. However, Lisa avoided saying so because she feared a lack of reciprocation, and Jason delayed saying anything because he didn't like feeling pressured to express his feelings. Although Lisa was happy to hear of Jason's feelings for her, she was also overwhelmed with questions about his intentions and motivations for expressing them. Her uncertainty, in turn, caused her not to reciprocate the expression, leaving Jason embarrassed and hurt. Ultimately, Jason's expression of affection for Lisa – which he intended to be a positive act and which they both wanted to occur – ended up inhibiting their relationship rather than advancing it.

The primary goal of this text is to discuss why affectionate communication is often so volatile: why it can produce very positive effects and why, even when it is enacted with benevolent intentions, it can produce quite negative outcomes. The reasons are many. Communicating affection to another person can elicit numerous benefits, including the establishment or maintenance of a significant relationship, the reciprocation of the affectionate feelings, and a host of salutary mental and physical effects. It also can entail substantial risks, including misinterpretation, misattribution, and the lack of reciprocation. Like many other social exchanges, the expression of affectionate feelings can lead to relational outcomes that are predicated on this cost–benefit ratio. For Jason and Lisa, even through the rewards of their affectionate behavior were evident to each of them, the costs – including Lisa's uncertainty and Jason's embarrassment at her lack of reciprocation – outweighed them, and a negative relational outcome was the consequence.

To understand the theories relevant to affection and the empirical research that has focused on its exchange, it is necessary first to disentangle the underlying emotion from its behavioral manifestations. Although affection and the expression of it often cooccur, they are, in fact, independent phenomena, and distinguishing between the two is particularly important given that people can experience either in the absence of the other. Detailed definitions of each term are offered subsequently.

Affection and Affectionate Communication

Any mission to understand a social phenomenon relies on the clarity of its conceptual definitions. This is especially important for a phenomenon such as affection, both to sort through the multiple ways in which researchers have defined it and to make clear the distinction between affection and the behaviors through which it is made manifest. Toward this end, this section begins by defining the *experience* of affection and then addresses the *expression* of affection, which is the major focus of this text.

The Experience of Affection

The term *affection* originally derived from the Latin *affectio* and its earliest appearances (c. 1230 A.D.) were in reference to "an emotion of the mind" or a "permanent state of feeling." In the late 14th century, its usage evolved from a mere "disposition" to a "good disposition toward" something, such as a person or an idea. Later, writers such as Descartes, Spinoza, and most of the early British ethical writers used *affection* to index a positive emotional disposition toward others that bore a resemblance to *passion* but was relatively free of its sensuous elements and volatile nature (e.g., parents' affection for their children as opposed to their passion for each other).

Contemporary theoretic and empirical work on affection has not retained this conceptual distinction from passion, but it has retained the focus on a positive emotional disposition that is externally directed. For instance, Floyd and Morman (1998) conceptually defined affection as an emotional state of fondness and intense positive regard that is directed at a living or once-living target. Although the target is often another human, people most certainly feel affection toward animals (especially pets) and perhaps even toward favorite plants. Several distinctions about the emotional experience of affection warrant discussion. First, unlike some emotions, affection is not evoked by a simple stimulus; a discrete event can elicit surprise, fear, or anger, for instance, but feelings of affection develop over time as a collective response to multiple stimuli from the same target.[1]

Second, affection is not an innate response. Rather, affection is innate only insofar as humans have an adaptive capacity for it, a point that will receive more focused attention in this text. The application of affection to a particular target is conditioned and target-specific. For instance, most people feel more affection toward their own children than toward the children of others (see Floyd & Morman, 2002). Similarly, one may feel affection toward a friend whom no one else appears to like. Moreover, people can develop affection for others whom they themselves previously disliked; first impressions, although powerful, are not irrevocable.

Finally, like many emotions, affection should be distinguished from the behaviors through which it is presented. This distinction is frequently not drawn in empirical research – researchers may purport, for instance, to study *affection* when in fact they are studying *affectionate behavior*. It

---

[1] Although people do have visceral experiences of attraction or even lust immediately upon interacting, these experiences are to be distinguished from genuine affection; indeed, they can, and often do, occur in the complete absence of fondness or positive regard.

is imperative to draw this distinction, however, for the simple reason that affectionate feelings and affectionate behaviors do not necessarily coincide. As this text will discuss in detail, most communicators have the capacity to feel affection without expressing it, and most can also express affection without feeling it. Thus, to truly understand affectionate communication, it is necessary to separate it from its underlying internal experience.

The Expression of Affection

The primary focus of this text is on the expression of affection, or the behaviors through which the experience of affection is presented. The term *presented* is used deliberately here, to acknowledge that one need not actually be experiencing affection in order to express it. Consequently, affectionate behaviors are defined herein as those that portray or present the internal experience of affection, whether accurately or not.

The goal of presenting or portraying affectionate feelings is therefore dependent on the enactment of behaviors that either denote or connote such feelings to the recipient. Whereas some affectionate behaviors are minimally equivocal (e.g., hugging, saying "I love you"), many others are far more indirect and some, such as idiomatic expressions, connote affectionate feelings only for a specific target who will interpret them in that manner. Communicators have many possible reasons for conveying affection equivocally; this text will discuss the strategic use of indirect affectionate gestures and the important relational purposes they serve.

Of course, the experience and the expression of affection are inextricably linked and I do not wish to suggest otherwise. However, for a number of reasons that will be discussed in this text, they do not *necessarily* cooccur. As empirical research has indicated, it is not uncommon for feelings of affection not to be communicated, for instance, or for expressions of affection to be insincere. Sometimes these incongruencies between experience and behavior are strategic; for example, one might fail to express felt affection in order to avoid appearing overly eager for relational escalation, or one might express unfelt affection in order to gain sexual access or other favors. In other instances, of course, incongruencies between experience and behavior may be purely unintentional. One might intend to say, "I love you," to one's spouse before leaving for work but get sidetracked and leave the expression unmade.

There is much to know about affection and affectionate communication:

- What verbal and nonverbal behaviors do people use to express affection to others? How is the encoding of affection influenced by age, sex, type of relationship, or situational context?
- What behaviors do people interpret as expressions of affection? How closely are these related to the behaviors used to encode affectionate messages?
- Under what conditions are people most likely to communicate affection to others, and for what reasons do they do so?
- Why might people express affection when they do not feel it? Why might they fail to express affection when they do feel it?
- How do people interpret expressions of affection when they observe them between others? Do observers make different interpretations than the receivers themselves?
- With what individual characteristics is affectionate communication correlated? Do highly affectionate people, as a group, differ from less affectionate people?
- When are people most likely to reciprocate affectionate expressions? What happens when they do not?
- What are the possible mental and physical health benefits associated with receiving affection? What benefits, if any, accrue to those who express affection, as opposed to receiving it?

A large and diverse body of research has addressed many of these questions. Other questions remain to be answered. The purpose of this text is therefore twofold: to summarize and critique the existing body of theoretic and empirical work on affectionate communication, and to acknowledge some of the questions about affection and affectionate behavior that have yet to be addressed. A more detailed preview of this text appears subsequently.

A Preview of the Chapters

Before examining the empirical research on affectionate communication, this text describes and critiques the major theoretic paradigms in which this research has been conducted, and identifies several specific theories within each paradigm that either have been empirically tested or espouse principles that are relevant to the experience or expression of affection. This critique comprises Chapter 2. As noted, most of the theories discussed in that chapter were not developed with the specific purpose of explaining affectionate behavior; however, many have been profitable for the advancement of knowledge in this area, and their contributions, as well as their limitations, are acknowledged in later chapters.

The subsequent four chapters are devoted to examining the empirical research on affectionate communication and to summarizing both what is known and what is yet to be learned. Chapter 3 details studies of affection encoding – those that have examined how affection is communicated and how individuals select from among their options for expressing affection to others. This chapter also discusses the effects of individual, contextual, and relational characteristics that influence how affectionate people are and what forms of encoding affection are considered appropriate for a given situation. Similarly, Chapter 4 focuses on studies of decoding and response. This chapter examines the behaviors that carry affectionate meaning for receivers and observers, and the manner in which people react to expressions of affection, both cognitively and behaviorally.

Chapter 5 addresses the benefits of affectionate communication, and Chapter 6 addresses the risks. Both sending and receiving expressions of affection are associated with a range of benefits, including physical and emotional benefits to the individuals involved and benefits to the maintenance and satisfaction levels of their relationships, and this research is reviewed in Chapter 5. In particular, this chapter details new research on cardiovascular and endocrine function that makes a compelling case for why affectionate communication is associated with the benefits that it is.

Despite these benefits, however, affectionate exchanges often also expose senders and receivers to multiple risks. For example, an expression of affection can easily be misinterpreted to be of either greater or lesser intensity than the sender intended (e.g., if a woman tells her friend that she loves him, she may have intended to express platonic love but he may interpret the statement as a romantic gesture). Moreover, recipients of affectionate gestures, even in established relationships, may run the risk that the gestures do not reflect genuine affectionate emotion but are enacted for ulterior motives. Chapter 6 discusses these and other potential risks for senders and receivers of affectionate communication.

As theory and research on affectionate communication have advanced and matured, new questions have arisen that await empirical testing. At various points in these four chapters, examples of such questions are identified in bold print; this is done both to acknowledge the limitations of existing research and to stimulate future inquiry along several important lines. It must be recalled that having unanswered questions is neither problematic nor undesirable, but is instead a normal characteristic of the scientific process.

Chapter 7 returns to the issue of theory by considering the adequacy of existing theoretic explanations in light of empirical findings and in light of questions that remain largely unanswered. This chapter observes that several extant theories have fruitfully advanced knowledge on various aspects of affectionate behavior; however, no single theory has as yet been able to explain all (or even most) of the empirical findings, or to address some of the most provocative theoretic questions about affectionate communication. The need for a more comprehensive theory of human affection exchange is identified, and this chapter details one candidate for such a theory, *affection exchange theory*. Its assumptions and principles are discussed in detail, and its abilities to account for existing empirical findings and to resolve apparent contradictions are identified.

This text ends in Chapter 8 with the identification of several general conclusions about affectionate communication that are explained by affection exchange theory and supported by existing empirical work. Where appropriate, this chapter also offers important qualifications on these conclusions, so that their proper application can be appreciated.

The study of affectionate communication presents social scientists, and consumers of their work, with a true challenge. It is imperative to physical and mental health that humans give and receive affectionate expressions, yet they can evoke uncertainty, discomfort, and even physical distress. Affectionate behavior is critical to the formation and maintenance of personal relationships, yet it also can be the demise of those relationships. It is a paradoxical human phenomenon and fertile ground for scientific inquiry.

2

Thinking about Affection

The Theories

They do not love that do not show their love.
– William Shakespeare

To fully appreciate the implications of social scientific research, one must begin with both a working knowledge and a critical assessment of the theory or theories in which that research is grounded. For two reasons, this is particularly important for understanding the research on affectionate communication. First, a great deal of the research has been exploratory and atheoretic. This is not problematic in principle, but it ought to encourage consumers of this research to consider the theoretic implications that findings from such studies might have. Second, the theory-driven research on affectionate communication has used multiple theories that represent considerable diversity in assumptions and foci. This requires that the conscientious reader exercise caution when comparing studies to each other.

The literature on affectionate communication is a theoretically eclectic one, and there are at least two reasons why. One is that researchers studying affectionate communication have directed their attention toward a diversity of questions, so theories that are useful in one area have not necessarily been useful in others. For instance, theoretic principles that can explain why a given affectionate behavior is or is not reciprocated during an intimate exchange may not be able to explain why highly affectionate people have greater immunocompetence than their less affectionate counterparts. The second, and perhaps more important, reason is that, before now, there has not been a comprehensive theory about affectionate communication to use. This necessarily limits the growth of an area of study, and this book will offer one possible remedy to this situation.

This chapter is divided into two major sections representing the primary theoretic paradigms within which research on affectionate communication (and indeed, much of human communication) has been conducted. I have labeled these the *sociocultural* and *bioevolutionary* paradigms. Each approach is described in terms of its history and paradigmatic assumptions, and then several specific theories grounded in each paradigm are described. Some of these theories, particularly those associated with the sociocultural paradigm, have been used in published research on affectionate communication, and representative studies are identified for each. Others are included because of their ability to illuminate aspects of affectionate behavior in ways that competing theories cannot.

An important caveat – one that will be reiterated later in the book where the theoretic status of the affectionate communication literature is scrutinized more closely – is that most of the theories described in this chapter were not developed for the purpose of explaining and predicting affectionate behavior. Rather, they were developed to account for other phenomena (e.g., behavioral adaptation, politeness) and their tenets have been applied to the study of human affection. This caveat is important because some critiques of these theories *as they have been applied in affection research* do not necessarily implicate the utility of the theories in total, but only of their abilities to account for affectionate behavior.

An additional caveat is that the lists of theories included under each paradigm are representative, not exhaustive. Rather than attempting to index all theories with implications for affectionate behavior, this chapter focuses on those that either have received empirical support in affection research or have clear, compelling, and testable implications for human affection exchange. Moreover, the theories discussed in this chapter vary in their level of specificity and the level of abstraction at which they are pitched. Some are aimed narrowly at specific phenomena (e.g., interaction adaptation theory), whereas others make broader theoretic statements from which more specific predictions can be deduced (e.g., need to belong).

Bioevolutionary Paradigm

In its most fundamental form, the bioevolutionary paradigm suggests that propensities for particular behaviors are rooted in the adaptive advantages those propensities would have conferred on our premodern ancestors and in the ways that such adaptive advantages are currently manifested in human physiological systems. For instance, to explain why men are more affectionate with biological sons than with stepsons (Floyd & Morman, 2002), the bioevolutionary approach would focus on the survival or reproductive benefits of receiving affectionate expressions and on the adaptive nature of benefiting one's genetic relatives (biological sons) more than nongenetic others (stepsons). Similarly, to explain why highly affectionate people have more differentiated 24-hour cortisol rhythms than nonaffectionate people (Floyd, in press), this paradigm would focus on the adaptive advantages of *giving* affectionate expressions and on the ways in which they may manifest themselves in the physiological stress response.

By referring to this paradigm as "bioevolutionary," I intend for it to be inclusive both of theories rooted in psychophysiology and of those grounded in principles of natural selection or sexual selection. Although theories of neither type necessarily reference the principles important to the other, all theories in this paradigm can be distinguished from those in the sociocultural paradigm by their relative emphasis on adaptive motivations or physiological processes rather than socially or culturally constructed explanations for behavior. Importantly, although theories in this paradigm by no means dismiss the influences of social context or culturally engrained motivations for behavior, they instead emphasize how propensities for behavior can be linked to health benefits related to the ability to survive or to procreate.

Central to the bioevolutionary paradigm is the Darwinian concept of natural selection. In their efforts to understand how species changed over time in apparent response to environmental challenges (e.g., extreme temperatures, access to food, evasion of predators), scientists have proposed various theoretic explanations, the most ubiquitous of which is Darwin's (1859) theory of evolution by means of natural selection. The underlying premise of Darwin's theory is that some organisms (e.g., some fish, some birds, some humans) are better adapted than others to the demands of their environments and are, therefore, more likely than others to survive and reproduce. To the extent that these organisms' advantageous characteristics are passed on to their offspring, these characteristics should recur with greater and greater frequency in each succeeding generation. In Darwinian terminology, these advantageous characteristics – which might include the ability of a fish to camouflage itself to evade predators or the ability of highly attractive people to entice reproductive partners – are *selected for*, because the survival or procreative advantages they confer will ensure that they are passed on to new generations at a greater frequency than less-advantageous characteristics.

Two extensions of this theory are particularly relevant to the bioevolutionary paradigm. The first is that advantageous characteristics need not be physical (e.g., strength, attractiveness, height) but also may be cognitive or psychological (e.g., intelligence, empathic ability). This is the premise behind the subdiscipline of evolutionary psychology (Buss, 1999; Workman & Reader, 2004), which focuses both on the adaptive advantages and the heritability (the extent to which characteristics are transmitted genetically) of various psychological abilities or attributes. The second important extension is that emotional or psychological activities (whether adaptive or not) often coincide with physiological processes; for instance, weak psychological attachment tends to covary with poor immunocompetence (Coe & Lubach, 2001), whereas the experience of positive, loving emotion often coincides with the release of analgesic hormones such as oxytocin (Uvnäs-Moberg, 1998). These relationships are the purview of the subdiscipline of psychophysiology (Andreassi, 2000; Cacioppo, Tassinary, & Berntson, 2000). As noted earlier, the principles of both evolutionary psychology and psychophysiology, along with those of classical Darwinian thought, are enveloped in the bioevolutionary paradigm. Extensive explications of Darwin's theory, principles of evolutionary psychology, or psychophysiology are beyond the scope of this chapter, although each of these areas is explicated more fully in subsequent chapters.

Some Specific Theories in the Bioevolutionary Paradigm

Darwin's Theory of Emotion Expression. In his seminal work on the expression of emotion, Darwin (1872/1965) proposed three general principles regarding forms of emotional expression. The first two of these have particular relevance for the study of affectionate expressions. The first, known as the *principle of serviceable associated habits*, suggests in essence that humans perform certain physical actions in order to meet particular needs or desires (e.g., plugging one's nose in the presence of a foul odor, to block that odor from the nasal passages), and that when humans experience states of mind similar to those they experience when they have these needs or desires, "there is a tendency through the force of habit and association for the same movements to be performed, though they may not then be of the least use" (p. 28). For example, when confronted with an offensive person or a particularly bad idea, one might plug one's nose to express contempt because one's state of mind in such a situation is similar to that experienced in the presence of an offensive odor, causing one to plug one's nose out of habit or association. The action is functional in the primary situation, protecting oneself from an offensive odor, but it is merely symbolic in the associated situations, conveying the message that "you [or your ideas] stink." The second principle, known as the *principle of antithesis*, builds on the first by suggesting that when we experience states of mind that are opposite those that lead to functional behaviors, we tend to perform the opposite behaviors (e.g., instead of plugging one's nose, one takes a long, deep breath in).

Inherent in these principles is the idea that emotional states approximate mental states associated with physical needs. The need for protection from physical threats mentally approximates the emotional desire to protect oneself from offensive or distasteful ideas, interactions, or social situations, according to these principles, and therefore the behaviors associated with each are similar. There are three important implications of this paradigm. The first is that one can identify a repertoire of behaviors associated with particular emotional states by identifying states of mind analogous to those emotions and considering the behaviors that functionally serve those states. Two other important implications of this approach are that the repertoire for each particular emotional state ought to be relatively stable across individuals and cultures, and that there ought to be relative consensus across individuals and cultures in recognizing the behaviors that convey each emotion. Darwin devoted much of his 1872 book to detailing the repertoire of behaviors associated with each major emotional state, and he posited a great deal of similarity across races and cultures in both the encoding and decoding of such emotions, a proposition that was later supported with cross-cultural comparisons conducted by Ekman, Friesen, and Ellsworth (1972), Eibl-Eibesfeldt (1972), Izard (1971), and others.

Darwin did not go into great detail about the repertoire of behaviors associated with expressing affection specifically, although he did offer an explicitly associative argument:

No doubt, as affection is a pleasurable sensation, it generally causes a gentle smile and some brightening of the eyes. A strong desire to touch the beloved person is commonly felt; and love is expressed by this means more plainly than by any other. Hence we long to clasp in our arms those whom we tenderly love. We probably owe this desire to inherited habit, in association with the nursing and tending of our children. (p. 213)

Tend and Befriend Theory. Developed in response to the fight-or-flight model of stress management, tend and befriend theory (TBT:

Taylor, Klein, Lewis, Gruenewald, Gurung, & Updegraff, 2000) challenges the primacy of fighting or fleeing as the most adaptive responses to environmental threats. Whereas males may have benefited evolutionarily from either fighting or fleeing from potential challenges, TBT argues that neither response would have been as adaptive for females, due to the peril to which either approach would subject the women's offspring. Specifically, if a mother is expending her energies and attention fighting a threat or fleeing from it, her children are more likely to be left unprotected in the process. Consequently, the theory predicts, these tendencies on the part of females will eventually be selected against.

As alternatives, TBT proposes that the complexity of protecting and caring for offspring (particularly under threatening circumstances) has made it adaptive for females to adopt two related strategies for responding to stress. The first, *tending*, involves "quieting and caring for offspring and blending into the environment" (Taylor et al., 2000, p. 412) and is thought to be adaptive particularly insofar as it reduces the offspring's own stress response, maximizing its capacity to survive to reproductive age. The second strategy, *befriending*, refers specifically to creating and maintaining social relationships that can provide resources and protection for the mother and her children, particularly under stressful circumstances. For example, women may have benefited from forming intimate social bonds with female relatives and female friends who were physically proximal and could therefore be a source of emotional or instrumental support.

Although tending to and calming children quite likely would have involved holding them in affectionate ways or speaking to them in affectionate tones, even for our evolutionary ancestors, befriending is the strategy of the two that most directly implicates affectionate communication. Given that befriending involves forming and maintaining positive, intimate social bonds – and given that affectionate behavior is one of the principal communicative means of relational development and maintenance – it is logical to conclude that TBT would predict a direct relationship between expressing affection and reducing stress, particularly for women.

One of the most innovative aspects of TBT is that is draws directly from both evolutionary psychology and psychophysiology. Specifically, it implicates a neurohypophyseal hormone, oxytocin, as the principal source of the stress-reducing effects of tending and befriending. In this way, TBT predicts that humans, and females in particular, have evolved a physiological mechanism whereby tending and befriending increase secretion of oxytocin, which counteracts many aspects of the physiological stress response, and that the evolution of such a mechanism follows the adaptive advantages of tending and befriending described above. Whereas many theories within the bioevolutionary paradigm focus either on the adaptiveness of a behavioral tendency or on its physiological correlates, TBT is one of the few that specifically implicates both lines of reasoning.

The Need to Belong. Perhaps the most succinct theoretic statement relevant to the importance of affection appears in Baumeister and Leary's (1995) explication of the *need to belong* as a fundamental human motivation. These authors offered that humans are innately prepared to seek, form, maintain, and protect strong interpersonal relationships, and that this drive is fundamental to the human condition. In their essay, Baumeister and Leary presented evidence from a wide range of literatures that humans habitually seek significant interpersonal bonds, that they suffer from relational deprivation, and that both the emotional experience and the behavioral expression of those bonds are necessary. On this latter point, the authors argued that the need to belong is so fundamental that it cannot be satisfied either by love without interaction (as in the case of long-distance romance or the military deployment or incarceration of one relational partner) or by interaction without love (as in the case of loveless marriages or sexual interactions with prostitutes).

In calling this motivation "fundamental," Baumeister and Leary contended that it met nine specifically articulated criteria: (1) it must operate in a wide variety of settings; (2) it must guide cognition; (3) it must guide emotion; (4) it must produce ill effects when it is unsatisfied; (5) it can be met by a variety of people and social groups; (6) it cannot be limited to certain people or circumstances; (7) it must not be derived from another fundamental motivation; (8) it must affect a wide and diverse range of behaviors; and (9) it should have implications that extend beyond psychological functioning. In their explication, Baumeister and Leary addressed each of these criteria to build the case for the fundamental nature of the need to belong.

Most relevant to the importance of affectionate communication is Baumeister and Leary's contention that the need to belong cannot be satisfactorily met in relationships that involve affectionate emotion but are deprived of interaction. In their discussion, Baumeister and Leary noted that even relationships characterized by permanent, unbreakable emotional bonds – such as those between mothers and their children – suffer when opportunities for interaction are curtailed (as when the mothers are incarcerated). Although this proposition refers to the lack of interaction, in general, rather than the lack of affectionate interaction, in particular, one could deduce from this proposition that people have a need to *express* and *exchange* feelings of love with those for whom they have them. That is, because people experience distress at the deprivation of interaction opportunities with significant others, one could argue that this partially reflects a need not only to *be loved* but to tell others they are loved and to be told one is loved in return.

Somatosensory Affectional Deprivation Theory. Somatosensory affectional deprivation theory (SADT: Prescott, 1970, 1975, 1976a, b, 1980; Prescott & Wallace, 1978) is founded on the premise that physically and psychosocially healthy infant development requires sufficient stimulation of at least three sensory modalities: (1) the vestibular–cerebellar system, involving postnatal continuation of constant movement; (2) the somesthetic system, involving frequent tactile stimulation; and (3) the olfactory system, involving smell and the ability to identify primary caregivers by smell. Prescott (1976a) noted that there is considerable evidence from animal and human studies (including cross-cultural studies) to support the principle that insufficient stimulation of these sensory modalities retards infant development. Working from this premise, SADT posits that these sensory modalities mediate experiences of somatosensory pleasure in infants' initial caregiving relationships, which are typically with their mothers, and that these pleasure experiences are necessary to the development of a primary affectional bond with the mother or mother-surrogate. SADT further proposes that sensory deprivation (in any or all of these modalities) experienced by infants in their initial caregiving relationships prevents the formation of a primary affectional bond with the mother, and that failure to develop a primary affectional bond during infancy has two detrimental effects later in life. First, it impairs the ability to form secondary affectional bonds, particularly sexual bonds, in adulthood. Second, it inhibits the ability to provide sufficient sensory stimulation to one's own offspring, resulting in the intergenerational transmission of affectional deprivation.

SADT has been used to explain a variety of behavioral outcomes, such as the pervasiveness of human violence (Prescott, 1979), the tendency toward drug and alcohol use and abuse (Prescott, 1980), and even sexual behavior among the blind (Prescott, 1973). For instance, Prescott has shown that the average degree of physical affection between mother and infant (holding, touching, carrying) characterizing a primitive culture predicts with nearly perfect accuracy the propensity toward violence in that culture (Prescott, 1976a, 1979). Similarly, he has theorized that the reduced ability to enjoy adult sexual pleasure (resulting from impaired somatosensory development) predicts the use of alcohol and other drugs, and has presented data that supports (although does not conclusively prove) this assertion (Prescott, 1980). SADT explains both behavioral patterns as the consequence of depriving the body of the affectional behavior it requires to fulfill humans' engrained needs for somatosensory stimulation.

Importantly, Prescott's theory gives primacy to physical manifestations of affectionate interaction: touch, smell, and motion. As such, it does not propose that infant development is arrested from a lack of love or emotional attachment on the part of the parent, but from a lack of intimate physical contact that stimulates the sensory modalities (behaviors like rocking a baby, touching the baby's skin, or holding the baby close to one's chest). As I noted in the previous chapter, although behaviors of those sort frequently derive from strong emotional experiences of love and commitment (i.e., experiences and expressions of affection often covary), there is no *necessary* relationship between the emotions and the behaviors. Whereas perspectives such as the need to belong give primacy to emotional experiences – indeed, Baumeister and Leary (1995, p. 513) explicitly provide that relational behavior in the absence of an emotional bond only partially satisfies people's affiliative motivations – SADT is unique among socioevolutionary theories in its focus on the behaviors themselves as causal agents.

In support of this assertion is the large literature on the therapeutic effects of touch among humans. Much of the best scientific research in this area has been conducted by the Touch Research Institute at the University of Miami School of Medicine, which has demonstrated the beneficial effects of tactile contact in a broad range of physical conditions, including anorexia (Hart, Field, Hernandez-Reif, Nearing, Shaw, Schanberg, & Kuhn, 2001), asthma (Field, Henteleff, Hernandez-Reif, Martinez, Mavunda, Kuhn, & Schanberg, 1998), dermatitis (Schachner, Field, Hernandez-Reif, Duarte, Krasnegor, 1998), diabetes (Field, Hernandez-Reif, LaGreca, Shaw, Schanberg, & Kuhn, 1997), HIV (Diego, Field, Hernandez-Reif, Shaw, Friedman, & Ironson, 2001), hypertension (Hernandez-Reif, Field, Krasnegor, Theakston, Hossain, & Burman, 2000), leukemia (Field, Cullen, Diego, Hernandez-Reif, Sprinz, Beebe, Kissell, & Bango-Sanchez, 2001), nicotine addiction (Hernandez-Reif, Field, & Hart, 1999), Parkinson's disease (Hernandez-Reif, Field, Largie, Cullen, Beutler, Sanders, Weiner, Rodriguez-Bateman, Zeleya,

Schanberg, & Kuhn, 2002), and sleep disorders (Field & Hernandez-Reif, 2001). In each case, the observed physiological, psychological, and behavioral benefits of therapeutic touch were unattributable to any emotional connection between the source and the recipient of the touch. Importantly, although Prescott's theory makes no dismissal of the assertion that somatosensory stimulation is often accompanied by intimate emotional bonds, the emotional bonds are neither necessary nor sufficient precursors to the outcomes SADT predicts. Rather, it is the behaviors themselves that are theorized to affect outcomes such as delayed physical development, propensity toward violence, and propensity toward drug and alcohol abuse.

Sociocultural Paradigm

In contrast to the bioevolutionary paradigm, the sociocultural paradigm focuses on the ways in which the meanings of behaviors are prescribed at social or cultural levels and the ways in which those meanings are learned and taught. I use the term "sociocultural paradigm" broadly, intending for it to be inclusive of social learning traditions (e.g., Bandura, 1971) and approaches focusing on the social construction of meaning (e.g., Burgoon & Newton's 1991 social meaning model).

An underlying assumption of the sociocultural paradigm is that a given behavior (e.g., a wink) conveys a specified meaning (e.g., an expression of affection) because, and only because, that meaning has been prescribed to it by the social or cultural group in which it is observed. The primary implication of this approach is that a behavior or repertoire of behaviors are used to encode particular meanings, and are decoded as having those meanings, only within the social or cultural group that has prescribed those meanings to them. Thus, unlike the bioevolutionary paradigm, the sociocultural paradigm does not necessarily assume consistency, either in how expressions are encoded or in how they are decoded, *between* social or cultural groups (which may be as broad as a nationality or as small as a specific organization, profession, or family). Rather, the sociocultural paradigm generally assumes consistency only *within* such groups.

At the heart of this paradigmatic approach is the idea that most communicative behavior is learned, either through observation, direct instruction, or both. For example, people learn what are considered to be appropriate ways of expressing affection within the culture or even the family in which they are raised. If the rules of appropriateness differ – as they often do from culture to culture (Ekman & Friesen, 1969) and family to family (Halberstadt, 1986) – then observed patterns of behavior would likewise be expected to differ. The means through which people acquire the knowledge necessary to guide their behavior are, therefore, of paramount interest to researchers working with this paradigm.

One example from the affectionate communication literature is a perspective that has been referred to, alternatively, as the *gendered closeness perspective* (Floyd, 1996; Morman & Floyd, 1999), the *male deficit model* (Doherty, 1991), and the *covert intimacy perspective* (Swain, 1989). This idea was formulated to explain the common finding that women's familial and platonic relationships are closer, more intimate, and more affectionate than men's, and is based on a concept of affectionate communication as a type of relational currency (see Wilkinson, 2000). The perspective posits that men's relationships are not inherently less affectionate or intimate than women's, but that men express their affection for each other using different relational currencies than women use. Whereas affection between women might be expressed primarily through verbal statements (e.g., saying "you're my closest friend") or through direct nonverbal gestures (e.g., hugging), affection between men is expressed primarily through the provision of instrumental support, such as helping with a project or loaning the use of a car. The reasoning is that men are socialized to value gestures of instrumental support – that is, men think of such gestures as being more valuable forms of relational currency – more so than do women, and also that using such behaviors as forms of expressing affection allows the affectionate message to be conveyed in such a way as not to call attention to it. Swain (1989) referred to these behaviors as "covert" because they may not be interpreted by observers as affectionate expressions, thereby mitigating the potential ridicule that more direct expressions might invite (for further reviews, see Parks, 1995; Wood & Inman, 1993).

As regards the communication of affection, then, this perspective predicts that men, particularly when communicating with other men, will use instrumental gestures of support more than direct verbal or nonverbal statements as means of expressing affection, and that they will use instrumental gestures of support to express affection more than women will. Morman and Floyd (1999) used this perspective to study affectionate communication between fathers and adult sons, and I have used it elsewhere to study manifestations of closeness and intimacy in friendships and between siblings (see Floyd, 1995, 1996; Floyd & Parks, 1995).

Importantly, sociocultural perspectives, such as the gendered closeness perspective, locate their causal and explanatory agents in socialization and cultural training and direct the researcher's attention to these influences. Compared to the bioevolutionary approach, the sociocultural approach has been more widely used in research on all aspects of affectionate communication, including encoding and decoding processes.

Some Specific Theories in the Sociocultural Paradigm

Social Exchange Theory. Social exchange theory (SET, which also has been called the theory of interdependence; Thibaut & Kelley, 1959) is founded on an economic model of human social interaction. It assumes that humans are continually driven to seek or maximize their rewards and to reduce or avoid their costs. More specifically, SET provides that humans assess the costs and rewards of their personal relationships when making decisions about maintaining them. Two types of comparisons are of primary importance here. The first is one's *comparison level* (CL); this represents one's abstract standard for a relationship, or one's idea of how costly and how rewarding a given relationship ought to be. For instance, one might expect romantic relationships to be highly rewarding, so if one's own romantic relationship is not so rewarding, this creates a low CL. The second comparison is one's *comparison level for alternatives* (CL_{alt}); this represents the lowest ratio of rewards to costs that a person is willing to accept in a relationship, given what the alternatives are (such as being in a different relationship or being alone). One would be willing to put up with an unsatisfying relationship, for example, when it is preferable to being alone and when no preferable suitors are available.

Social exchange theory has not been explicitly used in published research on affectionate communication. However, it provides a basis for deducing hypotheses about the exchange of affectionate expressions, if one conceives of affectionate expressions as a contributor to relational satisfaction. Comparison levels, and comparison levels for alternatives, could be measured with respect to the form or amount of affectionate communication characterizing a given relationship. People who desire a great deal of affection should consider relationships in which they receive few affectionate messages to have a low CL. Similarly, those who desire very little affection should consider relationships with highly affectionate people to have a low CL. In both cases, CL_{alt} may be influenced by the other types of rewards people perceive in such relationships, as well as by their own desired levels of affectionate behavior.

Interaction Adaptation Theory. Interaction adaptation theory (IAT: Burgoon, Dillman, & Stern, 1993; Burgoon, Stern, & Dillman, 1995) places people's desires, needs, and expectations in a central explanatory role. It supposes that people enter any given interaction with a mix of *requirements* (what they need from the interaction), *expectations* (what they anticipate from the interaction), and *desires* (what they want from the interaction). These elements combine to form an *interaction position*, which is then compared to the actual behavior enacted by one's interaction partners. According to IAT, when one encounters behaviors that match one's interaction position, or behaviors that are more positive than those initially required, expected, or desired, one will be apt to reciprocate those behaviors by behaving in a similar manner. Conversely, when one encounters behaviors that are more negative than those initially required, expected, or desired, one will be apt to compensate for those behaviors by acting in an opposing manner.

Two experiments have applied IAT to the task of predicting patterns of reciprocity and compensation of affectionate behavior. Floyd and Burgoon (1999) reasoned that, although affectionate behavior might be welcomed in many situations, it may be undesired in others. It also may be completely expected in one situation but totally unexpected in another. Using the expectation and desire elements of IAT, Floyd and Burgoon predicted that individuals will match increasing affectionate behavior, and compensate for decreasing affectionate behavior, when they desire and expect affection, and that they will demonstrate the opposite responses when they neither desire nor expect affection. More important, however, they also addressed (in the form of research questions) how people would respond to affectionate behavior when they desired one thing but expected another. Floyd and Ray (in press) used IAT to predict generalized patterns of response to increasing and decreasing affectionate behavior over time, hypothesizing that increases in affection are generally reciprocated and that decreases are generally compensated for, but that specific goals and expectations moderate these effects.

Expectancy Violations Theory. Expectancy violations theory (EVT: Burgoon, 1978; Burgoon & Hale, 1988; Burgoon & Le Poire, 1993; Burgoon & Walther, 1990; Burgoon, Walther, & Baesler, 1992) proposes that humans have expectations about their own and others' behaviors. EVT proposes that when people behave in ways that deviate noticeably from these expectancies, these expectancy violations heighten the arousal of the recipient or observer and initiate a series of cognitive appraisals that assess the meaning of the behavior and the reward value of the violator. At question is the overall valence of the violation, whether positive or negative. Some behaviors have a consensually shared meaning that dictates their valence, such as an obscene gesture. When the meaning of the behavior is ambiguous, attention is turned to the violator. Some people, because of their attractiveness, credibility, fame, wealth, familiarity, or power, are considered to be high-reward communicators; others who do not bear such virtues are considered to be low-reward communicators. EVT provides that when the meaning of a behavior is ambiguous, people will tend to judge it positively when enacted by a high-reward communicator and negatively when enacted by a low-reward communicator.

These assessments provide an overall valence to the violation. A positive expectancy violation is akin to a pleasant surprise, something that is better than what was expected. Conversely, a negative violation is akin to an unpleasant surprise. EVT predicts that communicators who commit positive violations will subsequently be evaluated more favorably, and those who commit negative violations will subsequently be evaluated more negatively, than communicators whose behaviors are expectancy-confirming. Since its introduction, EVT has engendered a good deal of empirical support in a number of content areas (for a review, see Burgoon, 1995).

As Floyd and Voloudakis (1999a) noted, EVT provides a basis for understanding not only why a recipient of an affectionate expression might judge it positively but also why he or she might judge it negatively. Specifically, negative evaluations should be elicited when the expression constitutes a negative expectancy violation, which could be the case for a number of reasons. Perhaps, for example, the expression comes earlier than expected in the developmental trajectory of a relationship. Or it may occur at an inappropriate time or place, or be delivered in an inappropriate manner. Perhaps it comes from someone the recipient finds to be unrewarding. In these or similar instances, the affectionate expression might be an unwelcome surprise, causing the recipient (as EVT predicts) to evaluate it negatively.

Social Meaning Model. The social meaning model (SMM: Burgoon & Newton; 1991) deals specifically with evaluation and interpretation of nonverbal messages. The model predicts that, within a given speech community, there are consensually recognized relational meanings for some nonverbal behaviors. That is, nonverbal behaviors "comprise a socially shared vocabulary of relational communication" (Burgoon & Newton, 1991, p. 96; see also Burgoon, Manusov, Mineo, &

Hale, 1985; Burgoon, Coker, & Coker, 1986). To that end, all observers of a given behavior should make similar interpretations of its relational meaning. According to Burgoon and Newton, support for the SMM requires attention to at least three issues. First, the range of meanings attributable to a given nonverbal behavior should be identified. For example, immediacy behaviors can signal involvement but also can be used to convey power. Moreover, matching another's nonverbal behaviors can communicate similarity and interconnectedness but also may signal dominance. Second, support for the SMM requires evidence that encoders and decoders converge in their interpretations of a given behavior. That is, senders' intentions for the meaning of an enacted behavior should be similar to receivers' interpretations of the behavior. Third, the congruence between the perspectives of participants and observers must be examined. The SMM predicts that, because behaviors have shared social meaning within a given community, conversational participants and third-party, nonparticipant observers should interpret the behaviors similarly.

Floyd and Erbert (2003) used the SMM to make predictions about the evaluation of nonverbal affection behaviors. In a laboratory experiment, confederates in an affectionate condition were instructed to maintain high amounts of gaze, smiling, touch, and proximity, and to maintain direct and open body postures. Floyd and Erbert derived three hypotheses from the SMM: (1) confederates' and receivers' interpretations of the confederates' behaviors would be linearly related; (2) receivers' and nonparticipant observers' interpretations of the confederates' behaviors would be linearly related; and (3) receivers would evaluate confederates' behaviors more favorably than would observers.

Politeness Theory. Politeness theory (PT: Brown & Levinson, 1987) espouses that all individuals have, and are concerned with maintaining, *face.* As first articulated by Goffman (1959, 1967), face refers to a person's desired public image. Politeness theory identifies two types of face needs to which individuals are posited to attend. *Positive face* refers to one's desire for acceptance and approval from others. *Negative face* refers to one's desire for autonomy and freedom from imposition or constraint. Behaviors that run contrary to people's face needs are called face-threatening acts, or FTAs. For instance, insults or criticisms can threaten people's positive face because they imply disapproval, whereas requests for favors can threaten people's negative face by constraining their behaviors and imposing on their autonomy.

Politeness theory articulates five forms of "facework," or strategies that senders of a message can use to mitigate the potential face threats of their messages. The facework strategies are ordered hierarchically on their degree of politeness, or the extent to which they mitigate face threats. The least polite strategy is to use a "bald-on-record" statement in which the message is encoded as directly as possible, with no attempt to mitigate potential face threats. The second and third strategies are called "positive politeness" and "negative politeness"; these involve crafting a message to minimize threats to the hearer's positive or negative face needs, respectively. A fourth strategy is to make one's statement "off the record," meaning that the message is implied but never directly stated; this allows the sender to deny the intention behind the message (e.g., to say "that's not what I meant") if he or she finds that a face threat has occurred. Finally, the most polite strategy is simply to forego the FTA altogether.

Erbert and Floyd (2004) applied PT to the task of predicting receivers' evaluations and assessments of affectionate expressions. Because affectionate behaviors communicate value for the receiver, Erbert and Floyd reasoned that these would support, rather than threaten, positive face, and that receivers would perceive greater positive face support from expressions that are more direct (e.g., bald-on-record) than from expressions that are less direct (e.g., off-the-record). They also reasoned, however, that affectionate messages could simultaneously threaten negative face, either by implying that the sender wishes to modify the status of the relationship with the receiver (e.g., a platonic friend wanting to become a romantic partner), or by making the receiver feel manipulated (i.e., that the sender was using the expression as a form of persuasion or manipulation). These threats to negative face were predicted to be greater with more direct messages (e.g., bald-on-record) than with less direct messages (e.g., off-the-record).

Cognitive Valence Theory. Cognitive valence theory (CVT: Andersen, 1983, 1984, 1989, 1992; Andersen, Guerrero, Buller, & Jorgensen, 1998) assumes that relational partners have a level of affection and intimacy display that is expected and comfortable for their relationship. When an increase in such behaviors on the part of one person is perceived by the other, the receiver responds with an increase in cognitive arousal. CVT predicts that small changes in behavior have negligible effects on arousal and thus would not be expected to influence a receiver's response. Large behavior changes are predicted to produce large changes in arousal that cause automatic reactive responses from the receiver, such as immediate flight.

CVT is concerned primarily with behaviors that lead to moderate arousal. According to the theory, such behaviors can lead either to reciprocity or compensation on the part of the receiver. The critical variable is the valence that the receiver attaches to his or her arousal. Positive arousal is hypothesized to generate reciprocity and negative arousal is hypothesized to generate compensation. Whether arousal is valenced positively or negatively depends on six cognitive schemata: (1) cultural schemata, including social and cultural norms; (2) relational schemata, including the history of the relationship and its specific norms for behavior; (3) interpersonal schemata, which encompasses the receiver's assessment of how rewarding the sender is; (4) situational schemata, including the environmental context and the types of behaviors appropriate to that context; (5) state schemata, dealing with one's physiological and psychological states at the time of the behavior; and (6) individual schemata, which encompass one's personality traits.

According to CVT, an increase in arousal will be positively valenced only if all six schemata yield positive valences. If only one of the schemata is activated negatively, then the increase in arousal will be negatively valenced and the behavior will be compensated for, rather than reciprocated. CVT has not been used in published research on affectionate communication, although Andersen and his colleagues have tested various parts of it in studies on nonverbal immediacy behaviors. However, it does provide a direct means of predicting whether affectionate expressions will be reciprocated or compensated for, warranting its inclusion here.

On the Status of Affectionate Communication Theory

Each of the theories and perspectives reviewed above provides something important in the way of explaining an aspect of affectionate communication: for example, how affectionate messages are encoded or when they are likely to be reciprocated. Some of these theories have proven fruitful in framing empirical investigations on these topics, and others have the potential to do so. All of these theories and perspectives have also garnered empirical support in research on other cognitive or behavioral phenomena.

Despite how useful these theories have been, or could be, to scientists studying affectionate communication, each is limited by the fact that it can explain or predict only one or two parts of the overall process of affectionate communication (although some, like SADT, are more specifically relevant to the expression of affection than others). Moreover, explanation and prediction from these theories (and particularly those of the sociocultural paradigm) reside largely at the level of the relationship, if not at the level of the interaction itself. Thus, a scientist can consider an affectionate act to be a type of relational currency, or an expectancy violation, or a form of negative politeness, but these theoretic properties are often particular to the relationship or the interaction in which the act occurs. For instance, an affectionate act that is a positive expectancy violation for one couple or in one conversation can be a negative violation for a different couple or in a different conversation. Few of these theories provide the type of higher-order explanation for affectionate communication that is necessary for an appreciation of its importance, utility, or functionality in a context larger than individual relationships or interactions.

Importantly, this is not a shortcoming of these theories, *per se*, as none of them, save for SADT, was *designed* to explain affectionate communication (and SADT focuses only on the behavioral components of affection exchange without considering its potent social and emotional influences). Rather, each was designed to explain other phenomena, and the reasoning inherent in each has been applied – or could be applied – to the study of affectionate behavior. Therefore, the limitations being raised here are not resident in the theories themselves, but in the application of these theories to affectionate behavior and in the lack of a more comprehensive theory about affectionate communication.

The consequence of these theoretic limitations has been a body of research that provides small and somewhat fragmented pieces of information about the process of affectionate behavior but has no over-arching framework that can pull the diverse (and sometimes contradictory) pieces of information into a comprehensive whole. A higher-order theory is needed, both to cohere the existing knowledge about affectionate communication and to allow this body of research to mature by addressing more sophisticated questions beyond the level of the relationship or interaction.

As noted, a principal goal of this text is to offer such a theory. Before considering what a higher-order explanation might require, however, it is instructive to review the body of empirical knowledge on affectionate behavior in human relationships. The subsequent chapters attend to such a task by describing research on the ways in which affection is conveyed, interpreted, and responded to, and on the benefits and risks associated with the communication of affection. Much of the research reviewed in these chapters was grounded in the theories described earlier. By noting both the strengths and weakness of how existing theories have fared in the empirical realm, one can better appreciate the increased understanding of affectionate communication that a more comprehensive theory can offer.

3

Encoding Affectionate Messages

Most people would rather give than get affection.
– Aristotle

Human communication is an extraordinarily diverse enterprise, and the communication of affection is no exception. Individuals use a broad range of behaviors to encode feelings of affection for each other. Some are verbal in nature, such as a spoken or written declaration of love. Others are nonverbal gestures, such as hugs or kisses or pats on the back. Still others consist of supportive behaviors that may not necessarily be thought of as affectionate expressions but have that connotative meaning within particular relationships. This chapter explores the different forms of encoding affectionate messages (including those that are idiomatic to particular relationships), and reviews research on what individual-, relational-, and contextual-level influences affect the encoding of affection. With respect to categorizing affectionate behaviors, one might offer that they can be most parsimoniously understood as comprising three separate but interrelated types.

A Tripartite Model for Encoding Affectionate Messages

Early work on the encoding of affectionate communication adopted, at least implicitly, a two-dimensional model wherein affectionate messages were either encoded verbally (e.g., by saying "I love you" or "I care about you") or nonverbally (e.g., by hugging, kissing, or holding hands). Many measurement models assessed verbal and nonverbal expressions without making an *a priori* distinction between them. For instance, Noller (1978) examined videotaped interactions of 87 parent–child dyads and coded "the number of instances of interactive behavior that would normally be

28

regarded as affectionate," including kissing, cuddling, or saying "I love you" (p. 317). (Other measurement models placed specific emphasis on nonverbal expressions of affection, such as kissing or hugging; see Acker, Acker, & Pearson, 1973; Acker & Marton, 1984.)

A more detailed assessment tool for the two-dimensional model was developed by Twardosz, Schwartz, Fox, and Cunningham (1979) as a system for live coding of affectionate behavior in preschool settings. This coding scheme emphasized both active (e.g., hugging, kissing, patting) and passive (e.g., smiling, sitting on another's lap) nonverbal expressions of affection, as well as verbal statements expressing love, praise, or friendship (see also Twardosz, Botkin, Cunningham, Weddle, Sollie, & Schreve, 1987). A similar approach was employed by Christopher, Bauman, and Veness-Meehan (1999) in their system for coding affectionate behaviors in neonatal intensive care units. Floyd (1997a, b; Floyd & Morman, 1997) retained the two-dimensional model in the development of a self-report measure used to ascertain affectionate behavior, as did Huston and Vangelisti (1991) in the development of their self-report measure of marital affection.

These two categories (verbal and nonverbal) are both mutually exclusive and exhaustive, and it would appear at first that they ought to capture fully the range of potentially observable affectionate messages. Largely unaccounted for in this two-dimensional model, however, is the notion that, within particular relationships, individuals may express affection through the provision of social and instrumental support, such as doing favors for each other, helping with projects, or loaning the use of resources. Although these behaviors may accompany other, more direct expressions of affection within these relationships, they often do not. Regardless, the critical point is that individuals in particular relationships both *use supportive behaviors for the purpose of expressing affection* to each other and *decode these behaviors as such.*

These types of social support behaviors seem to be outside of the realm of traditional affectionate behaviors; if they were not, they would have been included among those behaviors already being measured in two-dimensional models. This observation alone might lead researchers not to include such behaviors in an operational definition of affectionate communication. If, however, the behaviors are used (at least in some types of relationships) for the purpose of expressing affection, and are decoded as such within these relationships, then the decision to exclude such behaviors from one's operational definition necessarily entails the risk of failing to capture the construct at any level beyond its most overt.

Certainly, one need not incorporate every idiosyncratic form of expressing affection that it used within individual relationships; such a practice would, by definition, preclude generalizeability. However, if a behavior or set of behaviors is used by groups of people or relationships for the purpose of encoding affectionate messages and is decoded as such by those people or in those relationships, then it inhibits the scientist's understanding of that construct to ignore such behaviors.

Floyd and Morman (1998) thus proposed a tripartite model of affectionate behavior with the publication of the affectionate communication index (ACI). The ACI was designed with the goal of capturing native referents – those behaviors through which people actually express affection – rather than a set of behaviors imposed *a priori*. Admittedly, such an approach concedes some conceptual control at the outset, and some empiricists may find this a problematic concession. However, in light of the lack (at the time) of a comprehensive theory of affection exchange, and in consideration of perspectives suggesting that affectionate messages may intentionally be conveyed "covertly," Floyd and Morman opted to initiate scale development in an open-ended manner by asking groups of individuals to indicate how they communicated affection in their most affectionate relationships. This strategy mirrors that advocated by Berscheid, Snyder, and Omoto (1989), which is to investigate a construct within the context of the relationships in which it is most salient. After the elimination of items mentioned by fewer than 10% of the sample, a list of 34 items remained, which then comprised the initial version of the measure.

A second group of participants was asked to think of their most affectionate same- or opposite-sex relationship and to indicate, on a seven-point scale, how often they engaged in each of the 34 behaviors as a way to communicate affection in these relationships. Factor analyses (both exploratory and confirmatory) reduced the item load to three distinctive, although nonorthogonal, factors representing verbal, nonverbal, and social support forms of affectionate communication. Subsequent assessments of construct validity indicated that all three forms of affectionate behavior were directly related to psychological affection and relational closeness and inversely related to psychological distance characterizing these relationships. Later tests confirmed the scale's stability (test–retest reliability) and its ability to discriminate relationships known in advance to be highly affectionate from those known to be nonaffectionate. Supplemental studies also demonstrated that the scale's scores were directly related to closeness and communication satisfaction in father–son relationships and that they successfully predicted nonverbal immediacy and emotional expressiveness behaviors in conversations between adult friends.

Unlike other self-report measures of affectionate behavior (many of which are reviewed in Floyd & Morman, 1998), the ACI has successfully demonstrated multiple forms of psychometric adequacy (see, e.g., Floyd & Mikkelson, 2002). The availability of a practical and psychometrically sound instrument has been advantageous to those interested in furthering scientific knowledge on affectionate behavior.

This three-dimensional model continues to differentiate between verbal and nonverbal forms of encoding, but it further discriminates between *direct* nonverbal gestures and behaviors that indirectly encode affectionate messages through the provision of social support. A brief discussion of each of these three categories is provided below.

Verbal Statements

Included in this category are those verbal statements that convey one's affectionate feelings for another (whether accurately or not). Such statements come in several forms. Some convey the nature of the sender's feelings for the receiver; these include statements such as "I like you," "I love you," or "I am in love with you." Others establish or reinforce the status of the relationship between sender and receiver, such as "You're my best friend," "You are the most important person in my life," or "I could never love anyone as much as I love you."[1] Still others project dreams or hopes for the future of the relationship between sender and receiver; these include "I want us to be together forever" and "I can't wait to be married to you." Finally, other statements convey the value of the relationship by noting how the sender would feel without it, such as "I don't know what I'd do without you," "I can't stand the thought of losing you," or "My life would be empty if I hadn't met you."

The feature that clearly distinguishes verbal statements from the other two forms of affectionate communication in this model is their use of language, which makes verbal statements unique in their specificity relative to the other forms in this model. When people wish to be unambiguous about their feelings for each other, they may opt to put those feelings

---

[1] I do not intend my use of the term *sender* to imply an outdated transactional model of communication. Rather, I use this term instead of *speaker* because the latter term appears confined to senders of spoken verbal messages, whereas my remarks are also inclusive of those communicating through written messages and nonverbal behaviors.

into words, rather than convey them through nonverbal channels, so as to reduce the chances of misinterpretation. They may do this either to convey intense affection for each other (e.g., "I'm in love with you; let's get married") or to be clear that the affection is less intense (e.g., "I like you; let's be friends"). There is an enormous qualitative difference between saying "I like you" and "I'm in love with you," a distinction that may not be conveyed quite as accurately through nonverbal behaviors.

Certainly, this is not to suggest that verbal statements are unambiguous in an absolute sense. If a sender says "I love you" to another, he or she can intend to convey many different types of love and the intention may not be evident at first. Indeed, as addressed in Chapter 6, misinterpretation of affectionate expressions (even verbal expressions) is one of their more potent risks. Verbal statements are usually less ambiguous in their meaning than are direct nonverbal gestures or social support behaviors, however.

Language is, of course, both spoken and written, and both forms are included in this first category. The differences between these forms raise some compelling questions – for example, **What factors influence people's decisions to convey affection through written versus spoken means?** One might speculate, for instance, that senders prefer to express their affectionate feelings in writing, instead of by speaking, when they are more certain of those feelings, since the written word might seem to be more "permanent" than the spoken word. That is, because recall of the spoken word (if unrecorded) relies on memory, spoken expressions of affection may be easier than written statements for senders to deny later if their feelings change. Another speculation might be that senders prefer spoken to written statements when their goal is to be as unambiguous as possible. A written message of "I love you," for instance, could be interpreted as conveying either romantic or nonromantic forms of love. To reduce ambiguity, a sender may choose to speak the words, so that the cues as to their intended meaning can be conveyed through the sender's facial expressions, body language, or tone of voice. Both of these predictions are speculative, however; the question is presented here in bold type to denote that it awaits empirical attention.

Direct Nonverbal Gestures

The second category of affectionate behaviors in the model is direct nonverbal gestures. The term "gestures" is not used here in the specific sense of gesticulation (i.e., the use of hand and arm movements in an emblematic or illustrative fashion) but in a broader sense that simply denotes a social behavior (in the way that one might compliment another by saying "What you did for that person was a nice gesture"). Referring to the gestures in this category as "direct" indicates that they are limited to those nonverbal behaviors that are readily associated with the communication of affection within the social community in which they are observed. (As discussed elsewhere in this text, these will sometimes vary from culture to culture and sometimes not.) In North American cultures, for example, hugging, kissing, smiling, sharing prolonged mutual gaze, winking, holding hands, using "babytalk," putting one's arm around another, and sharing physical proximity are examples of behaviors that are commonly used to encode affectionate messages and are commonly decoded as such, at least by others in these cultures.

Although these gestures are referred to as "direct," their meaning is often more ambiguous than the meaning of verbal statements. This is partly because of the relative specificity of language, as noted earlier, and partly because of the fact that many direct nonverbal gestures of affection can be performed in a variety of ways, each of which may carry a somewhat different meaning. A good example is the kiss. Kisses can range in intensity from a perfunctory peck on the cheek to a prolonged, open-mouth-to-open-mouth encounter. Several aspects of a kiss might vary as a function of its intended meaning. Longer kisses may connote affection of a romantic nature, whereas shorter ones connote familial or platonic affection. A kiss on the mouth is often more intimate than a kiss on the cheek, and an open-mouth kiss more intimate than a closed-mouth kiss. A "dry" kiss (with no tongue contact) might be used when nonromantic affection is conveyed, whereas romantic or sexual affection might call for a "wet" kiss.

Another example is the embrace (Floyd, 1999). Hugs also can vary on a number of dimensions. One is their duration; longer hugs are often used to convey more intense affection than shorter hugs. Another is their intensity, which is a function both of the pressure and the amount of body contact. Intimates may engage in intense, full-body-contact embraces, whereas casual friends might prefer lighter hugs that are restricted to upper-body contact. Finally, hugs vary in their form, which is primarily a function of relative arm placement. Floyd (1999) referenced three forms of hugging: the "criss-cross hug," in which each person has one arm above and one arm below the other's; the "neck-waist hug," in which one person's arms wrap around the other's neck and the other person's arms wrap around the partner's waist; and, the "engulfing hug," in which one person's arms are held together on his or her chest and the other's arms are wrapped entirely around this person (some might call this a "bear hug").

These and other direct nonverbal gestures are provocative, in part, *because* their meaning is often more ambiguous than that of verbal statements. The verbal content of a message such as "I love you" is always the same; it always consists of these three words in this exact order. As noted above, this does not suggest that its meaning is always unambiguous, but it does suggest that variation in its meaning cannot be attributed to variation in its verbal form, because there is no such variation. The same is not true of many of the direct nonverbal gestures of affection. An important question, therefore, is: **How is variation in the form of direct nonverbal gestures of affection associated with variation in their intended meanings?** Given the differences in ambiguity – or at least, potential ambiguity – between verbal and direct nonverbal forms of expressing affection, one also might ask, **Under what conditions are people more likely to convey affection through direct nonverbal gestures than through verbal statements?**

Social Support Behaviors

The final category in this tripartite model includes behaviors that are provisions of social or instrumental support.[2] These behaviors convey affection indirectly, through acts of assistance, rather than through behaviors that directly denote affectionate feelings. As such, they often appear outwardly to be the least intense of the three forms of affectionate communication, although in fact they are often the most potent of the three. Moreover, in some relationships, they are the most common of the three forms to be observed (see, e.g., Morman & Floyd, 1999).

Behaviors in this category are characterized by their provision of some type of assistance. Some cases involve the provision of psychological or emotional support. For instance, relatives and friends might show their affection to a newly divorced young mother by providing a sympathetic ear, making themselves available to her at all hours, empathizing with

---

[2] Floyd and Morman (1998) used the term "social support" for the sake of brevity, not for the purpose of excluding instrumental support from this category. This is especially clear when one considers items from the affectionate communication index that are intended to measure social support, such as "helping with a project." For the sake of consistency (and brevity), the same terminology is used here.

her situation, and telling her that she is going to "make it through" the situation. This type of support is closest to what many researchers consider "social support"; however, the model also includes cases that involve the provision of more instrumental types of support. For example, the relatives and friends of the young mother also might show their affection by offering to baby sit, bringing her meals, taking care of her yard work, and sending her money to help with her financial needs.

None of the support behaviors mentioned here encodes an affectionate message directly, in the way that behaviors such as kissing or saying "I love you" do. Indeed, it is easy to conceive of situations in which many of these behaviors would have no affectionate connotations whatsoever – a therapist lending a sympathetic ear or a social service agency sending money, for instance. However, when these behaviors are done for the purpose of conveying affection, they may do so in a more profound way than verbal statements or direct nonverbal gestures do.

The provision of a resource, whether it be one's money, one's time and effort, a material resource (such as the use of a car), or merely one's attention, is significant both denotatively and connotatively to the recipient of such support. Such provisions denote that "I wish to meet the need you are experiencing" and connote that "You are so important to me that I am willing to use my own resources to meet your need." This characteristic of support behaviors as forms of encoding affection raises some interesting research questions concerning the connection between the value of the resource and the intensity of the affection that is expressed. Taking a social exchange orientation to the issue, for example, might lead one to ask, **Is there a relationship between the real or perceived value of a social support behavior and the intensity with which it connotes affection to the receiver?** Let us suppose that George needs $10,000 immediately or he will lose his house. All other things being equal, would he consider one friend's gift of $5,000 to be a more intense expression of affection for him than another friend's gift of $1,000? The first gift certainly benefits him more and represents a greater depletion of the friend's resources, so he might conclude that the first friend cares about him more. If he knew, however, that the first friend can easily spare the money whereas the second friend gave him all of his or her savings, he may then consider the second gift to be a more intense expression of affection.

Social support behaviors are distinguished from verbal and indirect nonverbal forms of affectionate communication not only by their provision of support, but also by the relative indirectness with which they encode affectionate messages. There are at least three reasons to believe this is the more consequential of their two characteristics. First, it makes them more likely to be overlooked by recipients as affectionate gestures. An example concerns a husband who was advised by a marital therapist to show more affection to his wife. In response, the husband went directly home and washed his wife's car. Later, he was astonished that neither his wife nor their therapist had recognized this instrumental behavior as an expression of affection, because to the husband, it clearly was. If the husband had instead rushed home and said "I love you" to his wife, no such problem would have ensued.

In the same vein, the relative indirectness with which support behaviors encode affectionate messages makes them more likely than verbal or direct nonverbal gestures to be overlooked by third-party observers. This is, potentially, one of their greatest assets, because it allows for people to express affection "covertly" if they choose, in ways that may not be evident to onlookers. Swain (1989) suggested that it is more common for men to express their affection for their male friends through instrumental support behaviors, such as helping with a household project, than for them to express affection more overtly. Swain offered that men do this so that their affectionate sentiment can be conveyed in such a way that protects them from possible ridicule or negative attributions from others, who might see more overt expressions of affection as feminine (see also Wood & Inman, 1993).

Finally, the relative indirectness of supportive behaviors as affectionate expressions is significant because researchers might overlook them. As noted earlier, this is not problematic if the researcher's goal is to study only overt expressions. For researchers who aim for a broader under-standing of affectionate communication within relationships, however, a more inclusive conceptual definition is clearly warranted. It was for this reason, more than any other, that support behaviors were included in Floyd and Morman's (1998) model.

Idiomatic Expressions of Affection

The tripartite model of affectionate communication was designed to refer to behaviors that are commonly used to encode affectionate messages and are typically decoded by recipients as such. Its companion operational definition, the ACI, captures specific behaviors within each of the three categories, but the list of behaviors is representative, not exhaustive. Of course, this is true of many operational definitions used in the social sciences, and the researcher aims, through careful selection of items and rigorous validity and reliability tests, to compile a list of referents for the variable being measured that will truly represent the variance to be captured. Science works to account for what is true of most people most of the time. By focusing on the broad picture, however, social science inevitably misses many of the idiosyncrasies that characterize people's behaviors in specific relationships.

There are several reasons why individuals may devise ways of expressing affection that are idiosyncratic to particular relationships. Perhaps people develop idioms that will allow them to express their affection to each other secretly. In the 1997 film, *Bent,* two prisoners in a Nazi POW camp discover feelings of affection for each other but are too afraid of repercussions from the guards to express their feelings openly. Instead, they developed a code system whereby one would simply scratch his eyebrow and both would recognize it as an expression of affection. These types of idioms allow relational partners to communicate their affection openly in public contexts without concern for how others in the same context might respond.

Idioms of this nature also may allow people to express affection in situations when it simply might not be appropriate to express it more overtly (for instance, during a business meeting or a church service). Moreover, as Oring (1984) suggested, individuals can use these types of idioms to underscore the intimacy of their relationships, because their use indicates that the users "know one another in ways unknown and unknowable to others" (p. 21).

Finally, physical distance or other constraints may restrict relational partners' means of expressing affection. Consequently, relational partners may elect to establish means of conveying affection that circumvent these constraints, such as through the use of computer-mediated communication (see, e.g., Parks & Floyd, 1996).

Although idioms defy generalization by definition, the social scientist can still study the patterns in their use and the purposes they serve. Bell, Buerkel-Rothfuss, and Gore (1987) examined idiom use in heterosexual romantic couples and reported that expressing affection was among the most common functions of personal idioms. They found that idioms for affection were slightly more likely to be verbal than nonverbal and were slightly more likely to be used in public contexts than in private. They also discovered that it was usually the man in the relationship who invented idioms for affection. Moreover, for both men and women, the number of idioms for expressing affection was linearly related to reported levels of love, closeness, and commitment in the relationship (see also Hopper, Knapp, & Scott, 1981).

Little other research has examined the use of idioms for communicating affection. However, the multiple risks associated with affectionate communication, which are discussed in greater detail in Chapter 6, may make this a profitable area of study. For instance, one might examine **whether idiomatic forms of expressing affection are more characteristic of particular people, or particular relationship types, than others**. Perhaps, for instance, there is a connection between the type of relationship in which an idiomatic expression is used and the reason for using the idiomatic expression in the first place. Perhaps, for certain reasons, people in some relationships communicate their affection *only* idiomatically. Future research on the use of idioms may illuminate one way in which relational partners mitigate some of the risks associated with affectionate communication.

Influences on Affectionate Communication

A number of influences at the individual, relational, and contextual levels affect the communication of affection. This section details the findings from the most commonly studied influences. Importantly, this is not an exhaustive list, and the items on this list are not mutually exclusive in their influence.

Sex, Sex Composition, and Gender

Numerous studies have examined the influences of sex, sex composition, and gender[3] on the amount of affection people communicate to others, and the findings have been remarkably consistent. For example, nearly every study examining the effect of sex has found that women express more affection than men do, and those that have not (e.g., Bombar & Littig, 1996; Floyd, 1997b; McCabe, 1987) have reported null findings.[4]

---

[3] I will use the term *sex* to distinguish between biological males and biological females, and the term *gender* to refer to the socially and culturally prescribed role orientations of masculinity and femininity. By *sex composition*, I will refer to the pairing or grouping of individuals within relationships by sex (e.g., male–male, female–female, and so on).

[4] It may be tempting to interpret these null effects as evidence that men and women do not differ from each other in their levels of affectionate behavior. One must bear in mind, though, that statistical probability is biased in favor of null results. Using the conventional alpha error rate of .05 entails a 95% probability of achieving a null result by chance alone. Thus, one cannot have any reasonable confidence that a null effect is evidence that men and women are the same; rather, null results appropriately call for the suspension of judgment.

To my knowledge, no published research has found that men, at any age or in any context, express more affection than women do.

Not only do women express more affection overall than men do, but they are cognizant of this sex difference as well. D. H. Wallace (1981), in his study of affection in the family of origin, reported that women perceived themselves as having been more affectionate in their families of origin than men did, and that women perceived that they were still more affectionate than men were. In a diary study of affectionate behavior, Floyd (1997b) also found that women perceived themselves as being more affectionate than men did. Interestingly, this was one of the few studies that did not show a sex difference in *actual* behavior; the significant difference was only in *perceived* behavior.

Instead of (or in addition to) main effects for sex, some studies have reported that affectionate behavior within dyads is influenced by their sex composition. In her research, Noller (1978) videotaped interactions between 87 Australian parents and their 3- to 5-year-old children as the parents were dropping the children off at a child-care center. She later coded the videotapes for the number of "instances of interactive behavior that would normally be regarded as affectionate (e.g., kissing, cuddling, hugging)" and compared these frequency scores according to the sex of the parent and the sex of the child (p. 317). Her results indicated that father–daughter pairs were significantly more affectionate than father–son pairs, whereas there was no such difference in pairs involving mothers. Mother–child pairs were more affectionate, overall, than father–child pairs, however.

Shuntich and Shapiro (1991), in their verbal affection experiment, found that male–male dyads were significantly less affectionate than female–female or male–female dyads, the latter two of whom did not differ from each other. Moreover, Floyd and Voloudakis (1999a) reported that, in conversations between same-sex friends, women displayed greater nonverbal immediacy, expressiveness, and positive affect (as coded from videotapes) than did men; however, no sex differences in these behaviors were observed in conversations between opposite-sex friends. Although these two experiments presented their findings somewhat differently, they amount to the same pattern: *men are less affectionate than women in same-sex interaction but not in opposite-sex interaction.* The same pattern emerged in Bombar and Littig's (1996) questionnaire study about affectionate babytalk; men and women did not differ from each other in their likelihood of using babytalk with opposite-sex friends, but women were more likely than men to use it with same-sex friends. The pattern in Noller's study was only slightly different: boys were less affectionate than girls when interacting with fathers but not with mothers. Father–son dyads (which are male–male pairs) were the least affectionate of the four types, however, which is consistent with the findings of Shuntich and Shapiro, Floyd and Voloudakis, and Bombar and Littig.

Finally, some studies have examined the extent to which gender influences the amount of affection one communicates. Gender refers to one's psychological sex role orientation (i.e., masculine, feminine) rather than to one's biological sex, and it has been conceptually and operationally defined in various ways. Early approaches to measuring gender dichotomized masculinity and femininity, meaning that the more of one orientation a person was seen to have, the less he or she had of the other orientation. Being more masculine thus meant being less feminine, and vice versa (see, e.g., Gough, 1957). Bem (1974) reconceptualized masculinity and femininity as independent constructs, therefore allowing that an individual could actually score high on both (a case she referred to as being *androgynous*), or could score low on both (which she referred to as being *undifferentiated*). In the Bem Sex Role Inventory (BSRI), masculinity is operationally defined as including assertiveness, competitiveness, and aggressiveness, whereas femininity is operationalized as including compassion, responsiveness, and gentleness. Although they eschew the terms "masculinity" and "femininity," later definitions of the constructs, such as Richmond and McCroskey's (1990) Assertiveness-Responsiveness Scale (ARS), retain largely similar operational indicators of each.

The potential effects of gender on interpersonal behavior are particularly interesting to those who take a strong social learning theory perspective. Such a perspective suggests that men and women are not inherently different from each other in ways that ought to affect their behavior, with the obvious exception of reproductive behaviors. Any sex differences in behavior that are observed are therefore attributed to differences in role socialization – that is, in the ways that culture and upbringing socialize girls and boys to act. According to this perspective, males act in predominantly "masculine" ways, and females in predominantly "feminine" ways, because (and only because) their social and cultural influences have taught them to. This conceptualization makes sex differences more pliable than if they are grounded in biological differences. Presumably, therefore, females who are more masculine than feminine ought to act more like males than like other females, and vice versa.

Morman and Floyd (1999) began looking at the influences of gender on affectionate behavior in a study of fathers and their young adult sons. Given the evidence that women tend to be more affectionate than men, and that they perceive themselves as more affectionate than men, it seemed logical to predict that affectionate behavior is directly related to psychological femininity and inversely related to psychological masculinity. Indeed, Rane and Draper (1995) reported that both men and women described in written scenarios were judged to be less masculine when engaging in nurturant touch with young children than when not engaging in such touch, by participants who read the scenarios. Morman and Floyd advanced these predictions for verbal affection and direct nonverbal affection. However, because supportive affectionate behavior may be less recognizable as affectionate, they were unsure whether it would follow the same patterns with respect to gender, and so this issue was addressed in an open-ended research question.

Using the BSRI to define gender operationally, Morman and Floyd discovered that sons' femininity was directly associated with their own nonverbal and supportive affection and with their fathers' verbal, nonverbal, and supportive affection. Fathers' femininity was directly related only to their own supportive affection. These results fit the predictions. However, they also discovered that sons' masculinity was directly (rather than inversely) associated with their own nonverbal affection and with their fathers' verbal, nonverbal, and supportive affection. Moreover, fathers' masculinity was directly associated with their own verbal, nonverbal, and supportive affection.

These latter results were unexpected. One would not necessarily anticipate that stereotypically masculine qualities (e.g., aggression, competitiveness) are positively related to affectionate behavior, *especially* verbal and direct nonverbal affection and *especially* in male–male relationships, such as a father–son pair. Speculating that the results might be an artifact of a potentially outdated measure of gender roles, Morman and Floyd opted to use Richmond and McCroskey's (1990) ARS and examined the relationships again in a different study of men's affection with their adult sons (Floyd & Morman, 2000a). They elicited only fathers' reports in this study, but again discovered that fathers' verbal, nonverbal, and supportive affection were all directly related to fathers' femininity *and* directly related to their masculinity.

This replication suggested that the findings were not artifacts of the measurement. Because no explanation was evident, the extent to which the findings were unique to male–male relationships (or perhaps to father–son relationships in particular) was examined in two new replications. The first involved data collected for the Floyd (2003) project, although these data are not reported in that paper. In this project, adults completed the ARS and then reported on their verbal, nonverbal, and supportive affection with three targets: their mothers, their fathers, and a sibling (who was randomly selected if participants had more than one). Results indicated that participants' femininity was directly related to their verbal, nonverbal, and supportive affection for all three targets. Participants' masculinity was directly related to their verbal affection with their fathers and to their supportive affection with their siblings. The coefficients for all of these correlations are reported in Floyd and Mikkelson (2002).

The second replication was conducted during the Floyd and Tusing (2002) experiment, which involved opposite-sex pairs of adult platonic friends or romantic partners. Again using the ARS as the operational definition of gender, Floyd and Tusing found that participants' nonverbal and supportive affection were directly related to their femininity and also directly related to their masculinity (coefficients appear in Floyd & Mikkelson, 2002).

Considered in concert, the findings from these four studies warrant several observations. First, affectionate behavior is positively associated with femininity, which is of little surprise given the tendency of women to be more affectionate than men. Second, affectionate behavior is positively associated with masculinity, which is more puzzling. Third, the associations between affectionate behavior and masculinity are neither measurement-specific nor relationship-specific. Fourth, masculinity showed fewer significant associations with affectionate behavior than did femininity, and the magnitudes of its correlations were generally smaller than those for femininity. Fifth, however, all of the significant correlations between affection and masculinity identified in these studies (and, indeed, all of the nonsignificant ones) were positive; not once did masculinity shown an inverse association with any form of affectionate behavior in any relationship, as Morman and Floyd (1999) had originally hypothesized.

Individual Differences Other than Sex or Gender

Other aspects of individuals, besides their biological sex or gender role orientation, also appear to influence their level of affectionate behavior toward others. Floyd (2003) examined a number of individual- and relational-level characteristics to ascertain which ones would discriminate between people who, as a trait, are highly affectionate, and those who, as a trait, are rather nonaffectionate. Undergraduate students were given pairs of questionnaires and were asked to give one to "one of the most affectionate people you know" and the other to "one of the least affectionate people you know." The questionnaires included measures of a number of individual-level characteristics, including self-esteem, comfort with closeness and intimacy, importance of relationships, attachment styles, stress, depression, and overall mental health.

The "high affection" group consisted of 55 adults (16 male and 39 female), and the "low affection" group consisted of 54 adults (29 male and 25 female). The two groups did not differ from each other in terms of their age, level of education, level of income, ethnicity, or area of the United States in which they lived. They did, however, differ on a number of other characteristics. The findings of this study are discussed in greater detail in Chapter 5, but in summary, compared to low affection communicators, high affection communicators were more self assured, more comfortable with closeness and intimacy, in better mental health, less stressed and depressed, more likely to have a secure attachment style, and less likely to have a fearful-avoidant attachment style.

In the Floyd (2003) study, no relationship emerged between participants' trait levels of affectionate behavior and their ages (recall that the high affection and low affection groups did not differ from each other with respect to age). However, other studies have reported associations between age and affectionate communication. In their study of communication motives, for instance, Rubin, Perse, and Barbato (1988) found that older respondents were more likely than younger respondents to report communicating for the purpose of conveying affection. Other studies have drawn more direct associations between age and actual affectionate behavior. In two studies with children and adolescents, Eberly and Montemayor (1999) discovered that 6th-grade students were more affectionate than 8th- and 10th-grade students (the latter of whom did not differ significantly from each other), but also that 6th- and 8th-grade students were less affectionate toward their parents than 10th-grade students.

Research on father–son relationships has also found associations between age and affectionate communication. In a study of men's relationships with their preadolescent sons (ages 7 to 12 years), Salt (1991) reported that the sons' age was inversely related to the fathers' self-reported affectionate touch behavior and also to the number of affectionate touches actually observed in the study. The same pattern emerged in Floyd and Morman's (2000a) study of men's relationships with their adolescent and adult sons (ages 12 to 53 years). This study, which used the ACI as the operational definition of affectionate communication, found that sons' age was inversely related to fathers' self-reported affectionate behavior. Both of these studies suggest that fathers are more affectionate with younger sons than with older sons. Floyd and Morman (2000a) also reported a significant direct relationship between fathers' affectionate communication and fathers' own age. Thus, older fathers communicated more affection to their sons than did younger fathers.

Comparatively fewer studies have examined the effects of ethnicity on affectionate behavior, and among those that have, most have focused on touch. In one such study (Regan, Jerry, Narvaez, & Johnson, 1999), Asian and Latino heterosexual romantic dyads were unobtrusively observed while walking across the campus of California State University at Los Angeles. Coders observed each dyad for a period of 2 minutes and recorded any instances of touching behavior. Only half of the couples engaged in any form of touch during the 2-minute observation window. Those who did, however, were significantly more likely to be Latino than Asian. With respect to particular forms of touch, the authors found that Latino couples were more likely than Asian couples to engage in "one-arm embracing" (i.e., one person's arm draped across the shoulders of the other as the pair walks), although there was no significant difference in hand-holding. Regan and her colleagues explained their findings as being reflective of the difference between the "contact culture" of Latin America (which emphasizes personal proximity and touch) and the "noncontact culture" of Asia (at least, some parts of Asia; see McDaniel & Andersen, 1998). Likewise, other research has reported that Hispanic parents are considerably more physically affectionate with their children than are Caucasian parents (e.g., Calzada & Eyberg, 2002; Escovar & Lazarus, 1982).

Research comparing the touch behaviors of black and white participants has produced somewhat mixed results. In a review of studies examining black and white touch, Halberstadt (1985) reported that, in eight studies (Hall, 1974; Rinck, Willis, & Dean, 1980; Smith, Willis, & Gier, 1980; Williams & Willis, 1978; Willis & Hoffman, 1975; Willis & Reeves, 1976; Willis, Reeves, & Buchanan, 1976; Willis, Rinck, & Dean, 1978), black participants exhibited more touch than did white participants, and that this difference was stable for all age groups, from early childhood through adulthood. Halberstadt suggested that this behavioral difference reflects a difference in the social meaning of touch. Specifically, she contended that black participants touched each other to convey messages of community and to develop and maintain a sense of pride and solidarity, more than did white participants.

Contrary to these findings, a ninth study reviewed by Halberstadt (Reid, Tate, & Berman, 1989) reported that white preschool children touched, and stood closer to, white babies than black preschool children did with black babies. By way of explanation, Reid and colleagues suggested that expectations for the appropriateness of touch, at least with infants, might be more stringent in black families than in white families, causing black children to shy away from touching infants more than white children of comparable ages did. To investigate this possibility, Harrison-Speake and Willis (1995) studied differences between black and white adult respondents in their ratings of the appropriateness of several kinds of parent–child touch within families. These researchers approached shoppers in a Kansas City, Missouri, market and asked them to read 18 short scenes depicting various forms of parent–child touch, ranging from a child sitting on a parent's lap to a parent touching the child's genitals while tucking him or her into bed. The children in the scenarios were described as being either 2, 6, 10, or 14 years of age. Respondents (41% of whom were black and 59% of whom were white) rated the appropriateness of each scenario.

Harrison-Speake and Willis found a main effect of ethnicity, whereby white respondents reported higher appropriateness ratings than did black respondents. This main effect was qualified by numerous interactions effects involving the sex of the parent in the scenarios, the age of the child in the scenarios, and the type of touch being described.[5] Among the findings Harrison-Speake and Willis reported were that touch initiated by fathers was particularly viewed as less appropriate by black respondents than by white respondents. However, the differences between black and white participants also varied with the age of the child being described. For 2-year-old children, black respondents approved of parental touch more than did white respondents; this difference was reversed for 6-year-old and 10-year-old children, and for 14-year-old children, no difference between black and white respondents was observed.

Relationship Type

Although affectionate communication is influenced by aspects of individuals, it is also influenced by aspects of the relationships in which they

---

[5] Genital touches were excluded from these analyses for a lack of variance: nearly every respondent rated them as highly inappropriate, regardless of the sex of the parent or the age of the child.

communicate. Several studies have compared different types of relationships to each other, in terms of their tendencies to communicate affection in particular ways.

In their study of babytalk in adult relationships, Bombar and Littig (1996) found that, as predicted, people were more likely to use babytalk as a form of affectionate communication in their romantic relationships than in their platonic friendships. However, slightly more than half of their respondents (50.4%) reported having used babytalk in a platonic friendship, which suggests that the behavior is by no means exclusive to romantic relationships. Bombar and Littig also found that women were more likely than men to use babytalk with same-sex friends, but among opposite-sex friends no such difference was observed.

Two studies have shown that relationship types within families differ in terms of their levels of affectionate communication. Floyd and Morr (2003) examined affection exchange in the marital/sibling/sibling-in-law system. They collected data from triads consisting of a married couple and the biological sibling of one of the spouses. All three participants in each triad reported on the extent to which they communicated affection to the other two, using the ACI. The reports for verbal, nonverbal, and supportive affection were aggregated within each relationship, to form an affection score for that relationship (e.g., the two siblings' scores were averaged to form a score for the sibling relationship). When they analyzed these scores by relationship type, Floyd and Morr discovered a clear pattern in which people communicated the most affection within their marriages, less affection within their sibling relationships, and the least affection within their sibling-in-law relationships. All of the relationship-type differences were statistically significant for each of the three forms of affectionate communication.

Similarly, as part of the data collection for the Floyd (2003) study, participants were asked to report on their affectionate communication with their fathers and with their mothers. These data are not reported in the Floyd (2003) paper, so I will provide more detail on the analyses here. The reports of affectionate communication were analyzed by parental type (father vs. mother), affection type (verbal, nonverbal, support), and sex of the participant, and a significant three-way interaction effect emerged, $F(2, 346) = 22.96$, $p < .001$, partial $\eta^2 = .12$. The interaction effect was completely ordinal, indicating that one can interpret the significant main effects for parental type, $F(1, 346) = 120.40$, $p < .001$, partial $\eta^2 = .41$; for affection type, $F(2, 346) = 313.75$, $p < .001$, partial $\eta^2 = .65$; and for participant sex, $F(1, 173) = 5.86$, $p = .017$, partial $\eta^2 = .03$.

Table 3.1. *Means and Standard Deviations for Affectionate Communication with Mothers and Fathers from Floyd (2003)*

	Men		Women	
Affection Type	Fathers	Mothers	Fathers	Mothers
Support	4.96 (1.50)	5.54 (1.21)	5.13 (1.32)	5.84 (1.11)
Verbal	3.88 (1.72)	4.64 (1.59)	3.90 (1.55)	4.97 (1.53)
Nonverbal	2.51 (1.16)	3.98 (1.61)	3.43 (1.39)	4.04 (1.34)

Notes: Means are on a 1–7 scale wherein higher scores indicate greater amounts of affectionate communication. Standard deviations are in parentheses.

The means and standard deviations appear in Table 3.1. The pattern of differences was one in which participants were more affectionate with mothers than with fathers. Moreover, participants were most likely to communicate affection through supportive behaviors, less likely to communicate affection through verbal behaviors, and least likely to communicate affection through nonverbal behaviors. Finally, women reported being more affectionate than men.

Two studies also have examined differences between biological and nonbiological family relationships in terms of their levels of affectionate communication. On the basis of affection exchange theory, Floyd and Morman (2003) reasoned that, if affection is a resource that contributes to long-term viability and fertility, then parents ought to give more affection to their biological children, on average, than to their nonbiological children (e.g., stepchildren or adoptees) because such discrimination will further the parents' own reproductive success. They tested the prediction in a survey of nearly 500 American fathers who reported on their affectionate communication with either a biological or a nonbiological son. The subsamples of stepsons and adopted sons were too small to analyze separately, so they were combined for purposes of the comparison. Using the ACI as the operational definition of affectionate communication, Floyd and Morman found that fathers reported expressing more verbal, nonverbal, and supportive affection to biological sons than to nonbiological sons.

There is some disagreement in the literature on parental solicitude as to whether predictions made for stepchildren should necessarily generalize to adopted children (see, e.g., Daly & Wilson, 1995). To examine these relationships separately, Floyd and Morman replicated their study in two new surveys, which are reported in Floyd and Morman (2002). The first survey included only fathers' self-reports, whereas the second survey included the reports of both fathers and sons about the fathers' affectionate behavior. Both surveys had a more equal distribution of biological, step-, and adoptive father–son relationships than was the case in the earlier study, allowing for separate examinations of the three relationships. Results from both surveys indicated that fathers were more affectionate with biological and adoptive sons than with stepsons, but that biological and adoptive relationships did not differ significantly from each other.

Other experiments have examined the influence of relationship type on people's perceptions of the *appropriateness* of affectionate behavior. Floyd and Morman (1997) compared platonic friendships with sibling relationships and found that, overall, respondents considered it more appropriate to be affectionate with siblings than with friends. However, relationship type also interacted with the sex of the participant, such that the difference between siblings and friends was nonsignificant for women. That is, women did not report a difference in the appropriateness of affectionate communication with siblings and friends. Male respondents did report that they felt affectionate behavior was more appropriate with siblings than with friends. On the same note, men in the Morman and Floyd (1998) experiment reported believing that it was more appropriate for them to communicate affection to their brothers than to their male friends. Patterns similar to these have emerged in my survey (nonexperimental) research with siblings (see, e.g., Floyd, 1995, 1997a, b, c), and I suggested in those papers that the pattern reflects the culturally ingrained fear, inherent in the North American concept of masculinity, that overt affection displays between men may be interpreted as sexual overtures. Because of equally strong cultural proscriptions against incest, however, men appear to be less concerned about the risks of expressing overt affection to family members than to unrelated friends, *even if they actually feel more affection for their friends*. This topic is addressed in greater detail in Chapter 6.

Contextual Characteristics

Finally, aspects of communicative contexts or situations can influence affectionate behavior. Research on contextual influences has focused primarily on privacy and has produced some mixed findings, depending on the behaviors being examined and on whether reports of behaviors or judgments of their appropriateness have been sought. Bell and Healey (1992), for example, reported that participants in their study were more likely to express affection through the use of idioms in private settings (such as at home) than in public settings (such as at work). Respondents in Bombar and Littig's (1996) study similarly reported that they were more likely to communicate affection to friends or romantic partners through the use of babytalk in private contexts than in public ones. Conversely, however, when Floyd and Morman (1997) asked respondents to report on their perceptions of the appropriateness of affectionate behavior with friends or siblings, they discovered that affectionate behaviors were judged to be more appropriate in public settings than in private ones, a finding that was replicated for male respondents in Morman and Floyd (1998).

Why should the privacy level of the context matter, either in terms of people's actual affectionate behavior or in terms of their perceptions of appropriateness? Floyd and Morman (1997) suggested that the answer has partly to do with the risks involved in overtly communicating affection, particularly in nonromantic relationships such as friendships or family relationships. Certain risks, such as embarrassment over nonreciprocity, are mitigated by saving affection displays for private settings. Other risks, however, are mitigated by expressing affection publicly. For example, if I wonder whether a friend's affection display might be a romantic overture, I may be less concerned if the display occurs in a public setting, where I know that my friend realizes he or she is being seen and heard by others. That is, if my friend appears unconcerned about how onlookers might interpret the affection display, then I may be similarly unconcerned, whereas if the display occurred in private, I might be led to wonder why my friend waited for a private setting before conveying his or her affection.

One other aspect of the context that Floyd and Morman (1997) studied was its emotional intensity. Specifically, they predicted that affectionate behavior in nonromantic relationships ought to be considered less appropriate in emotionally neutral situations than in situations that are emotionally charged in some way. The reasoning was that the emotional intensity of a situation like a wedding, a graduation, or a funeral would make affection displays more common – and thus would mitigate any potential risks of such displays – than in situations that were not particularly charged emotionally. To test the prediction, they used a scenario method involving descriptions of a positively charged situation (in this case, a wedding), a negatively charged situation (a funeral), and a neutral situation (an interaction in a classroom). As hypothesized, they found that respondents rated affectionate behavior as more appropriate in the emotionally charged situations than in the emotionally neutral one. There was no difference between the positively and negatively charged situations. This finding was replicated with male respondents in Morman and Floyd (1998).

Considered collectively, the research reviewed in this chapter indicates that the encoding of affectionate messages is subject to individual, relational, and contextual influences that are numerous and sometimes interact with each other in complex ways. Is this evidence against the idea that human communication behavior might be governed by underlying biological causes? It would seem at first glance to be; the fact that just one type of behavior, affectionate communication, could be influenced by sex, gender, sex composition, age, ethnicity, relationship type, *and* the social context in which it occurs would seem to suggest that it is malleable, fleeting, and subject only to the demands of the socially constructed moment. In fact, however, this is not evidence of any such sort. A key aspect underlying biological explanations of human behavior (evolutionary explanations, in particular) is the idea that adaptations provide people with tools that must interact properly with their environments to be effective. As useful as affectionate communication can be in serving one's goals, affectionate behavior that is encoded in ways that are improper for the individual, relationship, or social context will tend to elicit social censure and will tend not to further the evolutionary goals of the encoder. A common misconception is that biological explanations for behavior are one-size-fits-all propositions, and that is simply not the case.

The recognition that affectionate behavior is influenced, at a proximal level, by numerous variables does not negate the idea that it may have biological underpinnings that influence it on a more ultimate level. Of course, neither does it prove such an idea. Rather, the findings reviewed in this chapter merely delineate what the primary proximal influences are and how they operate. From this starting point, researchers can investigate some important questions, such as the extent to which influences on encoding overlap influences on decoding, and the ways in which these influences *could* interact with more enduring biological forces to shape the process of affectionate interaction. I will begin to address these questions in subsequent chapters, but that discussion will only scratch the surface. Many more important and intriguing discoveries await communication researchers in these areas of inquiry.

4

Decoding and Responding
to Affectionate Expressions

We may not return the affection from those who like us, but
we always respect their good judgment.

— Libbie Fudim

The focus in the previous chapter was on the formulation of affectionate messages from the point of view of the sender. However, expressions
of affection are provocative events for receivers as well. When individuals are the recipients of affectionate behaviors they are typically called
on to make at least two assessments: first, are they correctly decoding
these behaviors as affectionate messages, and second, how should they
respond to them? This chapter will review research that has addressed
each of these issues and will articulate new questions in this area that
await empirical attention.

Decoding Behaviors as Affectionate

Competence in telling friend from foe is perhaps one of the most useful
human abilities in terms of individual and group survival. Affectionate
communication most assuredly plays a part in forming and maintaining
pair bonds and other significant relationships, but only to the extent that
one's affectionate overtures are decoded as such by recipients. As will be
illustrated in Chapter 6, incongruence between a sender's intention with
an affectionate message and a receiver's interpretation of that message is
one of the major sources of risk in communicating affection in the first
place. For these reasons, this section will discuss research on the decoding
of affectionate behaviors.

The body of research on decoding is small, relative to the larger numbers of studies that have addressed how affection is encoded and how

people react to affectionate expressions. This could very well reflect a "social meaning" assumption, wherein researchers presume congruence between how people encode and decode a given relational message, and thus tend not to examine that congruence in detail (see, e.g., Burgoon & Newton, 1991). This is likely a safe assumption; one can easily imagine how disjointed communication efforts would be if there were large gaps in how the same messages were encoded and decoded. There is still something to be learned by examining the decoding of affectionate behavior in greater detail, however. The few studies that have done so can be divided into two focus areas. Those in the first group have examined congruence between particular behaviors and affectionate interpretations; thus, they indicate *which behaviors are the most likely to be decoded as affectionate*. Those in the second group have focused on intensity ratings for affectionate expressions; these studies indicate *which behaviors communicate affection the most intensely*. I will describe findings from each group of studies separately.

Congruence between Behaviors and Affectionate Interpretations

The previous chapter described a tripartite model of affectionate behavior in which expressions of affection were categorized as either being direct verbal statements, direct nonverbal gestures, or provisions of affectionate social support. Research on the congruence between specific behaviors and affectionate interpretations has thus far focused solely on behaviors in the second category, nonverbal gestures. This may be because direct verbal expressions are relatively unambiguous in their affectionate intentions (statements such as "I like you," "I love you," or "I feel close to you" are quite obviously gestures of affection), and because provisions of social support serve associated instrumental purposes (i.e., meeting whatever needs prompted them), and so their affectionate intentions are often secondary. Neither of these is a particularly *good* reason for failing to examine decoding in greater detail. On the contrary, I believe that more attention needs to be paid to decoding, particularly with affectionate social support (given that it is a relatively common means of communicating affection in many relationships), and will offer some specific research questions on this topic in this chapter.

The most direct examinations of the congruence between particular behaviors and affectionate decoding were provided in studies by Ray and Floyd (2000) and by Palmer and Simmons (1995). In the Ray and

Floyd study, pairs of college students (one of whom was induced to be a participant confederate) interacted with each other in two short conversations in a laboratory. Before the second conversation, confederates were instructed either to greatly increase, or greatly decrease, the extent to which they communicated messages of liking and affection to their partners, but they were not given any instructions as to the particular behaviors they should use to accomplish this task, except that they should enact the manipulation nonverbally, rather than verbally. The confederates' nonverbal behaviors during the second conversation were extensively coded and compared to their partners' reports of how affectionate the confederates were, and also to the reports of third-party observers who were watching the conversations on a closed-circuit television.

Most of the associations with nonverbal behaviors are reported in the Ray and Floyd (2000) paper. In line with the advice of Burgoon and Le Poire (1999), coding of the confederates included both their micro-level behaviors (e.g., smiling, head nodding, body orientation) and also macro-level perceptions of their behaviors (e.g., how friendly, pleasant, and involved confederates were being). Ray and Floyd then examined correlations between these behaviors and perceptions and participants' and observers' reports of how affectionate the confederates were being during the second conversation.

Two patterns evident in the results were noteworthy. First, several behaviors were significantly associated with reports of affection. The correlation coeffcients, including the nonsignificant correlations, appear in Table 4.1. With respect to discrete, micro-level behaviors, affection was directly related to facial animation, smiling, head nodding (as a type of backchanneling behavior), the use of illustrator gestures, eye contact, and vocal pitch variation. Participants' reports of confederates' affection were also directly related to the confederates' forward lean, and observers' reports of confederates' affection were inversely related to the confederates' use of other-adaptor gestures (behaviors like picking lint off of someone else's clothing). With respect to macro-level perceptions, affection was directly related to pleasantness, friendliness, warmth, involvement, and how participative and interested confederates appeared to be.

For exploratory purposes, Ray and Floyd also examined whether any linear combinations of the behaviors would predict assessments of confederates' affection levels better than the individual behaviors did themselves. They ascertained this by regressing reports of affection

Table 4.1. *Correlations between Confederates' Nonverbal Behaviors and Participants' and Observers' Reports of Confederates' Affection Level, from Ray and Floyd (2000)*[1]

Behavior	Participants' Report	Observers' Report
Animation	.34**	.32*
Smiling	.40**	.28*
Head nodding	.32*	.42**
Illustrators	.29*	.47**
Self-adaptors	.01	.11
Other-adaptors	−.22	−.32*
Gaze	.43**	.35**
Proximity	.23	.18
Forward lean	.26*	.14
Postural matching	−.19	−.01
Direct body orientation	.06	.03
Vocal pitch	−.17	−.19
Vocal pitch variance	.47**	.43**
Vocal intensity	−.03	−.04
Vocal intensity variance	.18	.00
Talk time	.06	.20
Pleasantness	.40**	.38**
Friendliness	.37**	.38**
Warmth	.40**	.29*
Involvement	.41**	.48**
Participativeness	.41**	.47**
Interest	.42**	.46**

Notes: $^*p < .05$; $^{**}p < .01$.
[1] Probability values are one-tailed for animation, smiling, gaze, proximity, forward lean, postural matching, vocal pitch variance, pleasantness, friendliness, warmth, involvement, participativeness, and interest. Probability values are two-tailed for the remaining behaviors.

level on the behaviors in stepwise analyses, which do not presume any hierarchical ordering of the predictor variables but test for all possible linear combinations. The regressions indicated that a combination of vocal pitch variance and warmth best predicted participants' assessments of confederates' affection level (adjusted $R^2 = .27$), whereas observers' assessments of confederates' affection level was best predicted by a combination of illustrator gestures and pitch variance (adjusted $R^2 = .25$).

The second aspect of the results that is noteworthy is the degree of correspondence between participants' and observers' reports. This follows from the social meaning orientation to nonverbal behavior, mentioned above. Participants' and observers' points of view diverged for only two behaviors (forward lean and other adaptors), and these differences were only in terms of statistical significance: the correlation between the behavior and the report of affection level was significant for one person but not for the other. In no case (including the nonsignificant correlations) was a behavior directly related to participants' assessments but inversely related to observers', or vice versa. Certainly, that doesn't mean that the distinction between participants and observers is a trivial one; as discussed below, the difference between these points of view has implications for reactions to affectionate behavior (especially cognitive reactions). It does, however, lend credence to the idea behind the social meaning orientation to nonverbal behavior by indicating that, with few exceptions, conversational participants and third-party observers converged in their decoding of confederates' behaviors.

Although acoustic analyses of confederates' voices were included in the behaviors reported in the Ray and Floyd (2000) paper, further analyses of these variables appear in a later paper by Floyd and Ray (2003). The latter paper contains hierarchical regression analyses using the participants' and observers' reports of confederates' affection levels as criterion variables. Control variables were the sex of the confederate and the confederates' talk time, measured in seconds. The predictor variables were confederates' vocalic fundamental frequency (F_0), variance in fundamental frequency, and vocalic loudness. Working from affection exchange theory, Floyd and Ray hypothesized that F_0 and variance in F_0 would both show direct relationships with participants' and observers' reports of confederates' affection levels, whereas loudness would show an inverse relationship with these outcome measures.

For F_0, observers' reports manifested the predicted linear relationship. Participants' reports were subject to a sex-by-F_0 interaction effect, however, which indicated that the predicted linear relationship held for female confederates only. For male confederates, F_0 was inversely related to participants' reports of their affection level, which was contrary to the hypothesis. Both participants' and observers' reports of confederates' affection levels were linearly related to confederates' variance in F_0, as hypothesized. Contrary to the prediction, however, neither participants' nor observers' reports were significantly related to confederates' vocal loudness (although both relationships were inverse, as expected).

The Palmer and Simmons (1995) experiment was designed to focus on expressions of liking, which is certainly implicated in affection. In their study, participant confederates were induced to show either increased or decreased liking for a naïve partner, using nonverbal behaviors. The partners were then asked to indicate their levels of liking for the confederates. Palmer and Simmons looked to see which nonverbal behaviors were most strongly associated with changes in participants' levels of liking for the confederates. They did not code for as many behaviors as did Ray and Floyd; however, their results were similar to those of the latter study. Specifically, Palmer and Simmons found that participants' judgments of liking for confederates were associated with increases in three of the confederates' behaviors: eye contact, smiling, and the use of object-focused gestures (which are referred to in the Ray and Floyd paper as "illustrator gestures"). They also had predicted that liking would be directly associated with head nodding and inversely associated with the use of self-adaptor gestures, although neither of these associations was significant.

Perhaps the most warranted conclusion to be drawn from these two studies is that there is a "core" set of behaviors that people tend to decode as expressions of liking or affection. These behaviors tend to be those that convey interest in, and attraction toward, the recipient (e.g., smiling, gaze), and those that convey involvement in the interaction (e.g., facial and vocal animation, head nodding). Certainly, just because each of these behaviors is decoded as an expression of affection, this does not suggest that the behaviors are equal in their intensity or in the magnitude with which they convey affectionate intentions. I take up the issue of intensity in the next section.

Ratings of Intensity for Affectionate Expressions

Although there are numerous ways to encode affectionate expressions, decoders tend not to attribute the same level of intensity to all of them. The statement "I like you" and the statement "I'm in love with you" are both affectionate verbal behaviors, but they clearly differ from each other in the *type* and *amount* of affection they convey. Thus, besides looking at which behaviors convey affection in the first place, it is also instructive to look at variation in intensity.

Two studies have elicited ratings of intensity for affectionate expressions. The first, by Shuntich and Shapiro (1991), focused on verbal behaviors only. The authors constructed a list of 10 verbal statements that were meant to convey to the receiver that "the person saying the statement feels positively toward her/him and is trying to convey this feeling" (p. 285). They then presented the list to a group of 102 undergraduate students (46 male, 56 female) and asked the students to rate each statement on a 7-point scale in which high scores meant "high intensity" and low scores meant "low intensity."

The means for each of the 10 statements appear in Table 4.2. The most intense statements on Shuntich and Shapiro's list were "I care for you very much" (mean intensity rating = 6.34) and "I like you very much" (mean intensity rating = 6.32). Because they intended to use these statements in later experiments with platonic pairs, Shuntich and Shapiro did not include statements dealing with love or being in love; presumably, these would have elicited higher intensity ratings. The least intense statements on the list were "I think you're OK" (mean = 3.51) and "I think you are sort of nice" (mean = 3.34). In a later experiment, Shuntich and Shapiro found that participants who were the receivers of affectionate statements from their list, as opposed to aggressive or neutral statements, judged the senders as being less hostile, less violent, less aggressive, warmer, and of course, more affectionate.

A later study by Floyd (1997b) expanded somewhat on Shuntich and Shapiro's efforts by asking participants to rate the intensity of a list of behaviors that included both verbal and nonverbal expressions of affection. The verbal statements included expressions of love, liking, and admiration, and the nonverbal behaviors included hugging, kissing, holding hands, and other affectionate gestures. As in the Shuntich and Shapiro study, undergraduate students (65 male, 71 female) rated each behavior for intensity; however, the Floyd study used a 5-point scale instead of a 7-point scale. Higher numbers indicated greater intensity. Means for all of the behaviors appear in Table 4.2.

In this study, the behaviors that elicited the highest intensity ratings were kissing on the lips and saying "I love you." Both earned a mean intensity rating of 4.64 out of a possible 5.00. Shaking hands was judged to be the least intense nonverbal affectionate behavior (mean = 1.27), and saying "I admire you" received the lowest intensity rating among the verbal statements (mean = 1.91).

Why is the issue of intensity consequential? Because it directly implicates the *value* decoders place on various affectionate behaviors.

Table 4.2. *Intensity Ratings for Verbal and Nonverbal Expressions of Affection from Shuntich and Shapiro (1991) and Floyd (1997b)*

Behavior	Intensity Rating
Verbal Statements from Shuntich and Shapiro[1]	
"I think you are sort of nice."	3.34
"I think you're OK."	3.51
"I think you are interesting."	4.29
"I think you are pleasant."	4.34
"I like you."	5.31
"I admire you."	5.35
"I value you a great deal."	5.77
"I'm very fond of you."	5.80
"I like you very much."	6.32
"I care for you very much."	6.34
Verbal Statements from Floyd[2]	
"I admire you."	1.91
"I value our relationship."	2.46
"I like you."	2.91
"I'm fond of you."	3.18
"I feel close to you."	3.64
"I care for you."	4.27
"I love you."	4.64
Nonverbal Behaviors from Floyd	
Shake hands	1.27
Put arm around shoulder	2.00
Hold hands	2.36
Kiss on cheek	3.63
Hug	3.73
Kiss on lips	4.64

Notes:
[1] Ratings from Shuntich and Shapiro (1991) were made on 1–7 scales.
[2] Ratings from Floyd (1997b) were made on 1–5 scales. In both cases, higher mean scores indicate greater intensity of the behavior.

Numerous theories in both the evolutionary and social learning paradigms capitalize on the concept of exchange: the give and take of things of value. Affection often functions as one such commodity; as discussed later (and also in Chapter 6), reciprocating one affectionate expression (e.g., "I'm in love with you") with another of lesser intensity (e.g., "I think you're neat") can cause distress for the sender, whose positive face is likely to be highly threatened by such a move. The "commodities" being exchanged in such an interaction are of unequal value; specifically, they are of unequal relational value. For this reason it is important for affection researchers to be cognizant not only of the *amount* of affection being communicated by study participants but also of the *intensity* being communicated.

The body of research that has examined the decoding of affectionate behaviors is small, but its findings are relatively consistent. By contrast, several studies have investigated how decoders react and respond to expressions of affection. This research is described subsequently.

Responding to Expressions of Affection

Expressions of affection are significant communicative events and they rarely fail to elicit some type of reaction from receivers. Of course, people do not always respond to affectionate behaviors in ways that senders wish; indeed, neither do they always respond in ways that senders can even perceive. Uncertainty about a receiver's response is one of the major risks to expressing affection in the first place. What determines how receivers of affectionate messages respond to them? This section reviews research that has addressed this question. Importantly, one must distinguish between two major types of responses: cognitive responses and behavioral responses. The former concerns judgments and interpretations that receivers make, and the latter concerns the behaviors that receivers enact in response to the message. Although these two types of responses are often complementary, it is important to discuss them individually because they do not necessarily covary.

Responding Cognitively to Affectionate Expressions

A good deal of research has addressed people's cognitive responses to affectionate behaviors. Participants in some studies acted as receivers, responding to expressions of affection that were directed at them. In other studies, participants acted as observers and responded to behaviors they witnessed. To make sense of this research, one must first distinguish between three types of cognitive responses (these apply to people's cognitive responses to all behaviors, not just affectionate messages). The first are *evaluations*, which deal with the valence of people's judgments about a behavior: is the behavior positive or negative? The second are *interpretations*, which pertain to people's sense-making judgments about a behavior: what does the behavior mean?[1] Finally, cognitions of the third type, *attributions*, pertain to people's inferences about the cause of a behavior: why did the behavior occur? Although most of the studies reviewed in this section have examined only one of these types of cognitive responses, those that have included more than one type have tended to find correspondence between them (i.e., positive evaluations coincide with positive interpretations or positive attributions).

This section reviews research that has investigated each of these three types of cognitive responses. The focus will be on identifying the antecedents of cognitive responses – that is, on what makes someone evaluate an affectionate expression negatively instead of positively, or attribute it to a favorable cause rather than an unfavorable one.

Evaluations. Several studies have examined how people evaluate expressions of affection, either as receivers of those expressions or as third-party observers. The question undergirding an evaluative response is one of valence: is the received (or observed) behavior good or bad, positive or negative, appropriate or inappropriate? Approaches to measuring evaluative responses have ranged from *ad hoc*, single-item bipolar adjective scales (such as a 1–7 scale on which the low end signifies "negative" or "inappropriate" and the high end signifies "positive" or "appropriate") to validated, multiple-item measures (such as the four-item evaluation measure developed by Burgoon, Newton, Walther, & Baesler, 1989).

As I discuss each study later, I will note how evaluation was assessed, because this can influence the appropriate interpretation of the findings. For instance, a rating of appropriateness may be more context-specific than a rating of positivity; some behaviors may be appropriate for certain individuals in certain situations, whereas other behaviors could be judged as inherently negative, regardless of the context. Thus, although ratings of appropriateness and ratings of positivity are both evaluative measures, they may tap different aspects of an evaluation.

Research on the evaluation of affectionate communication can readily be divided into two categories: those studies that have evaluated changes in people's overall levels of affectionate behavior, and those studies that

---

[1] When I speak here of *interpretations*, I am not referring to the act of decoding (e.g., waving means "hello"), but rather to the act of assigning broader relational meaning to a given message (e.g., waving means friendliness).

have evaluated specific affectionate expressions (and have examined the variables that influence those evaluations). Studies in the former category have been laboratory experiments in which participants evaluated the behavior of a confederate who behaved in an increasingly engaged, affectionate way during a conversation or else decreased his or her level of engagement and affection. Experiments by Floyd and Mikkelson (2004), Floyd and Ray (in press), and Floyd and Voloudakis (1999a), each of which used the Burgoon et al. (1989) evaluation scale, have all reported the same overall pattern: participants' evaluations of confederates become more positive as the confederates become more affectionate, and become more negative as the confederates become less affectionate.

This is certainly no surprise; given the importance of affectionate communication in relational interaction, one should absolutely expect that people will evaluate it positively *in the absence of reasons not to*. Notably, this does not mean there are no valid reasons to react negatively to affectionate behavior; indeed, the risks of affectionate communication are examined in detail in Chapter 6. Neither does it suggest that all affectionate behaviors in all contexts will be positively evaluated. Research has shown that several aspects of affectionate exchanges, including characteristics of the communicators and of the behaviors themselves, influence how those behaviors are evaluated. To identify those aspects, let us turn our attention to research on particular forms of affectionate communication.

Of the studies that have addressed evaluations of specific affectionate behaviors, most have focused on affectionate touch. Some have used the scenario method, wherein participants respond to written descriptions of a situation. Rane and Draper (1995), for instance, studied evaluations of men's and women's nurturant touching of young children, using written scenarios. The scenarios they created for the study varied according to whether (a) the subject of the scenario was a man or woman; (b) the subject did or did not engage in nurturant touching with children; (c) the children in the scenario were the subject's own children or were neighbor children; and (d) the context of the scenario was a bedtime setting or a playground setting. Nurturant touching included hugging, giving back rubs, holding a child on one's lap, putting an arm around a child's shoulder, and holding a child to comfort him or her. Participants in the study, who were undergraduate students, each read one of the scenarios and provided an evaluation of the "goodness" of the adult subject in the story. Rane and Draper measured evaluation by summing the ratings participants gave on three bipolar adjective scales: pleasant/unpleasant, well adjusted/maladjusted, and good/bad.

Two results were particularly noteworthy with respect to evaluation. First, story characters who engaged in nurturant touching were evaluated more positively than those who did not, and this difference was more pronounced for female than for male characters. Interestingly, although participants evaluated male characters who engaged in nurturant touching more positively than those who did not, they also rated the nurturantly touching males as being less masculine than the nontouchers.[2] The latter result replicated one identified earlier by Draper and Gordon (1986) in a study of men's perceptions of nurturing behavior in other men. Rane and Draper suggested that the inverse relationship between touching and ratings of masculinity could reflect men's unwillingness to engage in nurturant touching for fear of appearing feminine. Alternatively, one might speculate that, because men's nurturant touching was judged as *both* less masculine *and* more positive than the absence of touch, masculinity is not an especially prized quality when it comes to men's (and particularly, fathers') nurturant interactions with young children.[3]

The second finding of interest was that participants evaluated male story characters with their own children and female story characters with a neighbor's children more positively than they evaluated males with a neighbor's children and females with their own children. Rane and Draper interpreted this finding as reflecting a stereotypical view that women are better suited than men to provide care for young children who are not their own.

Harrison-Speake and Willis (1995) also studied adult-to-child touch within the context of the family using a scenario method. Unlike in Rane and Draper's study, their scenarios depicted adults interacting only with their own children, and they varied the sex of the child as well as the sex of the parent. They also varied the age of the child (2, 6, 10, and 14 years of age), and they separately described four different touch sequences: child sitting on parent's lap, parent kissing child on the lips, parents and

---

[2] The masculinity score was the sum of participants' ratings on two adjective pairs: masculine/feminine, and manly/womanly.

[3] Curiously, there is evidence that at least one physiological marker of masculinity, testosterone level, decreases in men as they become fathers. Gray, Kahlenberg, Barrett, Lipson, and Ellison (2002) reported such a decrease, speculating that it reflects nature's way of preparing men for the more nurturant role they would be required to play if their children were to have the best chances for survival (see also Storey, Walsh, Quinton, & Wynne-Edwards, 2000).

child sleeping together in the same bed, and parent giving child a bath.[4] Participants, who were adults approached at a shopping center, read all of the scenarios and provided an evaluation for each, using a single-item bipolar adjective scale with "very appropriate" and "very inappropriate" as the anchors.

Several main and interaction effects achieved significance in the Harrison-Speake and Willis study. For simplicity's sake I will focus here on the most relevant findings, the first of which was that participants evaluated mothers more positively than fathers in the kissing, bathing, and lap-sitting scenarios, and the differences between mothers and fathers were greater for older children than for younger children. Other research has suggested that, as their children age, men decrease their affectionate communication to their children more than women do (see, e.g., Morman & Floyd, 1999; Salt, 1991), and this finding supports that speculation. Harrison-Speake and Willis offered that men may especially curtail their affectionate touch as their children age, given the likelihood that male touch could be seen as sexual.

Moreover, participants evaluated the touch scenarios involving kissing and lap-sitting more positively when the child depicted was a girl rather than a boy. This was true regardless of the age of the child or the sex of the parent, and it confirmed Jourard's (1966) earlier finding that daughters receive more parental touch than do sons.

The findings from these two scenario studies are useful in that they identify specific influences on people's evaluative responses to affectionate expressions. Importantly – but perhaps not surprisingly – many of these variables parallel those that influence how affectionate people are in the first place: the sex of the person enacting the behavior, the sex of the person receiving the behavior, the nature of the relationship between them, the form that the affectionate behavior takes, and the context in which it occurs. This discussion will return to this point later.

Evidence that the form of an affectionate touch can directly influence evaluations of it also comes from an experiment that manipulated the form and duration of an embrace (Floyd, 1999). In that study, participants watched a videotape of two actors enacting one of three forms of an embrace (a "criss-cross" hug, in which each person has one arm over and one arm under the shoulder of the other; a "neck-waist" hug, in which one person's arms are around the other's neck, and the other person's

---

[4] Data from a fifth touch sequence, parents touching child's genitals, were excluded from analyses for a lack of variance on participants' evaluation scores.

arms are around the other's waist; and an "engulfing" hug, in which one person's arms are pulled to his or her chest and the other's arms completely envelop him or her) for one of three durations (1 second, 3 seconds, or 5 seconds). These conditions were crossed with the sex-pairing of the actors (either male–male or female–female) to create 18 experimental conditions. Participants evaluated the scenario they watched by completing the four-item evaluation scale developed by Burgoon et al. (1989).

These specific forms of the embrace were chosen to represent differing levels of egalitarianism in the behavior. That is, because the criss-cross hug was the most "balanced" in terms of the relative physical positioning of the two participants, I speculated that it would be judged by observers as being the most egalitarian. I further expected that the neck-waist hug would be seen as less egalitarian, and that the engulfing hug would be seen as the least egalitarian of the three. A manipulation check using the equality subscale of Burgoon and Hale's (1987) Relational Communication Scale confirmed these speculations.

Unlike in the Rane and Draper (1995) or Harrison-Speake and Willis (1995) studies, neither the sex of the actors nor the sex of the participants, alone or in combination, exerted any influence on evaluations in the Floyd (1999) study. However, both the form of the embrace and its duration had main effects on participants' evaluations. Specifically, participants evaluated the criss-cross hug the most positively, followed by the neck-waist hug and then by the engulfing hug. Expressed differently, evaluations declined in positivity as the embraces moved from more to less egalitarian. Participants also preferred shorter hugs over longer ones: the 1-second embrace was evaluated the most positively, followed (interestingly) by the 5-second embrace and then by the 3-second embrace (focused contrasts indicated, however, that only the 1- and 3-second hugs differed significantly from each other, whereas neither differed significantly from the 5-second hug).

Do these findings indicate that people are most favorably disposed to brief, egalitarian hugs? Perhaps in this particular context they are, although it is important to note that the actors in the videotapes were all students in their early -20s, interacting in same-sex pairs, and so participants probably attributed a good deal of egalitarianism to the relationships between the actors anyway. In fact, when asked to speculate as to what kind of relationship the actors in each videotape had to each other, participants were substantially more likely to conclude that the actors were friends, as opposed to relatives. This suggests the question:

**In relationships that appear to be less egalitarian by nature than friend-
ships (such as a parent–child or older sibling–younger sibling relationship), do observers evaluate longer and less egalitarian embraces more
positively than shorter, more egalitarian ones?** There is reason to suspect
that they would, although the question awaits empirical test.

Other studies have investigated the evaluation of affectionate behaviors other than touch. The Floyd and Morman (2000b) experiment, for
instance, looked at evaluative responses to verbal affection, specifically
the verbal expression of love. Participants in that study read a short transcript of a conversation occurring either between two females or two
males in which one communicator conveyed "I love you" to the other.
The transcript stimulus was chosen over an audio or video recording so
as to isolate the verbal channel and remove the possibility that nonverbal
cues, such as facial expression or tone of voice, would be rival explanations for the effects. As in Floyd (1999), participants provided their
evaluations of the interaction they read by responding to the evaluation
scale created by Burgoon et al. (1989).

Whereas no effects of actor or participant sex were found for evaluations of touch in the Floyd (1999) experiment, the Floyd and Morman
(2000b) results indicated that participants' sex interacted with the sex of
the communicators depicted in the transcripts to influence the participants' evaluations. The interaction effect is depicted in Figure 4.1. As the
figure shows, both male and female participants evaluated the conversations more positively when the expression of affection occurred between
two women than when it occurred between two men, and there was almost
no difference in the evaluations that male and female participants gave to
the female–female conversation. This is similar to the finding, reported
by Harrison-Speake and Willis (1995), that women engaging in affectionate touch were evaluated more positively than were men engaging in the
same touches.

Male and female participants disagreed more strongly in their evaluations of the male–male affectionate exchange, however. Female participants evaluated it only slightly more positively than they had evaluated the women's conversation. Male participants, by contrast, evaluated
male–male affection more negatively than they evaluated female–female
affection, and much more negatively than the female participants had
evaluated either conversation. An earlier experiment (Floyd & Morman,
1997) similarly found that women did not differentiate between female–
female and opposite-sex platonic relationships in terms of their evaluation of affection (measured in that experiment using a single-item bipolar

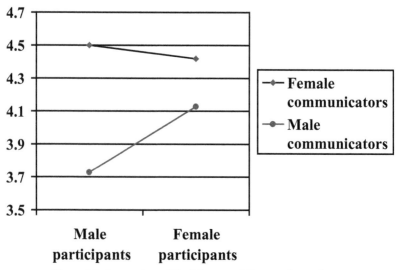

Figure 4.1. Interaction of Participant and Communicator Sex on Participants' Evaluations of Communicators' Affection Behaviors, from Floyd and Morman (2000b)

adjective scale with "very appropriate" and "very inappropriate" as the anchors). Men, however, reported that affectionate behavior was significantly more appropriate in opposite-sex platonic pairs than in male–male dyads. The 1997 experiment used a battery of verbal and nonverbal behaviors as the operational definition of affection, instead of a single touch or verbal behavior. Also found was that affectionate behavior was evaluated more positively when it occurred between siblings than between unrelated friends, and this difference between relationships was substantially more pronounced for men than for women.

Studying the evaluations that receivers assign to affection expressions provides one barometer for their cognitive reactions. In some ways, the judgment of whether a given behavior is positive or negative is the most basal of judgments one can make. However, it is often accompanied by other, perhaps more complex cognitive reactions, including interpretations and attributions. We turn our attention to interpretations next.

Interpretations. The issue of interpretations concerns the relational meanings that decoders ascribe to communication behaviors. Nearly 40 years ago, Watzlawick, Beavin, and Jackson (1967), in one of the foundational works of the human communication discipline, distinguished between the *content* and *relational* dimensions of messages. A given verbal message, for instance, conveys both a literal meaning and also an implied meaning about the relationship in which it is communicated. If one person says to a friend "I feel scared about the future," the content dimension of the statement is its literal message (the speaker feels scared about the future). However, the statement may also implicitly convey relational messages to the hearer, such as: "I trust you," "I feel I can be vulnerable with you," or "I want you to protect me." In truth, there are several types of relational messages that a given behavior can convey. In their seminal work on relational communication, Burgoon and Hale (1984) proposed that there are as many as a dozen conceptually distinct types of relational meanings that a given behavior might communicate, which include meanings of dominance, emotional arousal, composure, similarity, formality, task versus social orientation, intimacy, depth/familiarity, attraction/liking, inclusion, trust, and involvement. Most studies using Burgoon and Hale's (1987) measure have combined these relational messages, through factor analyses, into a smaller number of more conceptually and empirically orthogonal themes (typically between three and seven).[5] Other meanings that are often examined in this type of research include attraction and credibility.

What kinds of relational meanings do affectionate behaviors convey? One could certainly intuit that they would tend to communicate messages of interest, attraction, or intimacy, but do decoders attach other types of relational interpretations to them, as well? Four experiments have examined this question, the earliest of which was the Floyd and Voloudakis (1999a) study of adult platonic friends. In that study, friends interacted in the laboratory and one friend in each pair was induced to increase or decrease his or her affectionate behaviors toward the other. Before and after the manipulation, the naïve participants' relational interpretations of the confederates' behaviors were assessed using Burgoon and Hale's (1987) relational communication scale, McCroskey and McCain's (1974) interpersonal attraction scale (which measures both *social attraction*, or attraction to one's personality, and *task attraction*, or attraction to one's abilities), and McCroskey and Young's (1981) credibility scale (which measures both *competence* and the quality of one's *character*).

[5] In fact, Dillard, Solomon, and Palmer (1999) proposed that relational meanings can be collapsed into two superordinate factors: dominance and affiliation.

Several of these assessments were affected by the confederates' affectionate behaviors. Specifically, confederates who became more affectionate over time were judged by their friends as conveying more immediacy, being more receptive, being more composed, having more positive character, being more informal, and seeing themselves as more similar to the participants. Those confederates who became less affectionate over time received the opposite assessments. There were no significant effects in this study for dominance, equality, or attraction.

In the Floyd and Voloudakis study the participant confederates were instructed to increase or decrease their affectionate behaviors toward their partners but were not given any instruction as to the specific behaviors to manipulate. Numerous manipulation checks confirmed the efficacy of the manipulation; however, it is difficult to know *which* behaviors, in particular, contributed to changes in participants' relational message interpretations. Ray and Floyd (2000) examined the links between specific affection behaviors and relational message interpretations more directly, although this study looked only at the confederates' social attractiveness as an outcome measure. The design of the Ray and Floyd experiment was nearly identical to that used by Floyd and Voloudakis, except that strangers were used instead of friends and each dyad had a third-party observer who also provided assessments of the confederates. Ray and Floyd found that participants' social attraction to the confederates was directly related to how much the confederates smiled, nodded their heads, maintained eye contact, leaned forward, maintained proximity, and varied the pitch in their voices. Observers' social attraction to the confederates was likewise predicted by head nodding, eye contact, and vocal pitch variation, as well as to how much the confederates talked to the participants. These results are informative, and other research has investigated the links between specific behaviors and particular relational message interpretations (see, e.g., Burgoon & Le Poire, 1999). Further experimentation on this topic could address some intriguing questions. For instance, **how does variation in the context of an interaction influence the relational message interpretations of specific affectionate behaviors?** Might a given behavior, such as saying "I love you," elicit some types of relational message interpretations (e.g., intimacy, attraction) in one social context but other interpretations (e.g., dominance) in a different one? If so, then identification of those antecedent conditions could have important implications for understanding why the same affectionate behavior can sometimes be judged positively by a receiver and, other times, be judged negatively.

It is certainly the case, however, that expressions of affection often involve a combination of behaviors (e.g., smiling, touching, maintaining eye contact, increasing vocal warmth, and saying "I care about you" all in tandem), rather than single behaviors in isolation. Two other studies have examined relational message interpretations of affectionate behavior using multicue manipulations (i.e., those in which confederates manipulate several affection behaviors at once). Unlike the Floyd and Voloudakis study, both of these involved trained confederates interacting with strangers. In the first (Floyd, 1998), confederates were instructed to modify six behaviors during an experimental interaction with a naïve participant: smiling, gaze, touch, proximity, forward lean, and postural matching. Confederates in the "high affection" condition were specifically trained to smile a great deal, maintain moderate but consistent gaze with participants, touch participants during the interaction, sit close to participants, lean forward while speaking, and match the way participants were sitting (in terms of their arm and leg positions). Confederates in the "low affection" condition were given the opposite instructions. As in the other experiments, participants were asked to rate confederates in terms of their relational messages after the conversations.

In this study, significant differences between the high and low affection groups were observed for only three relational messages: competence, composure, and intimacy. In all cases, confederates in the high affection condition were rated higher than those in the low affection condition, as one might expect. Given the number of associations between affectionate behaviors and relational message interpretations identified in the Floyd and Voloudakis and the Ray and Floyd studies, it was surprising to find differences on only three such messages in the Floyd (1998) study. One methodological characteristic of the Floyd (1998) study that distinguished it from the others, however, was that it used a between-subjects design instead of a repeated-measures design. In the other studies, confederates all started out their laboratory conversations without manipulating any of their behaviors, and then changed their behaviors at specified points during the interactions. In the Floyd study, confederates behaved in either affectionate or non-affectionate ways through the conversations. Why should this design difference be consequential? Because confederates and participants in the Floyd study were strangers to each other, it could be that the lack of a baseline (nonmanipulated) portion of the conversations led participants to infer that the behaviors the confederates were enacting reflected their normative levels of immediacy, friendliness, and affection, and thus had little value as gauges for how the confederates might feel about the participants. In other words, without the baseline period for comparison, participants may have concluded that confederates were behaving as they would normally and were not, therefore, sending particular relational messages to the participants (at least, ones that would differ by condition).

This is speculation, of course, but the credibility of this explanation is bolstered by the results of a study by Floyd and Mikkelson (2004) that was nearly identical in design to the Floyd (1998) study, except that it used a repeated-measures design. This study also involved interactions between trained confederates and naïve participants who were strangers, and also manipulated the same behaviors that were manipulated in Floyd (1998). The difference was the inclusion of a baseline period before the start of the manipulation, and the comparison of participants' reports of confederates' behaviors during both the baseline and the manipulated portions of the conversation.

Unlike in Floyd (1998), several relational messages in the Floyd and Mikkelson study were influenced by confederates' behaviors. Specifically, those confederates who became more affectionate over time were seen as more socially attractive, more task attractive, more involved, more receptive to participants, as seeing themselves as more similar and equal to participants, and as having more positive characters. They also were seen as being less dominant and formal. Those confederates who became less affectionate over time elicited the opposite interpretations of their behavior.

Interpretations are important, of course, because they aid receivers in ascertaining the implications that a sender's behavior has for the relationship. When one receives an embrace from a platonic friend and interprets it as a romantic gesture, for instance, such an interpretation has implications for the friendship that are different than those associated with an interpretation of the hug as a social support gesture. Thus, it is in people's best interests to be cognizant of the relational meanings inferred from different behaviors, whether enacted by familiar or unfamiliar others.

Finally, in addition to evaluations and interpretations, humans make attributions about other people's behaviors (as well as about their own). Some studies have examined variation in the attributions made for affectionate behaviors, and that research is described next.

Attributions. Research on attributions for affectionate behaviors has focused on people's inferences for the causes of those behaviors. Attribution-making is a pervasive human activity; people continually make inferences about the reasons why things happen, often for the purpose of deciding on the most appropriate response (see, e.g., Heider, 1958; Kelley, 1972; Weiner, 1985). When snubbed by a friend, for example, people will typically respond differently if they perceive that it was deliberate than if they perceive that it was not. Specifically, they may feel more justified responding with hurt or anger in the former instance than in the latter, on the presumption that if the friend snubbed them on purpose, then the behavior was malicious and the friend should be held accountable for it. Contrariwise, if they infer that the behavior was accidental, they may attribute no malice or personal responsibility to it and feel less justified harboring hurt or anger as a result.

Three studies have focused on attribution-making for affectionate expressions. The first, by Booth-Butterfield and Trotta (1994), investigated the specific reasons that people used to explain a particular affectionate behavior, the verbal expression of love. Respondents in their survey were asked to think of a romantic relationship they had been in, in which the words "I love you" had been uttered. If they could identify such a relationship, they were asked to describe the first time love was verbally expressed in this way and to indicate *why* they thought the expression had occurred. Booth-Butterfield and Trotta content analyzed the responses and grouped them into five categories, the first of which was that *the expression reflected the speaker's true feelings.* Slightly more than half (54.8%) of the respondents provided this attribution, characterizing the verbal behavior as an accurate reflection of the speaker's feelings of love. The second most common attribution was that *the expression was motivated by situational influences.* This attribution explained the gestures as having been prompted by something in the environment – for instance, that the couple had just made love for the first time or that they were anticipating a temporary separation. Approximately a fifth (20.8%) of the respondents provided this attribution.

A third attribution was that *the expression had an ulterior motive.* The respondents who provided this attribution (13.2% of the sample) suggested that the speaker expressed love for an underhanded reason, such as convincing the recipient to engage in sexual activity, or for a type of "secret test," to find out whether the recipient would reciprocate the gesture or not. (The manipulative use of affectionate behavior, and why it is often effective, will be discussed in greater detail in Chapter 6.)

The final two attributions, which were each offered by only 5.5% of the sample, were that *the expression was meant to convey comfort or support, rather than love,* and that *the speaker was simply confused about his or her feelings.*

These attributions are similar in that, in both cases, the recipient does not believe the speaker's expression of love was genuine, even though the speaker may have felt that it was.

Two other studies have examined the form (rather than the content) of people's attributions for affectionate expressions. The first was the Floyd and Voloudakis (1999a) study, although the data on attributions are reported in a separate paper (1999b). In that study, participants were asked to provide causal attributions for the behaviors of confederates who had become either increasingly or decreasingly affectionate over the course of a laboratory interaction. The attribution measure, which had been adapted from an earlier study by Manusov, Floyd, and Kerssen-Griep (1997), first asked participants whether any of the confederates' behaviors "stood out" to them during the experimental conversations; if so, participants were instructed to describe those behaviors. (This first question had the dual purpose of focusing participants' thoughts onto the specific behaviors they would be asked to explain and also of allowing the researchers to discard attributions made about behaviors that were not manipulated in the study.)

If participants responded affirmatively to the first question, they were then asked to respond to the question, "How would you explain your partner's behavior(s)?" Their written responses were later coded along two dimensions: causality (indicating whether the cause of the behaviors was internal to the confederate or external) and responsibility (indicating whether the confederate was responsible for the behaviors or not) (see Bradbury & Fincham, 1992; Karney, Bradbury, Fincham, & Sullivan, 1994; Manusov, 1990).

As hypothesized, participants were significantly more likely to offer attributions about decreases in affectionate behavior than about increases. This difference was predicted on the presumption that, because the dyads in the study were pairs of platonic friends, decreases in affection would be more unexpected – and thus, more likely to invoke causal attributions – than would increases. For those participants (in both conditions) who did offer attributions, however, Floyd and Voloudakis then examined their scores for causality and responsibility, as coded from their written attributions, and two findings were particularly noteworthy.

First, Floyd and Voloudakis had hypothesized that, regardless of whether participants received increased or decreased affectionate behavior from the confederates, they would be more likely to attribute the behavior to external and uncontrollable causes than to internal, controllable ones. The justification for this prediction was that, in both conditions, attributing the change in confederates' affectionate behavior to external, uncontrollable causes would "shield" participants from having to attend to the potential relational implications of those changes. In close, but nonromantic, friendships, decreases in affectionate behavior could signal decreases in liking or interest, whereas increases in affectionate behavior could signal a desire to make the relationship romantic. Either implication could invoke psychological distress for the recipient (a point discussed in greater detail in Chapter 6). Thus, Floyd and Voloudakis reasoned that participants could avoid this potential distress by concluding that the behaviors were not done intentionally but were instead attributable to causes external to the confederates and beyond their control. The data supported this hypothesis.

Also hypothesized was that the intimacy level of the friendship would be influential, such that participants making external, uncontrollable attributions for changes in their friends' affectionate behavior would be from more intimate friendships than would those making internal, controllable attributions. Several previous studies had documented that patterns of attribution-making in established relationships are influenced by the intimacy or satisfaction of those relationships (for review, see Bradbury & Fincham, 1990). The Floyd and Voloudakis findings supported the hypothesis for causality but not for responsibility, although the mean difference for responsibility was in the predicted direction.

It is intriguing that the potential relational implications of affection behaviors might have an influence on the attributions receivers make for them. In the attribution literature, the principle of the *self-serving bias* suggests that individuals make attributions for their own behaviors so as to cast themselves in the most favorable light (see, e.g., Bradley, 1978; Luginbuhl, Crowe, & Kahan, 1975; Schopler & Layton, 1972). In particular, it predicts that individuals are most likely to attribute their successes to internal, controllable causes (e.g., I got an "A" because I'm so smart), and are most likely to attribute their failures to external, uncontrollable causes (e.g., I got an "F" because my child kept me awake all night). Assumed in this principle is the idea that attributions matter both to how we see ourselves and to how others see us. That is, it is much less threatening to one's self image (or "positive face"; see Brown & Levinson, 1987) to say that good behaviors reflect one's inherent goodness, whereas bad behaviors are anomalies, caused by external forces over which one has no control.

The self-serving bias, as it has been applied and studied in the attribution literature, has dealt only with people's attributions for their own behaviors. In a 2000 paper (Floyd, 2000b), I suggested that the principle behind the self-serving bias – that people's attributions for behaviors have implications for themselves – ought also to apply to their attributions for others' behaviors, at least in cases when those behaviors would have implications for the self. For example, if one observes a man acting rudely to someone else, one might attribute his behavior to his personality ("he's a jerk") without engaging in more involved cognitive activity. (Indeed, this is precisely the response predicted by another principle of attribution-making, the *fundamental attribution error*; see Ross, 1977.) However, if the man were a friend and the rude behavior were directed at oneself, then the behavior – and one's attribution for it – could carry personal implications for oneself. If, in this situation, one concludes that "he's a jerk," then one must deal with the attendant questions of what this implies for the friendship, what one has done to deserve this treatment, and indeed, why one is friends with a jerk in the first place. In such a context, one might therefore be motivated, at least subconsciously, to find a more external attribution for the friend's behavior that will allow one to sidestep those implications. If, for instance, the friend's behavior is attributed to a temporary situational influence (e.g., "he's been under a lot of stress at work lately"), then one can forgive and forget the behavior without attending to whatever personal or relational implications it might have.

This idea was the basis for the *extended self-serving bias*, proposed in Floyd (2000b). Floyd tested the model with respect to affectionate behavior, using an augmented version of the Floyd and Burgoon (1999) dataset. In that study, participants interacted with trained confederates whose non-verbal behaviors conveyed either liking and affection or disliking and a lack of affection. After the interactions, Floyd and Burgoon elicited participants' attributions for the confederates' behaviors, using the same procedure as in the Floyd and Voloudakis (1999b) study described above. Subsequent to the data collection, Floyd recruited a new sample of participants to watch the videotapes of the laboratory conversations and to provide their own attributions for the confederates' behaviors. He had the attributions from the participants and from the videotape observers coded on causality and responsibility dimensions, and then compared them to each other. Since the participants actually received the expressions of liking or disliking, whereas the observers merely witnessed them, Floyd expected their patterns of attribution-making to differ, on the principle that the behaviors ought to have carried more personal implications for the participants than for the observers.

Two comparisons were of particular interest. First, it had been predicted that participants would attribute liking behaviors to causes that were more internal and controllable than the causes to which they attributed disliking behaviors. Because affectionate behavior has direct personal implications for receivers, then receivers ought to be motivated to explain those behaviors in the most positive way possible. This prediction was supported using both the causality scores and the responsibility scores. Second, Floyd hypothesized that, for expressions of disliking, observers would make more internal and controllable attributions than participants would. Again, because disliking behaviors would not carry the personal implications for observers that they would for participants, he speculated that observers would opt for what is often the less cognitively demanding route and attribute them to the confederates' personalities ("he's acting that way because he's a jerk"), whereas participants would be motivated to look for external causes that would assuage any negative implications the disliking behaviors might have carried for them. This hypothesis was also supported. As anticipated, observers and participants did not differ from each other in their attributions for liking behavior; they were equally likely to attribute such behavior to internal, controllable causes.

What should one conclude from the research on cognitive responses? At least two conclusions are warranted from these data. First, *people's default mode is to respond to affectionate behavior positively, in terms of their evaluations, interpretations, and attributions.* Given its numerous and substantial benefits to individuals and their relationships, this is unsurprising. Referring to this as a "default mode," however, is intended to suggest that people respond to affectionate behavior positively *unless there is a compelling reason not to.* This qualifier is important, because although humans need affection, they also have other physical, mental, and emotional needs that may be superordinate. When competing needs are strong enough in magnitude, individuals will react negatively to expressions of affection if such expressions are seen as interfering with the individuals' abilities to satisfy their competing needs. This was evidenced in the Floyd (1998) study, which demonstrated that threats to negative face need (or the need to avoid being unduly encumbered) can override affection needs and cause people to evaluate affectionate behaviors negatively.

This is significant in an evolutionary sense, because motivations that are adaptive individually can often compete with each other. For example, parents can advance their reproductive success by investing resources in their children, but because such a move diverts resources from the parents themselves, it can actually be detrimental to the parents' own survival. Evolutionary success, in the larger term, therefore relies partly on people's abilities to simultaneously manage competing motivations. This explains why people can welcome affectionate behavior under most conditions, but can react negatively to it when competing needs take precedence. This idea will underlie the discussion of the risks of affectionate communication in Chapter 6 and will be central to the theoretic framework advanced in Chapter 7.

The second conclusion to be drawn from the research on cognitive responses is that *many of the same characteristics that influence how affectionate people are also influence how people react cognitively to affection displays.* These include the sex of the person enacting the affectionate behavior, the sex of the person receiving it, the point of view of the evaluator (whether a recipient of the affection display or a third-party observer), the form of the behavior itself, and the context in which it is displayed. This similarity in sources of influence may not be surprising, but it, too, may be important in an evolutionary sense. Adaptations, whether physical or psychological, are equipped to function only in response to particular environmental triggers. As I will suggest in subsequent chapters, affectionate behavior can serve one's motivations for viability and fertility motivations, but only if it is enacted in such a way that elicits favor from others. That is, affection expressed in a manner that causes negative reactions on the part of the receiver is not likely be of benefit to the sender (or to the receiver, for that matter). It is strategically useful, therefore, for individuals to be sensitive to the interpersonal and contextual variables that influence receivers' reactions to affectionate behavior. It is thus rather efficient that those variables are so similar to the ones that influence individuals' affectionate behavior in the first place.

Thus far, this chapter has examined receivers' cognitive responses in detail. Of course, as pointed out in the first chapter, people do not always behave in ways that are consonant with their thoughts or emotions. Let us therefore turn our attention to behavioral responses.

Responding Behaviorally to Affectionate Expressions

Receivers of affectionate expressions have three principal options for their behavioral responses. The first option is to *reciprocate the expression.* This can take the form of direct reciprocity, wherein the receiver displays the same behavior as was directed to him or her (e.g., hearing "I love you" and saying "I love you, too" in return). This might also take the form of indirect reciprocity, wherein the receiver replies with a similar, but not the same, behavior (e.g., hearing "I love you" and then hugging or kissing the sender). Of course, as mentioned earlier, one of the primary risks of expressing affection is that the gesture will not be reciprocated. In the case of indirect reciprocity, however, mere reciprocation is not necessarily sufficient. Rather, one tends to desire a behavioral response that is of approximately the same intensity as the original expression. Hearing "I'm in love with you" and saying "I really like you a lot" in reply qualifies as indirect reciprocity, but the sentiment implied in the response is clearly of a lesser intensity than that implied in the first expression. Likewise, one may not desire a response that implies a greater intensity, either. Therefore, although reciprocity is generally the most preferred behavioral response to an affectionate expression, its positivity is likely to be moderated by the extent to which the response matches the intensity level of the original expression.

A second option is to *compensate for the expression.* This consists of responding to the affectionate expression with negatively valenced behaviors. An extreme example would be hearing the words "I love you" and saying "Well, I hate you" in reply. A more common example would involve a sender acting increasingly affectionate toward a receiver who becomes increasingly withdrawn and disengaged from the conversation in response. Behavioral compensation was a key component of Argyle and Dean's (1965) equilibrium theory, which posits that increases in affiliative behavior (such as eye gaze or proximity) induce the receiver to compensate by reducing the level of affiliation. As with reciprocity, compensation can be done directly, by changing the same behaviors that were changed behavior (e.g., taking a step back in response to a partner's step forward), or indirectly, by changing other behaviors that have a similar effect on the interaction (e.g., frowning or crossing one's arms in response to partner's step forward). Empirical research has largely failed to support the primacy of compensatory adaptation that equilibrium theory predicts. However, it would be reasonable to hypothesize that compensation for expressions of affection is a likely response in cases when the expressions are particularly threatening to the receiver and when the receiver wants to be clear that the affectionate sentiment is not shared.

Finally, a third option is to *fail to respond to the expression.* In this case, the affectionate expression is simply ignored, at least behaviorally. This may be a common response when the receiver finds the expression to be somehow threatening but does not wish to hurt or embarrass the sender.

For example, suppose that Sarah sends a note to her friend Jake in which she conveys a romantic interest in him. Jake likes Sarah as a friend but is not interested in her romantically. He does not wish to compensate for her affectionate expression, because he fears that would hurt her, but neither does he wish to reciprocate her expression, because he does not share her feelings. Of course, he could reciprocate indirectly with a behavior of lesser intensity, but he fears that would embarrass her. So, he decides that his best course of action is to ignore the expression, at least initially. He hopes that Sarah will "take the hint" by his failure to respond, allowing her to save face and allowing their friendship to continue as though the romantic overture were never made.

In this example, the failure to respond is used strategically for the purpose of steering the outcome of the interaction. In other cases, receivers may fail to respond simply because they are uncertain about *how* to respond. Receivers might be unsure how to respond because they haven't yet ascertained the meaning of the affectionate expression or perhaps because they are uncertain whether they share the sender's affectionate sentiments.

Certainly, there is a good deal of variation within each of these three types of behavioral responses. However, if we accept these as constituting the three principal options for responding behaviorally to affectionate expressions, then we can turn our energies toward identifying the variables that predict when each type of response is likely to be observed. Thus far, three experiments have addressed this question. These studies used different theories and therefore examined different types of variables as potential predictors of behavioral responses, but taken together, their results begin to answer the question.

The first of the experiments was that conducted by Floyd and Voloudakis (1999a), which examined affectionate behavior in adult platonic friendships and tested hypotheses drawn from expectancy violations theory (EVT). EVT provides reason for expecting that behaviors that constitute a positive expectancy violation ought to be reciprocated, whereas behaviors that constitute a negative expectancy violation ought to be compensated for, or at least, ignored. In the experiment, pairs of friends reported to a laboratory where they were told that they would be engaging in two short conversations with each other. The first conversation served as a baseline, with no behaviors manipulated. In between the conversations, one friend from each pair was made a confederate and was induced either to increase or decrease his or her affectionate behaviors toward the partner during the second conversation. The conversations were videotaped and were subsequently coded for the participants' and confederates' behaviors.

Floyd and Voloudakis reasoned that, because their participants were friends (which is generally a rewarding relationship), participants should judge increases in their friends' affectionate behavior positively, and should judge decreases in their friends' affectionate behavior negatively. Using EVT, Floyd and Voloudakis predicted behavioral reciprocity (in the form of increased immediacy, expressiveness, and positive affect) in the former condition and behavioral compensation in the latter condition. Importantly, both predictions call for the same behavioral display from the participants; that is, in both conditions, participants were expected to become more affectionate.

The hypothesis received little support. Due to their intercorrelation, the behaviors of immediacy, expressiveness, and positive affect were analyzed together in a MANOVA that produced a significant multivariate effect for time (the difference between the first and second conversations). At the univariate level, only the effect for positive affect was significant, and an examination of the means revealed that participants actually *decreased* their positive affect from the first conversation to the second one. A *post hoc* analysis revealed, however, that the effect was attributable only to participants who received decreased affection. They decreased their positive affect in response (a reciprocal response), whereas participants who received increased affection had nearly identical levels of positive affect in both conversations.

The analyses also produced a significant effect for the interaction between time and confederate behavior. Follow-up tests showed that participants who received decreased affection increased their expressivity from the first conversation to the second (a compensatory response). Participants who received increased affection had nearly identical levels of expressivity in both conversations. There were no significant effects for immediacy.

Clearly, these were not the expected behavioral responses. There are a number of reasons why the predictions may have failed. Perhaps not all participants judged increases in affectionate behavior positively, and decreases negatively. Perhaps EVT is incorrect in its reasoning – or perhaps Floyd and Voloudakis reasoned from it improperly to arrive at the hypotheses advanced. Two features of the method are particularly suspect, however. First, confederates were not instructed as to the particular behaviors they should modify to manipulate their affection levels. Rather, they were asked to increase or decrease their levels of affection using whatever behaviors seemed most appropriate to them. This feature of the method did allow Floyd and Voloudakis to examine what behaviors confederates enacted in order to convey affection; however, it virtually guaranteed variance in those behaviors, such that participants in each of the two conditions were not always responding to the same behavioral changes. Second, the coders in the study rated participants' behaviors only once for the first conversation and once for the second conversation. This was done so that the behavioral data would match participants' self-report data (which was elicited once for each conversation) in terms of the size of the "data window." However, the conversations both averaged approximately four minutes in length, and levels of immediacy, expressivity, and positive affect can fluctuate considerably in that period of time. Given that likely variation, requiring coders to aggregate in their minds all of the behaviors they witnessed during a four-minute period was likely an unwise strategy.

These two methodological problems (as well as the small number of dyads in the Floyd and Voloudakis study) were remedied in the second experiment, by Floyd and Burgoon (1991). This study differed from the Floyd and Voloudakis study in a number of ways. First, pairs of strangers were used instead of pairs of friends. Second, trained confederates were used instead of participant confederates. Third, participants' and confederates' behaviors were coded in 30-second windows at eight points in the conversations. Fourth, the design was a between-subjects design, meaning that confederates did not increase or decrease their affection behaviors over time but were either highly affectionate or unaffectionate throughout the laboratory interaction. A fifth difference was that only same-sex pairs were used in the Floyd and Burgoon study, whereas the Floyd and Voloudakis experiment used both same- and opposite-sex dyads.

Perhaps the most important difference is that the Floyd and Burgoon study derived its hypotheses from interaction adaptation theory (IAT), which differs from expectancy violations theory in the specificity with which it predicts patterns of behavioral adaptation. Specifically, IAT proposes that people compare their needs, expectations, and desires to the behaviors of their conversational partners, and reciprocate behaviors that match, or are more positive than, those needs, expectations, and desires. Behaviors that people judge to be more negative than what they need, expect, and want are compensated for. These predictions are relatively straightforward when people's needs, expectations, and desires are all the same. However, it is not uncommon for people to desire one thing but expect another, or to need something that is undesired. The Floyd and Burgoon experiment not only tested IAT's ability to predict behavioral responses under conditions of congruent expectations and desires (needs were not manipulated in this experiment), but also examined how people respond to behaviors that match either their expectations or their desires, but not both.

In this experiment, naïve participants were paired up with trained confederates of their same sex. When a participant reported to the laboratory to check in for the study, a confederate (whom the participant thought was simply another student doing the study) was already present in the waiting area. During this check in and orientation period, the confederate was behaving either very positively toward the participant (smiling, maintaining eye contact, sitting close with an open posture, asking the participant questions, etc.) or very negatively (not smiling or looking at the participant, sitting far away with a closed posture, not saying anything to the participant). This was intended to manipulate participants' expectations, inducing them to expect either a positive or a negative conversation with the confederate during the interaction portion of the experiment.

Participants and confederates were told that the experiment was about how strangers interact with each other, that they would be taking part in a semistructured conversation that would be videotaped, and that they would be completing measures afterward that would ask assess their perceptions of their partner. Before the conversations, participants and confederates were briefly separated to complete some pre-measures. During this time, participants were informed that the conversation was being observed by a researcher, unconnected with the current study, who was looking for pairs of new acquaintances to invite as participants in a longitudinal study of relationship development. Specifically, participants were told that the new study would be a long-term, labor intensive project, and that the researcher was particularly looking either for pairs of people who seemed to like each other a great deal during their initial conversation or who seemed to dislike each other quite a bit. This served as the manipulation of participants' desire to be liked or disliked by the confederates. By describing the prospective study as long-term and labor intensive, Floyd and Burgoon intended to induce participants to want to avoid being invited to take part in it,[6] and by describing the type of relational

---

[6] This part of the manipulation was tested by asking participants if they wanted to go ahead and volunteer for the prospective study, on the understanding that if participants were actually interested in the study, this would reverse the effect of the desire manipulation. No participants volunteered.

interaction the prospective researcher was looking for, they intended to induce participants either to want the confederates to like them or to want the confederates to dislike them.[7] The efficacy of both the expectation and desire manipulations was confirmed in pilot studies.

For the experimental interaction, participants and confederates went through a conversation exercise in which they were presented with descriptions of moral and ethical dilemmas and instructed to discuss options for dealing with them. During the interaction, confederates were trained to behave either as though they especially liked participants (smiling, leaning forward, maintaining eye contact, using facial and vocal animation, sitting with open posture) or especially disliked them (not smiling, maintaining little eye contact, lacking facial and vocal animation, sitting rigidly with a closed posture). Confederates maintained either the "liking" or "disliking" behaviors throughout the interaction.

Thus, the study employed a three-way crossed factorial design with desire, expectation, and behavior manipulations. Drawing on IAT, Floyd and Burgoon hypothesized that participants would behaviorally match confederates when they expected, wanted, and received liking behavior, and also when they expected, wanted, and received disliking behavior. However, IAT does not specify the relative potency of desires and expectations, so there was no basis for making directional predictions about the behavioral responses of people who expected to be liked but wished not to be, or of people who wanted confederates to like them but did not expect that they would. There were, therefore, four cells of the design in which directional hypotheses could be advanced and four cells in which only research questions were appropriate. A depiction of the conditions appears in Table 4.3.

Results indicated that participants with congruent expectations and desires (represented in cells 1–4 of Table 4.3) matched the behavior of confederates who acted in accordance with those expectations and desires, but compensated for the behavior of confederates who acted against them. That is, participants who wanted and expected to be liked matched the behavior of confederates who enacted liking behavior and compensated for the behavior of confederates who enacted

---

[7] Certainly, it is not difficult to induce people to want to be liked by others; researchers such as Maslow (1970), Goffman (1959), and Brown and Levinson (1987) have pointed out that this is a fairly fundamental human desire. The challenge was in inducing people to want to be disliked. The manipulation drew on the principle of negative face, or the desire to avoid obligation. We reasoned that if one's negative face were sufficiently threatened, one's desire to be liked could be overridden.

Table 4.3. *Experimental Conditions in Floyd and Burgoon (1999) Study*

Cell	Desire	Expectation	Behavior
1	Liking	Liking	Liking
2	Disliking	Disliking	Disliking
3	Liking	Liking	Disliking
4	Disliking	Disliking	Liking
5	Liking	Disliking	Liking
6	Disliking	Liking	Disliking
7	Liking	Disliking	Disliking
8	Disliking	Liking	Liking

Notes: "Desire" and "Expectation" refer to the manipulations of naïve participants' desires and expectations for the confederates' behaviors (i.e., whether they desired and expected confederates to behave as though they liked participants or disliked them). "Behavior" refers to the confederates' actual manipulated behaviors.

disliking behavior. Moreover, participants who wanted and expected to be disliked matched the behavior of confederates who enacted disliking behavior and compensated for the behavior of confederates who enacted liking behavior. These findings provided direct support for the hypotheses derived from IAT.

When Floyd and Burgoon examined the behaviors of those participants with incongruent expectations and desires (represented in cells 5–8 of Table 4.3), they discovered that their responses to confederates' behaviors were largely in line with their desires, rather than their expectations. The general pattern was one in which participants matched the behaviors they desired and compensated for the behaviors they did not desire, irrespective of their expectations. This does not imply, of course, that desires are always more potent than expectations in determining people's behavioral adaptation to others; that was simply the case in this experiment.

Although they bolstered the predictive utility of IAT, these findings would otherwise be unremarkable were it not for their demonstration that friendly, affiliative behavior is not always welcomed, considered positive, or reciprocated. Rather, all four groups of participants who had been induced to want to be disliked actually compensated for liking behaviors when they received them, and matched disliking behaviors. The most important aspect of this finding is not the abstract pattern – people matching behavior that they desire – nor even the fact that people reciprocated negative affect behaviors. What is notable is the demonstration that *people can be induced into compensating for expressions of liking.* This runs directly counter to the intuitive notion that humans always strive to be liked and appreciated by others (see Goffman, 1959; Maslow, 1970). Instead, as this experiment suggested, when affectionate behaviors have implied obligations (or even potential obligations) attached to them, those obligations may be sufficient to override natural desires for liking and affection. The Floyd and Burgoon study is notable because it is the first to demonstrate a pattern of compensation for affectionate behavior.

Despite the significance of this finding, however, the Floyd and Burgoon experiment was limited in two important ways. First, confederate behavior was a between-cells manipulation only. That is, the confederates in each condition enacted their assigned behaviors (whether expressing liking or disliking) throughout the interactions, rather than starting with a baseline, nonmanipulated period and then changing their behavior over time (as in the Floyd and Voloudakis study). This makes it difficult for the researcher to observe behavioral adaptation occurring, because the comparison of interest is simply between conditions, not over time within conditions. Second, although manipulating expectations and desires provides the researcher with greater experimental control and a greater ability to examine causal relationships than would be gained by simply measuring them, it generally limits the researcher to studying only one type of expectation or desire at a time. As other studies have indicated, people can enter interactions with *multiple* expectations and desires (see Burgoon, Allspach, & Miczo, 1997). Therefore, manipulating one of each precluded examining the effects of other expectations and desires that participants may have had, and also from examining how multiple expectations and desires might operate in tandem. In the Floyd and Burgoon study, for instance, only participants' expectations of how confederates would behave during the laboratory conversations were manipulated. However, other expectations, such as how similar the confederate would be to oneself or how quickly the conversation would go, might also have been influential.

Floyd and Ray (in press) designed an experiment to address these limitations. Their design involved a mix of the elements of the Floyd and Burgoon study and the Floyd and Voloudakis study. Floyd and Ray used interactions between strangers and induced one of the strangers in each pair to be a participant confederate (instead of using trained confederates). Each pair engaged in a 4-minute baseline (nonmanipulated) conversation in which they discussed how they might deal with various moral and ethnical dilemmas.[8] After that conversation, the participants were separated and one was instructed to act, during a second conversation, either "as though you really like your partner" or "as though you really dislike your partner." This instruction was similar to that given to the trained confederates in the Floyd and Burgoon study; however, as in the Floyd and Voloudakis study, the confederates were given no instructions about particular behaviors to manipulate, nor were they provided with examples of behaviors that could be used. Rather, Floyd and Ray instructed confederates to express liking or disliking using whatever behaviors they believed would convey that message appropriately.

Earlier in this chapter, I discussed the specific behaviors confederates enacted in this study. The focus here, however, is on the behavioral responses of the participants to the changes in confederate behavior that they observed during a second 4-minute conversation. Like Floyd and Burgoon, Floyd and Ray used IAT to predict behavioral responses. In this study, however, expectations and desires were not manipulated, but were measured instead. Specifically, Floyd and Ray measured the extent to which participants expected the conversations to be pleasant and comfortable, expected themselves to be relaxed, engaged, and extroverted, and expected that they would like their partners (the confederates). They also measured the extent to which participants wanted to manage their images, their relationships with the confederates, and the flow of the conversations themselves. Certainly, these are not all of the expectations and desires one might measure, but other research has suggested that they are among the most pertinent expectations and desires with which strangers enter conversations (see, e.g., Burgoon et al., 1997).

The overall pattern of behavioral response was one in which participants reciprocated confederates' "liking" behaviors with increases in their own behavioral involvement and pleasantness. In response to "disliking" behaviors, participants tended not to change their own behaviors, maintaining their previous levels of involvement and pleasantness. Importantly, however, these patterns were moderated by participants' expectation about whether or not they would like the confederate. In particular,

---

[8] The dilemmas, adapted from Hale and Burgoon (1984), dealt with (a) the theft of a friend's valuables by a sibling; (b) one's Catholic friend who is contemplating abortion; (c) the infidelity of a best friend's fiancée; and (d) the impending visit of a cohabiting couple's unsuspecting parents. The topics were presented in a cyclical, counterbalanced order within conditions.

participants reciprocated both liking *and* disliking behaviors more if they expected (before the conversation) to like the confederates than if they expected not to. As Floyd and Ray pointed out, the fact that the expectation to like confederates moderated participants' reciprocity of liking behavior is in line with IAT's reasoning that liking behavior, even though it may have some inherent positivity, can be judged negatively by people who are not expecting it.

IAT's reasoning was contradicted, however, by the finding that the expectation to like confederates also moderated participants' reactions to disliking behavior. If participants expected that they would like the confederates, then disliking behavior on the part of the confederate should have been judged less positively than the expected behavior and should have, according to IAT, elicited compensatory behavior from participants (in the form of increased pleasantness and involvement, not decreased).

What should one conclude about behavioral responses to affectionate expressions from these three experiments? One evident conclusion is that *several variables can influence whether people reciprocate, compensate for, or fail to respond to affectionate behavior.* It is too simplistic to predict that people reciprocate positive behavior and compensate for negative behavior, as a number of other things can moderate that outcome, including the extent to which it supports or contradicts people's expectations. A second important conclusion is that, *although affectionate behaviors may carry some inherent positivity, their valence is also determined by the extent to which they are congruent with a recipient's desires.* If affection is expressed in an inappropriate manner or in an inappropriate situation, for instance, it may contradict the receiver's desires and be more likely to evoke compensatory than reciprocal responses.

The previous two chapters addressed the processes involved with encoding, decoding, and responding to expressions of affection. Toward what ends do individuals engage in these processes, however? As discussed in the next chapter, affectionate communication is associated with a number of physical, social, and emotional benefits that affect people at both the individual and relational levels.

5

Benefits of Expressing and Receiving Affection

> Affection is responsible for nine-tenths of whatever solid and durable happiness there is in our lives.
>
> – C. S. Lewis

Thus far in this book, the focus has been on the *process* of affectionate communication: how it is encoded, how it is decoded, and how it is responded to. In this and the subsequent chapter, the focus will instead be on the *outcomes* (or, in many cases, the *potential outcomes*) of communicating affection: the benefits of giving and receiving affection, and the various risks of giving and receiving affection. Nearly every other topic addressed thus far in this book has received more research attention than have the benefits and risks of affectionate behavior. Various lines of research offer much to draw on, however, and this chapter will address two fundamental questions. First, what are the benefits associated with affectionate communication? This chapter will engage this question first by examining research on the individual and relational benefits of receiving affectionate messages and then by examining the benefits of giving affection to others.

The second, and perhaps more provocative, question, is: why is affectionate communication beneficial? To address this question, this chapter reviews research and theory on the physical and social dimensions of affection (or at least, on what they *may be*) that can provide convincing and empirically testable answers. I will return to this topic in later chapters by suggesting that this will be one of the most important areas for future research on affectionate communication to address.

The discussion on the benefits of affectionate communication is divided into three separate, but strongly interrelated, areas. First reviewed is literature on the individual-level benefits of receiving expressions of affection. Some of the studies in this area have focused on the long-term effects of receiving affection – that is, the extent to which people who receive more affection from others, in general, are advantaged relative to people who receive less. Other studies have focused more on the effects of individual expressions of affection, such as a touch.

Next addressed is a smaller and newer body of research on the individual-level benefits of expressing affection to others. Affection exchange theory, which is explicated in detail in Chapter 7, suggests that individuals benefit not only from receiving affectionate expressions but also from conveying them, and I will describe the few but consistent findings in this area. Finally, the discussion will address the relational benefits of affectionate communication, or the extent to which relationships that are characterized by high levels of affectionate behavior are advantaged relative to those that are not.

Describing the Benefits of Affectionate Communication

Benefits Associated with Receiving Affection

It makes clear intuitive sense that receiving affectionate expressions from others invokes positive feelings. Indeed, the motivation to *be* loved and appreciated is among the most deeply engrained drives in the human experience (Brown & Levinson, 1987; Maslow, 1970), so it is only a minor deductive leap to the idea that the motivation to *be shown* that one is loved and appreciated is equally strong. However, does receiving expressions of affection actually benefit individuals in meaningful ways, besides simply making them feel loved and appreciated? The findings of a number of studies have suggested that it does.

The research in this area has tended to examine three different types of individual-level benefits associated with receiving affection, and so this section will discuss the research on each type of benefit separately. The first concerns research on the physical benefits associated with receiving affection, and specifically on the physical benefits associated with touch. The second encompasses research on the psychological and emotional benefits of receiving affectionate behavior, and the third involves the benefits associated with one's social experience (a topic addressed in greater detail below under the section on the relational benefits of affectionate communication).

A small number of studies have investigated associations between affectionate communication and one's individual health. In a multi-wave longitudinal study, Schwartz and Russek (1998) reported that the amount of love and caring college students had expressed to them by their parents significantly, and inversely, predicted their physical and psychological distress as many as 42 years later. Komisaruk and Whipple (1989) likewise reported that those who receive fewer expressions of love than they desire tend to be more susceptible to psychosomatic illness (see also Janov, 2000), whereas Shuntich, Loh, and Katz (1998) found affection to be negatively related to alcohol abuse and physical aggression toward family members.

Indeed, much of the research in this area has concentrated on affection received from family members as a correlate of individual health benefits. In a random sample of Dutch adults, for instance, Kerver, van Son, and de Groot (1992) found that the amount of affection participants reported receiving from their fathers during their upbringing was inversely associated with their likelihood of suffering clinical depression at the time of the study (although it was not significantly predictive of depression symptoms experienced one year later). Similarly, in a sample of over 2,400 Australian adults, Jorm, Dear, Rodgers, and Christensen (2003) reported that affection received from both mothers and fathers during upbringing was significantly associated with lower anxiety, less susceptibility to depression, and lower neuroticism. These collective findings suggest that receiving affectionate behavior, particularly from parents, coincides with a number of mental and physical health outcomes.

Some of the research in this vein has looked specifically at the link between physical health and affectionate touch, which has been shown to be critical even for the survival of newborns (Montagu, 1978, p. 79). In a review of such literature, Spence and Olson (1997) reported that touch can have significant effects on the reduction of pain as well as psychological anxiety. Krieger (1973) also reported that therapeutic touch can directly affect physiological well-being by increasing the production of white corpuscles, which enhance the body's ability to heal itself (see also Olson & Sneed, 1995; Whitcher & Fisher, 1979).

Some research suggests that the benefits of receiving touch are not just physical, but intellectual as well. Steward and Lupfer (1987) reported that college students who were touched lightly on the arm by their instructors during a one-on-one conference scored more than half a standard deviation higher on a subsequent examination (in either introductory psychology, American history, or government courses) than did students who were not touched by their instructors during the same type of conference (see also Foa, Megonigal, & Greipp, 1976).

Receiving affectionate communication also appears to have numerous effects on psychological and emotional well-being. In a general sense, it is traumatic for humans to be denied social contact with others (whether affectionate or not) for prolonged periods. Research on solitary confinement in prisons (Bonta & Gendreau, 1995; Zinger, 1999) and on political imprisonment or captivity (Bauer, Priebe, Haering, & Adamczak, 1993; Sanchez-Anguiano, 1999) confirms their damaging psychological effects. More specifically with respect to affectionate behavior, several studies have demonstrated positive relationships between received affection and individuals' overall psychological well-being (Downs & Javidi, 1990; Green & Wildermuth, 1993; Prager & Buhrmester, 1998; Quinn, 1983). Other research has linked affection to particular emotional or psychological outcomes, such as self-esteem (Barber & Thomas, 1986; Roberts & Bengtson, 1996), interpersonal competence (Rubin & Martin, 1998; Rubin, Perse, & Barbato, 1988), life satisfaction (Barbato & Perse, 1992), and satisfaction in therapeutic settings (Rabinowitz, 1991). Still other studies have documented that the lack of affection is associated with loneliness (Downs & Javidi, 1990) and depression (Mackinnon, Henderson, & Andrews, 1993; Oliver, Raftery, Reeb, & Delaney, 1993).

In the social realm, received affection is directly related to the quality of interpersonal and group relationships. Dainton (1998) and Parrot and Bengtson (1999) have both suggested that affectionate behavior is the interactional type that has the greatest influence on marital relationships. Indeed, affectionate communication has significant direct effects on relational quality and satisfaction in marriages (Schultz & Schultz, 1987; Spanier, 1976; Waring, McElrath, Lefcoe, & Weisz, 1981), parent–child relationships (Barber & Thomas, 1986; MacDonald, 1992; Morman & Floyd, 1999; Russell, 1997), friendships (Floyd & Morman, 1998; Floyd & Voloudakis, 1999a), caregiver relationships (Parsons, Cox, & Kimboko, 1989), small-group relationships (Anderson & Martin, 1995; Schutz, 1958), and even among those meeting for the first time (Floyd & Burgoon, 1999). In several studies, for instance, Floyd and Morman have demonstrated that communication satisfaction, relationship satisfaction, closeness, and positive relational involvement are all significantly related to the amount of affectionate communication people report receiving in their relationships (Floyd & Morman, 2000a, 2002, 2005; Morman &

Floyd, 1999, 2002; see also Bell & Healey, 1992; Prescott & Wallace, 1978).

There is some evidence that the relational benefits of affection operate partly through a buffering effect; that is, by attenuating the effects of otherwise adverse influences. In a 2-year longitudinal study of 105 newlywed couples, for instance, Huston and Chorost (1994) found that affectionate communication communicated from husbands to wives buffered the effects of their negativity on their wives' marital satisfaction. That is, when husbands were highly affectionate, their emotional negativity was uncorrelated with their wives' relational satisfaction. Contrariwise, when husbands were low in affection, their negativity was inversely associated with their wives' satisfaction (the same associations were not observed between wives' affection and husbands' satisfaction, however). Gulledge, Gulledge, and Stahmann (2003) likewise reported that physical affection in romantic relationships – in particular, kissing, hugging, and cuddling – is associated with the ease of conflict resolution, despite being unrelated to the amount of conflict. Both studies suggest that, in addition to whatever relational benefits affectionate communication may be directly associated with, affectionate behaviors also convey benefits via indirect relational pathways, by attenuating the effects of negativity or easing the process of conflict resolution. Unsurprisingly, these effects are influential in the long-term stability of marital relationships. As Huston, Caughlin, Houts, Smith, and George (2001) reported, overt expressions of affection shared between spouses during the first 2 years of marriage significantly predicted lower rates of divorce 13 years later.

A notable aspect about the research on the benefits of affectionate communication is that the vast majority of studies have focused on the benefits of *receiving* affection, rather than giving it. More recent research has begun to address the latter issue.

Benefits Associated with Communicating Affection

If one conceives of affectionate communication as a type of resource, then it make intuitive sense that individuals would benefit from receiving it, but it seems counterintuitive that people would benefit from giving it away. There is evidence that they do, however, and I will speculate later in this chapter as to the reasons why. As with receiving affection, the benefits associated with giving affection deal both with physical health and with emotional well-being.

The first and most direct study done to date regarding the benefits of communicating affection was reported in Floyd (2003). Working from AET, Floyd hypothesized that individuals who are, as a trait, highly affectionate people would be advantaged relative to those who are relatively nonaffectionate. Importantly, this study addressed not one's level of affectionate communication within a given relationship (as most previous research had done) but, rather, one's trait level of affectionate behavior – that is, at how affectionate one *typically* is with others. This variable (and also the amount of affection one typically receives from others) was measured with a two-part Trait Affection Scale (TAS). The TAS-G is a 10-item measure assessing how much affection one typically gives to others (scale items include "I am always telling my loved ones how much I care about them," and "Anyone who knows me well would say that I'm pretty affectionate"). The TAS-R is a 6-item measure assessing how much affection one typically receives from others (items include "I get quite a bit of affection from others," and "People are always telling me that they like me, love me, or care about me"). Reliability and validity data for both scales are summarized in Floyd, Hess, Miczo, Halone, Mikkelson, and Tusing (2006).

In the Floyd (2003) study, undergraduate research assistants were distributed pairs of questionnaires with instructions to recruit once of the most affectionate people they knew and one of the least affectionate people they knew to take part in the study. The questionnaires in each pair were identical except that their identification numbers indicated that one questionnaire was to be given to the affectionate person and the other was to be given to the nonaffectionate person. Participants were told nothing about why they were being selected to take part; rather, the research assistants simply asked them to complete the questionnaire to help the assistants with a class project. Participants mailed their completed questionnaires directly to the researcher.

The questionnaires contained a battery of measures assessing individual- and social-level variables. On the basis of AET, Floyd predicted that the high and low affection groups would not only differ from each other but also that the affectionate communicators would be advantaged relative to the nonaffectionate communicators. At the individual level, he hypothesized that highly affectionate people would be happier, have higher self esteem, be less stressed and less depressed, and have better overall mental health than would the less affectionate people. He also proposed that they would be more comfortable with interpersonal closeness and less fearful of intimacy. At the social level, Floyd predicted that highly affectionate people would be more socially outgoing, would receive more affectionate communication from others, would be more likely to be in a romantic relationship, and among those who were in romantic relationships, would be more satisfied with those relationships than would less affectionate people. The sample consisted of 109 adults who ranged in age from 10 to 60 years.

Despite the relatively small sample size, comparisons between the high and low affection groups confirmed each of these predictions. Specifically, compared to low affection communicators, high affection communicators were happier, more self assured, more comfortable with interpersonal closeness, less fearful of intimacy, less likely to view relationships as being unimportant, less stressed, less likely to be depressed, in better mental health, more likely to engage in regular social activity, more likely to be in an ongoing romantic relationship, and (among those in a romantic relationship) more satisfied with their relationships. Notable were the effect size (partial η^2) estimates, which ranged from .19 for depression and social activity to .56 for comfort with closeness (average partial η^2 values were .37 for individual-level variables and .32 for social-level variables).

These findings have since been replicated twice, once in conjunction with the Floyd and Mikkelson (2004) experiment and once in conjunction with the Floyd, Hess et al. (2005) online study (both of which are detailed in the latter paper). These replications differed from the Floyd (2003) study only in the sense that target groups of high and low affection communicators were not specifically recruited to take part. Rather, all participants in the studies were given similar batteries of individual- and social-level measures, and their scores on these measures were correlated with their TAS-G scores.

As in the Floyd (2003) study, the pattern of results from both replications was clear and unequivocal: in every case, the amount of affection people typically expressed to others was associated with individual and social benefits. The more affectionate people were, the happier, more socially active, less stressed, less depressed, and more satisfied with their romantic relationships they were. It is critical to point out that no causal inferences are warranted from the findings of these studies. Perhaps it is the case that communicating affection engenders the rewards of happiness, less stress, more relational satisfaction, and so on. Perhaps it is instead the case that being happy, un-stressed, and satisfied prompts one to be more affectionate to others. One might even surmise that the benefits of giving affection are only those associated with the affection one receives in return – thus, highly affectionate people are advantaged only because they get more affection from others. I will take up this point in greater detail later.

Relational Benefits Associated with Affectionate Communication

One can think about the relational benefits of affectionate communication in two ways. The first is to ask whether affectionate individuals are more likely than nonaffectionate individuals to have relational success. Second, one can investigate whether specific relationships that are characterized by more affectionate behavior are benefited relative to relationships that are characterized by less affection. Social scientists have taken up both questions, and the results have been consistent.

As mentioned earlier, individual affection level and its association with relationship success was examined in both the Floyd (2003) and the Floyd, Hess et al. (2005) studies. The predictions advanced in both studies were straightforward. First, people who are affectionate (as a trait) are more likely to be in an ongoing romantic relationship than are people who are less affectionate. Second, among those who are in an ongoing romantic relationship, their trait level of affectionate behavior predicts their satisfaction with those relationships. The predictions were confirmed in both studies. Specifically, in both cases, individuals' trait affection levels reliably discriminated between those who were in an ongoing romantic relationship (going steady, engaged, cohabiting, or married) and those who were not, with more affectionate people being more likely to be in such a relationship. Moreover, among those participants in both studies who did have a romantic relationship, their trait affection levels showed direct linear associations with their satisfaction in those relationships.

Let me reiterate the caveat that one cannot derive causal inferences from these findings. Affectionate people are more likely than nonaffectionate people to be in satisfying romantic relationships, but such a finding does not indicate that being affectionate *leads to* the establishment of such relationships. Certainly, it doesn't disprove such a cause-and-effect relationship, either, and one might suspect that such a relationship in fact exists. These data are simply silent on the issue of causality. They do, however, allow one to conclude that being affectionate is *associated* with the benefit of being in a satisfying romantic relationship. Future research can take up the important questions of **whether trait affection level predicts later involvement in romantic relationships**, and **whether trait affection**

level predicts romantic relationship satisfaction, or satisfaction predicts affection level, or the two are mutually causal.

A second way to address the relational benefits of affectionate communication is to investigate whether specific relationships that are characterized by more affectionate behavior are benefited relative to relationships that are characterized by less. There is ample evidence that this is the case. My research has addressed romantic relationships, platonic friendships, parent–child relationships, sibling relationships, and relationships between cousins and between siblings-in-law, and others, such as Hess (2003), have studied a variety of adult relationships (see also Tolstedt & Stokes, 1983). In all instances, the amount of verbal, direct nonverbal, and support-based affectionate communication characterizing the relationships was directly associated with such outcome measures as relational closeness, liking and love, relationship satisfaction, and communication satisfaction. Most of these findings are summarized in Floyd and Mikkelson (2002). Importantly, when one looks across studies at the correlations between affection and the outcomes of closeness, liking, love, and relational and communication satisfaction, one finds that moderate to large effect sizes are the norm. Of these outcomes, closeness as been the most frequently studied. As reported in Floyd and Mikkelson (2002), closeness manifests average correlations (averaged across numerous datasets) of .51 with verbal affection, .46 with direct nonverbal affection, and .58 with supportive affection. Love manifests even stronger average correlations: .77 with verbal affection, .79 with nonverbal, and .82 with supportive. It is worth noting, too, that the studies that produced these associations varied not only in the type of relationship on which they focused but also in their methodology and sometimes in their operational definitions of the outcome measures.

The conclusion to be drawn is a simple (and likely intuitive) one: *humans feel more love, closeness, and satisfaction in their more affectionate relationships than in their less affectionate relationships.* Indeed, a noticeable reduction in affectionate communication over time can be indicative of problems in a relationship; that is not *necessarily* the case, but it is *often* so.

Thus far this discussion has acknowledged that affectionate communication is associated with a number of positive states: individual health, happiness, and well-being, and relationship satisfaction and success. If such a conclusion is intuitive, it begs a more thought-provoking query: *why* is affectionate communication associated with positive outcomes? Curiously, much less is known about the source(s) of affection's benefits than about the nature of those benefits. The next section addresses three different possibilities for why the communication of affection is beneficial, posing additional research questions as appropriate.

Attributions for the Benefits of Affectionate Communication

From whence do the benefits of giving and receiving affection come? This is among the most important questions posed in this book, because an understanding of where the benefits of affection come from is not only informative to social scientists but could be useful in clinical and therapeutic settings as well.

The question of why affectionate communication is beneficial is an important one but, like most important questions, not a simple one, as there are probably several valid answers. This section addresses three propositions regarding the source of affection's benefits: (1) the idea that affectionate communication one receives is solely responsible for those benefits; (2) the idea that the benefits have physiological causes; and (3) the idea that the benefits are rooted in pair bonding and its socioevolutionary benefits.

The Respective Influence of Affection Given and Affection Received

The first and most parsimonious of these answers is not really an answer at all, but rather an important reframe of the question. This is the idea that the benefits of affection all lay in *receiving* it, and that giving affectionate communication is beneficial only because it elicits affectionate expressions from others. This perspective refocuses the original question by taking attention away from expressed affection, but it does not explain *why* receiving affection is beneficial. Nevertheless, this idea merits investigation because the relationship between affection given and affection received is strongly reciprocal. It is unsurprising that it should be; Gouldner's (1960) moral norm of reciprocity explains that humans expect one good turn to be followed by another, and theories of behavioral adaptation, such as interaction adaptation theory (Burgoon, Stern et al., 1995), acknowledge that dyadic communication operates in a patterned manner that tends, more often than not, to elicit behavioral reciprocity. The relationship between affection given and affection received has been investigated in two studies, both of which have used measures of participants' trait levels of affection given and affection received (rather than measures of affection given and received in particular relationships). The measures were strongly correlated with each other in both data sets ($r = .65$ and $.70$; see Floyd, 2003; Floyd, Hess et al., 2005).

This correspondence is important because received affection might moderate the effects of expressed affection on various benefits. That is, some of the benefits of communicating affection that were identified, for instance, in the Floyd (2003) study of trait affection level could have been dependent on the amount of affection participants received from others. Floyd, Hess et al. (2005) took up this issue in a study that used data from an online survey of more than a thousand undergraduates from schools around the United States. They first looked at the correlations between trait affection given and several individual and relational benefits; they then re-examined those correlations after having controlled for trait affection received.

All of the correlations with affection given that were significant when affection received was not controlled for continued to be significant when affection received was controlled for. Specifically, affection given showed linear associations with social activity, extraversion, comfort with interpersonal closeness, the likelihood of being in a romantic relationship, and relational satisfaction (for those in romantic relationships), and an inverse association with fear of intimacy. Most (but not all) of the correlations decreased in magnitude when received affection was controlled for, however, indicating that *some* of the variance in the beneficial effects of giving affection was accounted for by the effects of receiving affection, but not *all* of it.

To investigate the issue further, Floyd examined correlations between trait affection given and a number of individual and relational benefits from the Floyd (2003) dataset (more variables were measured in this study than in the Floyd, Hess et al., 2005, study), and then reconfigured the correlations having controlled for trait affection received. Both sets of correlation coefficients appear in Table 5.1. As in the Floyd, Hess et al. (2005) paper, significant linear associations emerged between affection given and social activity, comfort with closeness, and relationship satisfaction, and an inverse association between affection given and fear of intimacy. Direct associations also emerged with self-esteem, happiness, and general mental health, and inverse associations were observed with stress, depression, and the perception of relationships as being unimportant. Importantly, all of the correlations with affection given that were significant before controlling for affection received remained significant afterward.

Table 5.1. *Bivariate and Partial Correlations between Trait Affection Given and Individual and Relational Benefits, from Floyd (2003) Data*

Variable	Bivariate Correlation with Affection Given	Correlation Controlling for Affection Received
Depression	−.26***	−.15*
Self-esteem	.40***	.25**
Social activity	.38***	.14*
Stress	−.39***	−.31***
Comfort with closeness	.67***	.50***
Fear of intimacy	−.53***	−.37***
Happiness	.53***	.37***
Relational satisfaction	.36***	.25**
Mental health	.42***	.20***
Relationships as unimportant	−.50***	−.20*

Notes: Probability estimates are one-tailed. $df = 126$. $*p < .05$; $**p < .01$; $***p < .001$.

To investigate the possibility that the benefits of receiving affection are likewise moderated by the amount of affection given, Floyd computed correlations between affection received and the various individual and relational benefits from the Floyd (2003) and the Floyd, Hess et al. (2005) datasets, and then recomputed them after controlling for affection given. Both sets of correlations appear in Table 5.2. From the Floyd (2003) data, received affection was directly related to self-esteem, social activity, happiness, comfort with closeness, mental health, and relationship satisfaction, and inversely associated with depression, stress, fear of intimacy, and the perception that relationships are unimportant. When expressed affection was covaried out, these correlations remained significant, with the exceptions of depression, stress, fear of intimacy, and relationship satisfaction. The significant partial correlations were all reduced in magnitude relative to the original bivariate correlations. Similar results emerged from the Floyd, Hess et al. (2005) data. In that study, affection received was directly related to social activity, comfort with closeness, extroversion, likelihood of being in a romantic relationship, and satisfaction with that relationship. All of these correlations,

Table 5.2. *Bivariate and Partial Correlations between Trait Affection Received and Individual and Relational Benefits, from Floyd (2003) Data*

Variable	Bivariate Correlation with Affection Received	Correlation Controlling for Affection Given
Depression	−.24***	−.06
Self-esteem	.42***	.20*
Social activity	.48***	.33***
Stress	−.32***	−.11
Comfort with closeness	.53***	.19*
Fear of intimacy	−.39***	−.11
Happiness	.52***	.32***
Relational satisfaction	.27**	.06
Mental health	.42***	.22**
Relationships as unimportant	−.49***	−.25**

Notes: Probability estimates are one-tailed. $df = 126$. *$p < .05$; **$p < .01$; ***$p < .001$.

although attenuated, remained significant when expressed affection was controlled for.

One can conclude from these findings that affection given and affection received share some variance in the individual and relational benefits they are associated with, but also retain statistically significant, independent proportions of that variance in many cases. As noted earlier, this observation does not explain why either affection given or affection received is beneficial. It does indicate, however, that their benefits are at least partly orthogonal – that is, one can benefit from receiving gestures of affection even if one does not give them, and can benefit from giving gestures of affection even if one does not receive them. Based on theories of social exchange and the norm of reciprocity, one might posit that the *similarity* between one's levels of affection given and affection received should be influential in predicting benefit. In other words, are people who give and receive approximately the same amounts of affection advantaged over those who give more than they receive, or receive more than they give? To investigate this possibility, using the Floyd (2003) and Floyd, Hess et al. (2005) data sets, I computed deviation scores by taking the absolute value of the difference between participants' scores for affection given and affection received, and correlated those deviation scores with all of the individual and relational benefits measured. Significant inverse correlations would have suggested that people are better off giving and receiving approximately the same levels of affectionate communication, whereas significant direct correlations would have suggested that giving more than one receives, or receiving more than one gives, are advantageous strategies. None of the correlations with any of the benefits measured in either of the two data sets was significant, however, suggesting that while the *absolute levels* of affection given and affection received are associated with various benefits, their *relative levels* are not.

The fundamental question is left unaddressed, however: from whence do these benefits come? To begin to address the question more directly, let us now turn our attention to the second of the three propositions acknowledged earlier, which is the idea that the benefits of affectionate communication may reside partly in physiological processes.

On the Physiology of Affectionate Communication

As noted in various places in this book, sharing affectionate communication can induce positive responses, and in some circumstances, it can also induce negative responses. There is some evidence to suggest that those responses – whether positive or negative – are not purely cognitive, but also physiological. Therefore, an examination of physiological processes that are, at least potentially, related to the expression and receipt of affection can yield some important insights into why affectionate communication is as beneficial as it is.

Before discussing some of the potential physiological correlates of affectionate communication, it is important to acknowledge two caveats regarding the research reviewed in this section. First, only a few of the studies reviewed herein were conducted for the purpose of exploring affectionate communication. Instead, most have examined the physiological aspects of constructs that are closely related to affectionate communication, such as love, attachment, social support, and positive emotion. On the basis of this work, I pose the question of whether **similar physiological processes are also related to the expression of affection**, although this question requires empirical testing that has only recently begun to be conducted.

Second, some of the research reviewed in this section (particularly research on endocrinology) was conducted on animals rather than (or, in addition to) humans. For instance, scientists have commonly conducted research on the hormonal aspects of attachment using mammals known as prairie voles (*Microtus ochrogaster*) because, like humans, prairie voles are monogamous mammals that form enduring pair bonds and cooperate within those pairs to raise and nurture their offspring. I will be clear in my discussion on physiology about which findings have come from animal studies. Obviously, there is always some legitimate question about the extent to which discoveries about animal physiology can generalize to humans, and this, of course, is an empirical question that can be addressed only through replications with human subjects. Even when such replications have not yet been conducted, however, the animal research does provide a focused starting point for understanding the potential connections between physiology and the experiences of love, attachment, and affection.

The research in this section is divided into two parts. The first covers studies on endocrine system activity, particularly as it interrelates with neuroanatomy. Several researchers have suggested that particular neurohormones are implicated in systems for behavioral activation and reward, functioning to encourage and reinforce certain adaptive behaviors by making them rewarding to enact. The second part covers research on autonomic nervous system activity, particularly studies that have examined the connections between heart rate and blood pressure reactivity and various psychological and communicative stimuli. Neither of these sections comprises an exhaustive review of the research literature on endocrinology or nervous system activity. Rather, I have included those studies whose findings, particularly when considered together, offer compelling hypotheses about how humans might react physiologically to various aspects of affection and affectionate communication.

Endocrine Response and the Brain's Reward System. The human endocrine system regulates and integrates the body's metabolic activities and is, among other things, responsible for the production of hormones. Hormones are chemical substances that are secreted by various endocrine glands in response to particular stimuli (Becker & Breedlove, 2002; Greenspan & Baxter, 1994). The major glands of the endocrine system include, among others, the thyroid gland, the pituitary gland, the adrenal gland, the pancreas, the hypothalamus, and the gonads (testes or ovaries). Each gland produces and secretes specific hormones in response to various stimuli (Nelson, 2000).

Several hormones have been implicated in systems of behavioral activation and reward. Here, I will discuss five that have been studied for their potential connections to love, attachment, social support, and/or positive emotion: cortisol, oxytocin, vasopressin, dopamine, and endogenous opioids.

Cortisol. Cortisol is a steroid hormone that is secreted by the adrenal cortex in response to the release of corticotropic releasing hormone (CRH) by the hypothalamus. Cortisol is often thought of as a "stress hormone" because it is released in response to stressors, whether physical, mental, or emotional. When secreted, cortisol causes a breakdown of muscle protein, leading to the release of amino acids into the bloodstream. The liver uses these amino acids to synthesize glucose for energy. Cortisol also depresses physiological systems nonessential during stressful situations, such as the digestive and reproductive systems. It also stimulates immune organs in case the body must deal with injury, yet it also suppresses the immune system to prevent it from overreacting to injury and needlessly damaging tissues. In these ways, cortisol fortifies the body to deal with a stressor in the short term (McEwan, 1999; Sapolsky, 2000). In the long term, however, chronically high levels of cortisol are very damaging to the body because of immunosuppression and inhibition of bone formation (See Porterfield, 2001).

Two aspects of cortisol are particularly illustrative of the body's ability to handle stress. The first concerns the magnitude of variation in cortisol levels over the course of the day. In healthy individuals, cortisol follows a diurnal (i.e., 24-hour) rhythm wherein it peaks in the hour after awakening and drops continually during the day, reaching its lowest point around midnight (Kirschbaum & Hellhammer, 1989, 1994). "Flattened" diurnal curves, showing little change in cortisol values from morning to evening, are associated with dysregulation of the hypothalamic-pituitary-adrenal axis and are indicative of chronic stress (Chrousos & Gold, 1992; Giese, Sephton, Abercrombie, Duran, & Spiegel, 2004). A second important aspect concerns the magnitude of cortisol reaction to acute stressors and the period of time it takes cortisol to return to a normal level once the stressor has subsided.

Recent studies have examined both aspects of cortisol as correlates of affectionate communication. Working from affection exchange theory, Floyd (in press) predicted that individuals with high trait levels of expressed affection would experience less chronic stress – and, therefore, would have more differentiated diurnal cortisol rhythms – than those with lower trait levels. In this study, 20 healthy young adults completed measures of trait affection given and received, and then collected four saliva samples over the course of a day (on awakening, at noon, in the late afternoon, and right before bed). Controlling for trait received affection, Floyd found that trait expressed affection was strongly related to the degree of morning-to-evening change in salivary cortisol levels.

Of course, these findings indicate a relationship between affectionate communication and cortisol, but they permit no causal inferences. It may have been that expressing affection kept the participants' cortisol rhythms well differentiated, or it may have been that those with well differentiated rhythms were more likely to be affectionate. To look more directly at the *effect* of affectionate behavior on cortisol levels, Floyd, Mikkelson, Tafoya, Farinelli, La Valley, Judd, Haynes, Davis, and Wilson (in press) induced acute stress in participants by having them undergo a series of stress-inducing activities. These included, among others, a cold pressor test (holding the forearm submerged in ice water), mental math tests, and a stroop color word test (a timed test that presents participants with names of colors that are spelled out in letters of a different color – the word "yellow" appearing in blue letters, for instance – wherein participants must identify the color of the letters in rapid succession). Thirty participants had their saliva sampled before, during, and after the stress inductions. Once the stress inductions were completed, participants were randomly assigned either to an experimental condition or one of two control groups. Those in the experimental condition were instructed to write a letter to the person with whom they currently had the closest relationship, in which they expressed their feelings of love and affection for that person. Participants in one control group were asked to think of such a person (but not to write out their affectionate feelings), and those in the other control group were instructed simply to sit quietly. The researchers continued to sample saliva during the 20-minute period following the stress induction, in order to ascertain the rates at which participants' cortisol levels returned to their baseline values after having been elevated by the stress induction.

Working from affection exchange theory, the authors hypothesized that participants in the written affection experimental group would show the sharpest declines in cortisol levels, and this was the result. For both women and men, expressing affectionate feelings to a loved one (in writing) caused cortisol levels to drop sharply after the stress induction. Merely thinking about the loved one, without expressing one's feelings, did not engender the same stress-reducing benefits. These findings suggest that affectionate communication is not only correlated with healthy variation in cortisol levels, but that expressing affection to a loved one in the wake of acute stress can actually accelerate stress recovery.

Oxytocin. *Oxytocin* is a peptide hormone that is produced in the hypothalamus (Hedge, Colby, & Goodman, 1987). It is released into the circulatory system via the pituitary gland and is also projected to other parts of the brain, including the amygdala, the striatum, other parts of the hypothalamus, and the vagal motor and sensory nuclei (see Argiolas & Gess, 1991). Oxytocin is perhaps best known for the two important functions that it serves with respect to childbirth (Uvnäs-Moberg, 2003). First, it initiates the delivery process by stimulating uterine contractions. (The word *oxytocin* in fact means *swift birth,* and synthetic oxytocin, called *pitocin,* can be injected to initiate contractions.) Second, it is responsible for the let-down reflex, stimulating milk ejection in lactating women (McCarthy & Becker, 2002).

Oxytocin is also secreted during human sexual interaction and appears to play a role in making sex rewarding. Several studies have found that oxytocin is released into the circulatory systems of both men and women at sexual orgasm (Carmichael, Humbert, Dixen, Palmiana, Greenleaf, & Davidson, 1987; Murphy, Seckl, Burton, Checkley, & Lightman, 1990; Richard, Moos, & Freund-Mercier, 1991). Moreover, the amount of oxytocin released into the bloodstream is linearly related to the subjective intensity of orgasm, at least for women (Carmichael, Warburton, Dixen, & Davidson, 1994). It is also elicited by touch and massage, even when the touch is nonsexual (Turner, Altemus, Enos, Cooper, & McGuinness, 1999).

Oxytocin's primary effect on the body (besides initiating delivery and lactation in women) is a long-term reduction in the stress response: it reduces blood pressure and resting heart rate, increases anabolic metabolism, and inhibits the production of cortisol (Altemus, Deuster, Carter, & Gold, 1995; Amico, Johnston, & Vagnucci, 1994). It promotes a feeling of calmness, pleasantness, and mild euphoria. Simply put, it makes people feel really good.

A number of researchers have acknowledged a provocative parallel with respect to oxytocin. First, *it is secreted at relationally significant moments.* That is, the peripheral events that cause oxytocin to be secreted are significant in terms of relational bonding and attachment. It is produced at sexual climax, which is important for the maintenance of pair bonds (Carmichael et al., 1987), and it is produced in women when they deliver and nurse their babies, which is important for a nurturant parent–child attachment (Uvnäs-Moberg, 2003). There is also evidence that oxytocin release is associated with flirting behavior, which is often a precursor to the formation of pair bonds (see Carter, 1992). Second, as noted above, *it imparts feelings of pleasure.* It promotes relaxation, lowers the heart rate, and inhibits stress (Carter & Altemus, 1997; Chiodera, Salvarani, Bacchi-Modena, Spallanzani, Cigarini, Alboni, Gardini, & Coiro, 1991). Oxytocin has even been identified as the hormone responsible for the "afterglow" effect that couples often experience after lovemaking (Arletti, Benelli, & Bertolini, 1992).

The juxtaposition of these two observations has fueled speculation that oxytocin plays a critical role in bonding and attachment processes, both in humans and in other mammals. That is, there is reason to believe it is an important part of the brain's reward system, the neurological function that promotes behaviors that are important to survival and reproduction by making people feel good when they engage in those behaviors. Several theoretic perspectives have drawn explicit connections between oxytocin release and the formation and maintenance of pair bonds and sexually and emotionally intimate relationships. Porges's polyvagal theory (1995, 1996, 1997, 1998), for instance, offers that oxytocin release can facilitate a conditioning process that can help explain the importance of friendship and parent–child bonding, as well as the grief people feel at the loss of loved ones (see Porges, 1998, p. 852). Proposed is that oxytocin release facilitates a type of conditioning response that bonds people to significant others; that is, our brains produce oxytocin when we interact with loved ones, which makes us feel good in their presence and, therefore, makes us desire their presence more often.

Other theories offer similar proposals. Uvnäs-Moberg's (1998) theory on social support proposes that oxytocin, and its associated long-term reductions in heart rate and blood pressure, may be partly responsible for the benefits of social support behavior. Taylor's (2002) tend and befriend theory, which explains that women react to stress more by drawing on their social bonds than by engaging in fight-or-flight responses, suggests that tending and befriending behaviors are rewarding and stress-reducing partly because they elicit oxytocin secretion. Panksepp has written extensively on the connections between oxytocin and human attachment (see, e.g., Nelson & Panksepp, 1998; Panksepp, 1998). He suggested that "A straightforward emotional prediction is that brain oxytocin may evoke warm positive feelings of social strength and comfort when aroused by peripheral stimuli" (Panksepp, 1992, p. 243; see also Insel, 1997).

Barber (2002) went so far as to refer to oxytocin as the *cuddle hormone*, in reference to its apparent role in forming and maintaining pair bonds.

Several studies with nonhuman mammals have indicated that oxytocin does, in fact, increase affiliative behavior. These studies are often conducted by administering doses of either oxytocin or oxytocin antagonists (substances that prevent oxytocin from binding to its intended receptor sites) to animals and observing changes in their behaviors. This research has reported that oxytocin induces sexual and maternal behavior in rats (Pedersen, Caldwell, Walker, Ayers, & Mason, 1994; Witt & Insel, 1991), increases physical contact among rats and prairie voles (Witt, Carter, & Walton, 1990; Witt, Winslow, & Insel, 1992), and elicits grooming behavior among male squirrel monkeys (Winslow & Insel, 1991).

On the basis of both theory and research on oxytocin, it appears to be the case that the secretion of oxytocin (especially during relationally significant events) is a part of what makes love, and loving relationships, rewarding. It may be the reason why being in love is so rewarding, not just intellectually but also physically. And, as Porges (1998) has suggested, when oxytocin is repeatedly secreted in response to stimuli from particular people (e.g., interacting with a specific loved one), it may play a part in conditioning us to maintain social and personal bonds that we have already developed.

In light of these observations, there is reason to believe that oxytocin may also play a role in making the communication of affection such a rewarding experience. Perhaps it is the case that oxytocin secretion can be elicited not only by the loving touch of a friend or intimate partner, but also by his or her loving words. If true, this would help to explain why receiving affectionate expressions from loved ones commonly elicits such positive feelings. Perhaps oxytocin is even secreted when people express affection to others, as well as when they receive it. It may also be the case that affectionate messages do not elicit the same levels of oxytocin release when they are received from people the recipient does not care about, which could explain why people tend not to react as positively in these situations (unwarranted affectionate expressions may also engage physiological stress responses, further explaining the negative reactions).

In perhaps the first experimental investigation to test these predictions with humans, Grewen, Girdler, Amico, and Light (2005) had heterosexual romantic couples engage in a 10-minute affectionate interaction in which they sat close to each other, held hands, talked about times when they felt particularly close to each other, watched a romantic video together, and hugged. Using an indwelling catheter, the authors drew

blood samples during a baseline period prior to the affectionate interaction and again three times during a recovery period afterward. Each
participant also provided a self-report of the level of support he or she
received from the romantic partner.

Two findings were particularly noteworthy with respect to oxytocin.
First, for both men and women, baseline levels of oxytocin were directly
related to the amount of support participants reported receiving from
their spouses, suggesting that those with more satisfying, supportive relational bonds have higher average levels of blood oxytocin than do those in
less supportive relationships. Second, and more important to the current
discussion, plasma oxytocin levels increased over baseline levels following the affectionate interaction, but only for women. Moreover, participants of both sexes had a corresponding decrease in serum cortisol, a
hormone that is secreted in response to stress (Nelson, 2000; Sapolsky,
2002). Although it is impossible to know which aspect of the affectionate
interaction had the greatest effect on oxytocin levels, these findings are
the first to demonstrate that affectionate, warm contact between romantic partners increases plasma levels of oxytocin, at least for women. This,
along with the corresponding decrease in cortisol, suggests that affectionate communication in supportive romantic relationships may contribute to long-term mental and physical health benefits associated with
the downregulation of stress. Additional experimental work on the associations between affectionate communication and oxytocin will further
illuminate this relationship.

Vasopressin. Vasopressin (which is also referred to as *antidiuretic
hormone*, or ADH) is a peptide hormone that is very similar in structure
to oxytocin (in fact, the two differ by only two amino acids; Carter, 2002).
Although fewer studies have been conducted on vasopressin than on
oxytocin, the research suggests that vasopressin may have similar effects
on affiliation and attachment (Baum, 2002; Winslow, Hastings, Carter,
Harbaugh, & Insel, 1993). Like oxytocin, vasopressin is produced in
the hypothalamus (although in separate neurons) and is implicated in
human sexual response, although more so for men than for women.

Specifically, vasopressin appears to play a part in sexual initiation. In
human males, vasopressin levels are elevated during foreplay and sexual
arousal; however, they decline rapidly at orgasm (Baum, 2002). Oxytocin,
by contrast, remains low during arousal but is strongly released at orgasm
and remains relatively high for some time afterward (Nelson, 2000). It
thus appears that vasopressin promotes sexual eagerness and receptivity

in men, whereas oxytocin promotes sexual pleasure (Carmichael et al., 1987; Murphy et al., 1990). Porges (1998) suggested that the interplay between vasopressin and oxytocin could facilitate a powerful conditioning process that contributes to the maintenance of significant human bonds, whether sexual or not.

Animal research sheds more light on the roles that vasopressin might play in promoting sexual interaction, at least for males. Research on prairie voles suggests that vasopressin promotes sexual jealousy, which is certainly adaptive in terms of males' abilities to maintain their pair bonds and prevent copulation between their mates and other males. Winslow et al. (1993) reported that male prairie voles who copulated with females exhibited jealousy behaviors, but not if a vasopressin antagonist was placed in their brains before copulation. Moreover, they found that if vasopressin is introduced into the brain, male prairie voles will exhibit jealousy behaviors even without having copulated. They also reported that male prairie voles spent more time with females in whose company they experienced elevated vasopressin, suggesting that vasopressin secretion can promote the same types of conditioned responses as have been identified with oxytocin.

To the extent that research on vasopressin in prairie voles can be generalized to humans, it appears that vasopressin contributes both to precopulatory receptivity and to postcopulatory attachment and jealousy behaviors, both of which are important for the formation and maintenance of pair bonds. This research has focused on male humans and prairie voles. Less is known about the effects of vasopressin in females; this is partly because less research has been done on females, since males produce more vasopressin than females do (Panksepp, 1998). Sodersten, Henning, Melin, and Ludin (1983) did report, however, that although vasopressin promotes sexual eagerness in men, it appears to have the opposite effect on women. They indicated that, when vasopressin is artificially increased in women's brains, their sexual receptivity decreases, in contrast to the response observed with males. This suggests that vasopressin may play a larger role in the formation and maintenance of attachment bonds for males than for females.

Dopamine. Dopamine is a catecholamine released in the nucleus accumbens (Porterfield, 2001). It appears to be involved in several important functions, including attention, learning, and movement (Becker, 2002; Robbins & Everitt, 1996). More important for the present discussion, dopamine serves to create feelings of pleasure associated with various stimuli (Wise, 1989); indeed, a good deal of research on dopamine has focused on its relationship to addiction (e.g., Samson, Hodge, Tolliver, & Haraguchi, 1993). Addictive drugs, such as nicotine and alcohol, appear to stimulate rewarding experiences partly because of their abilities to promote dopamine release (Wise, 1996). Research on laboratory animals confirms that both nicotine (Damsma, Day, & Fibiger, 1989) and alcohol (Gessa, Muntoni, Collu, Vargiu, & Mereu, 1985) increase dopamine release in the nucleus accumbens. Moreover, injecting a dopamine antagonist directly in the nucleus accumbens inhibits alcohol intake (Samson et al., 1993).

Dopamine is also implicated in the experiences of love and sex. As noted earlier, vasopressin is secreted in men during sexual arousal, whereas oxytocin is secreted at sexual climax. Research suggests that, during sexual interaction, dopamine may function more like vasopressin than oxytocin, contributing more to the reward level of sexual arousal than sexual climax (see Larsson & Ahlenius, 1986). Indeed, Damsma, Pfaus, Wenkstern, Phillips, and Fibiger (1992) found that, in male rats, more dopamine was released during foreplay than during copulation itself (see also Pfaus, Damsma, Nomikos, Wenkstern, Blaha, Phillips, & Fibiger, 1990).

The possibility that dopamine is implicated in the experience of love and relational attachment was addressed in a unique study by Kurup and Kurup (2003). The authors recruited samples of East Indian adults from two populations: those who were currently in love and in non-arranged marriages, and those who had never been in love and had conventional arranged Indian marriages. Using plasma extracted from fasting blood draws, the researchers analyzed participants' basal levels of dopamine and found, as predicted, that plasma dopamine levels were significantly higher in "in love" participants than in those who were not in love. Results also indicated that the former group had higher levels of morphine and norepinephrine, and lower levels of serotonin, than did the latter group.

There is an interesting parallel between the involvement of dopamine in sustaining drug addiction and the idea that dopamine is implicated in relational bonding. Scientists who study dopamine as a reinforcing agent for drug addiction note that dopamine can function to produce both *positive reinforcement* and *negative reinforcement*. Positive reinforcement occurs when a stimulus (e.g., a drink of alcohol) is associated with a reward (e.g., a surge in dopamine). By contrast, negative reinforcement involves the termination of an aversive stimulus; for instance, drinking is negatively reinforced when we discover that consuming alcohol will relieve anxiety, emotional pain, or boredom, at least temporally. One might suggest that both processes could also be implicated in the formation and maintenance of human relationships. If dopamine (or oxytocin, or vasopressin) is secreted in response to affectionate exchanges with others, then this could act to positively reinforce those relationships, making individuals feel good in the presence of those other people (see, e.g., Pfaff, 1999). Likewise, one may find that dopamine production negatively reinforces relational attachment by diminishing the emotional pain of loneliness (thereby terminating, or at least reducing the force of, an aversive stimulus). Future research on the involvement of dopamine in human relational interaction will help to illuminate these possibilities.

Endogenous Opioids. Endogenous opioids are neuropeptides that, like the hormones discussed earlier, act to impart pleasure and reward. They are called opioids because their physical effects are similar to those of exogenous opiates such as morphine, which include the relief of pain and feelings of elation (Panksepp, 1998; Sapolsky, 2002). There are three families of endogenous opioids: β-endorphins, proenkephalins, and prodynorphins (Akil, Watson, Young, Lewis, Khachaturian, & Walker, 1984). Many people, particularly athletes, are already familiar with the analgesic effects of β-endorphins. These are the peptides credited with producing the "runners' high": the sensation of painlessness, energy, and elevated mood that runners sometimes experience toward the end of a long run (Sapolsky, 2002). The prefix *endo –* is short for *endogenous* (meaning that it refers to a substance produced internally), and the suffix *– orphin* is a variant of the word *morphine* (indicating that the physical effects of endorphins are similar to those of exogenous morphine).

Like the hormones discussed earlier, endogenous opioids are also implicated in sexual pleasure (see, e.g., Davis, 1984). Research conducted by Murphy, Checkley, Seckl, and Lightman (1990) found that, when men were given an endorphin antagonist (a drug that occupies the endorphin receptors, blocking the effects of endorphins when they are released), it affected their experiences at sexual climax. Specifically, men who were given the antagonist reported less arousal and pleasure at orgasm than did men who were given a placebo. Moreover, those in the placebo group had a 362% increase in their oxytocin levels at orgasm (compared to baseline readings taken before sexual arousal), whereas those men who had taken the endorphin antagonist showed no increase in oxytocin levels at orgasm. These findings suggest that endorphin release plays an important role, at least for men, in making copulation pleasurable. Research on other mammals, such as rats, has found that endorphin antagonists similarly inhibit the pleasure associated with sex (see, e.g., Ågmo & Berenfeld, 1990).

Cortisol, oxytocin, vasopressin, dopamine, and endogenous opioids are only five hormonal agents that may be implicated in the benefits of affectionate interaction. Others, such as serotonin or acetylcholine, also may play important roles. All of these possibilities await empirical investigation. However, the existing research on these hormones suggests that social scientists would do well to study their effects in interpersonal processes. Indeed, this is one of the most promising areas for future research on affectionate communication.

The endocrine system is not the only anatomical system whose functions are implicated in interpersonal processes. Arousal, in particular, is largely governed by the activities of the autonomic nervous system, to which we now turn our attention.

Autonomic Nervous System Activity. The nervous system can be divided into two inter-related parts: the central nervous system and the peripheral nervous system. The central nervous system is comprised of the brain and the spinal cord and has primary responsibility for all functioning in the body. As its name implies, the peripheral nervous system regulates behavior and reactivity that are peripheral to the central nervous system's activities but are still essential for health and survival, such as digestion, blood pressure, and thermoregulation. The peripheral nervous system consists of two main parts: the somatic nervous system, which controls skeletal muscle movement, and the autonomic nervous system (ANS), which maintains regulatory functions in the body. The ANS is responsible, for instance, for regulating heart beat, blood flow, skin temperature and perspiration, and other functions that are necessary to keep the body running efficiently. (For additional discussion on the structure of the nervous system, consult Marieb, 2003.)

The focus in this section will be on the ANS, which can be further divided into two parts: the sympathetic nervous system and the parasympathetic nervous system. The sympathetic nervous system governs excitation and arousal; the parasympathetic nervous system deals with relaxation and rest. When individuals feel excited by seeing or hearing from a loved one, it is activation of the sympathetic nervous system that they experience; contrariwise, the waning of such excitement is directed by parasympathetic nervous system activation.

There are several potential pathways through which sympathetic nervous system arousal can facilitate the formation, maintenance, and quality of significant affectionate relationships (thereby exposing individuals to the benefits of those relationships). This section describes some of these mechanisms. The sympathetic nervous system generates arousal partly through release of two chemical agents known as catecholamines: *epinephrine* (also referred to as adrenaline) and *norepinephrine* (or noradrenaline). Both are secreted into the bloodstream by the adrenal gland. Epinephrine is responsible for the increased heart rate that accompanies arousal. (It produces the physical sensation that is referred to in common parlance as an "adrenaline rush.") Norepinephrine increases blood pressure through vasoconstriction. Besides being released in tandem, these hormones are also released quickly following exposure to a stimulus. They have the effect of preparing the body for increased demands on its energy; for example, epinephrine and norepinephrine are secreted during sexual arousal to provide excess energy to be expended during copulation (Sapolsky, 2002).

The ANS also regulates pupil dilation and contraction. Normal pupils can dilate to approximately 8 to 9 mm, can contract to approximately 1.5 mm, and can react to stimuli in a fifth of a second (Guyton, 1977). Pupil dilation and contraction are influenced by a number of factors, including ambient light, use of stimulants or depressants, and the distance of an object of focus. Perhaps more interestingly for communication researchers, sympathetic nervous system activation can also initiate pupil dilation in response to an attractive other (Aboyoun & Dabbs, 1998). Pupil dilation is implicated in interpersonal attraction and pair bonding, in two separate but interrelated ways. First, pupils dilate when people look at others they find attractive (Andersen, Todd-Mancillas, & DiClemente, 1980). Of course, other sympathetic nervous system activities often cooccur with pupil dilation when people interact with attractive others, including increases in heart rate, blood pressure, and perspiration. Second, having dilated pupils makes people more physically attractive to others, all other things being equal (Hess, 1975).[1] Each of these processes initiates the other: a woman's pupils dilate if she finds a particular man attractive, and he therefore finds her more attractive because her pupils are dilated, which causes his pupils to dilate, which causes her to be

---

[1] In fact, it has been a common practice in times past for women to use the drug *belladonna* (which means, literally, *beautiful woman*) to cause their own pupils to dilate, thereby making them more attractive.

more attracted to him, and so forth. There is also evidence that auditory stimuli can initiate pupil dilation; Dabbs (1997) reported that listening to sexually charged sounds caused pupil dilation in participants and that this effect was enhanced for people with high testosterone levels. Pupil dilation and contraction are difficult for untrained observers to consciously appreciate without instrumentation. However, humans appear to be able to appreciate changes in pupil size at a subconscious level, which is adaptive for mating owing to its reliable association with attraction.

There is additional evidence that sympathetic nervous system arousal facilitates the formation and maintenance of affectionate relationships. In a now classic experiment, Dutton and Aron (1974) had a female confederate approach young men who had just walked across either a wobbly suspension bridge over a 230-foot drop, or a sturdy cedar bridge over a 10-foot drop, and invite them to complete a short questionnaire that included parts of the Thematic Apperception Test (TAT: Murray, 1943). The TAT item used was a photograph of a young woman covering her face with one hand while reaching with the other. Participants were instructed to write a brief dramatic story involving the woman in the picture, and their stories were later coded for the amount of sexual imagery and content, on a scale of 1 to 5 in which higher numbers indicate more sexual content. Participants who crossed the suspension bridge wrote stories with an average sexual content of 2.99, whereas those who crossed the sturdier wood bridge wrote stories with an average sexual content of 1.92, a statistically significant difference. The confederate also gave participants her telephone number and invited them to call with any questions about the study. Of those who crossed the suspension bridge, 65% subsequently called the confederate, whereas only 30% of those who crossed the wooden bridge subsequently called.

Why are these findings notable? Dutton and Aron surmised that the physiological arousal induced by fear of crossing the suspension bridge would cause participants to have greater sexual attraction to the confederate than would those who crossed the safer, less fear-arousing wooden bridge. (Sexual imagery in their TAT stories, and the instances of calling the confederate after the study, were taken as indirect measures of sexual attraction.) Their explanation was one of misattribution: crossing the suspension bridge produced arousal because of its danger, but participants, having experienced their arousal in the presence of the female confederate, misattributed their arousal to her. Thus, the researchers argued, participants felt sexual attraction because they were physiologically aroused in the confederate's presence, even though their arousal had been induced by the danger of crossing the bridge. The fact that participants who crossed the safer wooden bridge showed less attraction to the confederate than did those who crossed the suspension bridge added credence to this explanation.

The link between arousal and attraction suggests some practical applications. In their model of romantic love as expansion of the self, Aron and Aron (1986) proposed that the relationship quality of marriages and other significant romantic attachments could be enhanced through shared participation in exciting, novel, and arousing activities. That is, by taking part in activities together that activate sympathetic nervous system arousal, such as skiing, hiking, dancing, or going to concerts, couples might actually enhance the quality of their relationship (assessed through their reports of their marital satisfaction) more so than by doing activities that are pleasant but not arousing (such as going to a movie, attending church, or eating out). Aron and Aron speculated that shared participation in arousing activities may enhance relationship quality partly because such arousal amplifies positive feelings for the partner in much the same way that Dutton and Aron found that arousal increased sexual attraction. Sympathetic nervous system arousal heightens the senses, which may increase relational partners' attunement to each other. Moreover, insofar as the arousal is not accompanied by negative affect (such that it might be attributed to fear or anxiety, for instance), it might function, as the neurohormones discussed earlier have been theorized to, to create a reinforcement effect whereby one associates feelings of excitement and exhilaration with interaction with the specific relational partner.

Initial research by Reissman, Aron, and Bergen (1993) provided evidence for the effect of shared participation in arousing activities on increased marital satisfaction. In their 10-week study, 53 married couples were divided into three conditions. Couples in the first condition were instructed to spend an hour and a half each week doing something exciting and novel; those in the second condition were asked to spend an hour and a half each week doing something pleasant but not exciting; and those in the control condition were given no particular instructions. Pre- and posttests of marital satisfaction revealed that couples in the "exciting activity" condition had a significant increase in their marital satisfaction over the course of the 10 weeks, whereas those in the control condition did not. Importantly, those in the "pleasant activity" condition did not differ significantly from those in the control condition; that is, they did not experience an increase in their marital satisfaction. The only such increase was associated with doing exciting, arousing activities.

Aron, Norman, Aron, McKenna, and Heyman (2000) replicated the Reissman et al. findings in five studies. In three of the five studies, the researchers had dating and married couples take part in a laboratory procedure in which they were bound to each other at the wrists and ankles with Velcro straps and instructed to make their way across a set of gymnasium mats while holding a pillow between their heads and climbing over barriers. Couples in a parallel experimental condition took part in a mundane, nonarousing activity that involved rolling a ball back and forth across a gymnasium mat.[2] In all three studies, couples in the "exciting activity" condition manifested significant increases in their perceptions of their relationship quality, whereas those in the corresponding "mundane activity" condition did not. This finding is particularly noteworthy given that the interval between the pretest and posttest on relationship quality was not 10 weeks, as it had been in the Reissman et al. study, but only the hour it took couples to complete the laboratory protocols.

The collective implication of these studies is that sharing activities that facilitate physiological arousal has positive effects, not only on the formation of potential relationships (through increased sexual attraction) but also on the quality and maintenance of existing relationships. A logical derivation is that sympathetic nervous system activity is consequential for the formation and quality of pair bonding. If giving or receiving expressions of affection can induce physiological arousal, this may be an additional mechanism through which affectionate communication elicits benefit – at least, the benefits associated with being in satisfying, significant relationships.

The critical question, therefore is: **to what extent does giving or receiving affectionate messages increase nervous system arousal?** Anecdotal evidence clearly suggests an association; people often speak, for instance, of having sweaty palms and racing heartbeats when hearing the words "I love you" and reciprocating them in kind. Systematic research on the connection between affectionate behavior and nervous system arousal has yet to be conducted, however. Such research could address a number of important questions. For instance, **under what conditions do giving or receiving affectionate messages increase one's heart rate, blood pressure, or secretion of epinephrine and norepinephrine?** Such responses

---

[2] Manipulation checks confirmed that the activities in the "exciting activity" condition were more exciting and arousing than were those in the "mundane activity" condition.

might, for example, be more common in younger relationships than in more established ones, or more common in romantic relationships than in platonic ones. Similarly, one might ask, **how does nervous system arousal associated with giving affectionate communication compare with arousal associated with receiving affectionate communication?** Indeed, multiple aspects of the physiology of affectionate communication, including endocrine system activity and ANS arousal, as well as neurological activity, await systematic investigation.

The previous discussion has addressed two major propositions as to why affectionate communication is beneficial. A third proposition considers the direct connection between affectionate behavior and the formation of pair bonds, and it is to this idea that we turn our attention next.

The Adaptive Advantages of Pair Bonding

A third possible response to the question of why affectionate communication is beneficial is that its benefits derive from the pair bonds that it helps to create and maintain. This line of reasoning provides that affectionate behavior is indirectly beneficial; that is, affectionate behavior promotes the development of pair bonds (whether romantic or platonic), and pair bonds entail a number of physical, financial, emotional, and psychological advantages for individuals (see Gove, Hughes, & Style, 1983; Hu & Goldman, 1990; Hughes & Gove, 1981; Waite, 1995). This may be an unsatisfying answer for why affectionate communication is beneficial because, in some respects, it simply advances the question. If one argues that affectionate behavior is beneficial because it promotes pair bonding, then one needs merely to ask "*why* does it promote pair bonding?" to find that one's understanding has not been advanced much. And, if the benefits one seeks to account for by this explanation are those associated with pair bonding, then the explanation can appear to be tautological, as well: affectionate behavior elicits the benefits associated with pair bonding because it promotes pair bonding.

Progress toward a more adequate answer can be achieved by considering *why* affectionate behavior, among all human behavioral options, is so efficient and effective at establishing, maintaining, and nurturing pair bonds. Why is it, for instance, that humans attract friends and mates more efficiently with affection than with other behaviors (aggression, for instance)? As noted earlier, physiology may very well play a role; when humans give and receive affection, the accompanying physical and emotional experiences tend to be positive ones, and those positive feelings may well serve to condition people to seek out the presence of certain others.

It also may be the case that affectionate communication serves higher-order needs that have evolved to be adaptive in human mate selection. Specifically, *affectionate communication may facilitate pair bonding by conveying intentions of relational commitment and emotional investment, which qualities are adaptive to seek in a potential mate.* According to such a perspective, it is adaptive to concern oneself with commitment and emotional investment when pair bonding because the fundamental purpose of a pair bond is procreation, and the ability to rear healthy children is enhanced when both partners in a pair bond are committed to that task. It is advantageous, therefore, to be keen to signs of commitment and investment in a potential partner and wary of their absence. In the long term, in fact, one would expect that those who are more attuned to those signs are better positioned to select apt partners and exclude poorer options, and should therefore accrue more procreative success than those who are less cognizant of such signs.

There is ample evidence that humans do, indeed, discriminate in the selection of long-term and short-term romantic partners. Buss (1989) investigated patterns of mate selection among more than 10,000 people in 37 cultures worldwide and reported a high degree of consistency across cultures in the qualities people seek in potential mates and sexual partners. Specifically, he found that, when seeking potential mates, men across cultures look for physical attractiveness and cues to health and youth, whereas women across cultures seek cues to wealth, status, and markers of commitment. In a review of the research on mate preference, Grammer (1989) also noted that women typically consider a larger number of cues than men do when selecting potential mates. When selecting short-term sexual partners as opposed to long-term mates, however, men appear willing to adjust their standards fairly dramatically. Buss and Schmidt (1993) asked college students to indicate what would matter to them in selecting a short-term sex partner as opposed to a long-term mating partner. Their results indicated that men were substantially more willing than women to relax their typical standards when choosing a short-term sexual partner. Specifically, men relaxed their standards with respect to the age, education level, level of honesty and independence, intelligence, and emotional stability of a potential sexual partner, along with a number of other characteristics. Conversely, Buss and Schmidt found that men were less willing than women to accept sex partners who were physically unattractive, who had a high need for commitment, who had high amounts of body hair, and who had a low sex drive. On all of the other 61 characteristics Buss and Schmidt measured, however, men showed relaxed standards for sex partners as opposed to long-term mates more so than did women.

The differences in what men and women seek in mating partners may reflect a sex difference in minimal parental investment. Bearing even one healthy child and raising it to sexual maturity requires a substantial investment of time, labor, energy, and other resources on the part of a woman. At minimum, she must carry the fetus in utero for approximately nine months, incurring the accompanying costs of the physical strain on her body, the mental and emotional strain associated with her hormonal fluctuations, and the physical and financial stress of her restricted mobility and activity. Those who then rear their child must also attend to his or her substantial and oft-changing physical, emotional, and financial needs for many more years, if the child is to reach sexual maturity and be able to pass the mothers' genes on to succeeding generations.

By stark contrast, men's minimum investment consists of the time required to impregnate the woman and the resources he spent in the pursuit of that mating opportunity. His physiological part in this process is then complete. Certainly, most men invest enormous emotional and financial resources in rearing and caring for their children, and one should not minimize the significant role that fatherhood plays in human family dynamics. The point, however, is that the *minimum* investment of resources required to produce and raise a child to sexual maturity is substantially different for men and women.[3]

In humans and many other species, this difference manifests itself in different strategies used by men and women to attract mates. In his theory of parental investment, Trivers (1972) suggested that the sex whose minimum investment in offspring is greater will be the most selective when choosing sexual partners, because a poor decision is more consequential for that sex than for the other. Because women's minimum parental investment is so substantially greater than men's, therefore, Trivers predicted that women would be more selective than men when choosing mating partners, and indeed that is the case (see Bateman, 1948).

Importantly, however, differential minimum investment does not suggest only that women are more selective than men when identifying

---

[3] This is also true for males and females of many other species, particularly species characterized by internal gestation.

potential mates. It also suggests that the sexes ought to emphasize different qualities when seeking mates. Earlier, I described Buss's finding that, in numerous cultures, men seeking mates value physical attractiveness more than women do, whereas women seeking mates value both markers of status and markers of commitment more than men do. In his sexual strategies theory, Buss (1994) explained this robust sex difference within the framework of differential minimum investment. Specifically, he offered that men emphasize women's physical attractiveness because attractiveness signals health and youth, and these are markers of fertility. By mating with attractive women, men therefore increase the chances that any resulting offspring will be healthy enough to survive to sexual maturity. This strategy thus maximizes the evolutionary return on men's investment. Buss's theory suggested that women, by contrast, emphasize status because status typically translates into economic resources for the woman and her offspring; further, he suggested that women emphasize markers of relational commitment, because of the greater efficacy in raising a healthy child *with* the father's involvement as opposed to *without*. Women's attunement to signs that men (1) have resources to invest in them and their offspring, and (2) are committed to actually providing those resources in the long term, is therefore adaptive. Importantly, Buss's theory suggests neither that women are indifferent to physical attractiveness nor that men are indifferent to signs of status or commitment; rather, it provides only that women and men will favor these traits differentially.

How does this discussion relate to the use of affectionate communication in the establishment of pair bonds? Expressing affection to a potential partner does not likely make individuals appear wealthy or physically attractive. By contrast, it is efficient at conveying relational commitment. The use of verbal statements such as "I love you" or "I care about you," accompanied by nonverbal gestures that signal intimacy (such as kissing) and relational exclusivity (such as hand holding), can encode messages of commitment in new or ongoing relationships, perhaps more effectively and more efficiently than any other types of behavior. Because it is adaptive to be attuned to signals of commitment when forming new pair bonds (and to attend to *continued* signals of commitment in ongoing relationships), displays of affection often play a substantial role in relationship development and relationship maintenance. Indeed, as King and Christensen (1983) reported, using affectionate names and making verbal declarations of love are two of the most significant turning points in new romantic relationships.

This discussion comprises the third answer to the question of why affection displays are so beneficial: because they convey something that it is adaptive for humans to seek in pair bonds, and therefore contribute to the formation and maintenance of such bonds, exposing the partners to the benefits of pair bonding. Whether affection displays convey *genuine* relational commitment or not is, of course, a different matter. As noted in the first chapter, the experience of affection and the expression of affection do not necessarily covary. This, coupled with the importance of affection in newly developing relationships, creates the possibility that one could use affectionate communication in a manipulative way, perhaps to elicit sexual interaction or premature relational commitment. These possibilities receive more detailed attention in the next chapter.

This chapter has reviewed research on the benefits of giving and receiving affection and of being in affectionate relationships. It has also taken up the question of why affectionate communication is so beneficial, and has explored three possible answers to the question. The evidence suggests that there is merit in each of the answers. In particular, Floyd, Hess et al. (2005) indicated that, although not *all* of the benefit of giving affection is because of the affectionate expressions elicited in return, *some* of the benefit is. Moreover, current research suggests that there is physiological activity in both the endocrine and nervous systems that accompanies affection exchange and partly accounts for its benefit, and that the pair bonds that affectionate behavior helps to establish and maintain are the source of additional benefit.

Lest one believe that affectionate behavior is *always* beneficial, however, one must take stock of its potential risks and downfalls. These issues are taken up in detail in the next chapter.

6

Risks Associated with Affectionate Communication

The hardest of all is learning to be a well of affection, and not a fountain; to show them we love them not when we feel like it, but when they do.
                                                              – Nan Fairbrother

Perhaps the aspect of affectionate communication that challenges human intuition more than any other is the fact that it sometimes produces negative outcomes. Intuition – and indeed, human social experience – suggest that affectionate behavior characterizes our most positive, intimate relationships; that it is a pleasing aspect of those relationships; and that it advances the welfare of those relationships and their participants. It is largely counterintuitive, therefore, to think of affectionate behavior as an instigator of distress, one that could even precipitate the demise of an otherwise positive relationship. Counterintuitive though it may be, there are very real risks and potential problems associated with the communication of affection, and an adequate understanding of affection exchange would elude researchers if they failed to acknowledge them.

Although the potential pitfalls of affectionate communication comprise one of its most intriguing aspects, they are also among the least studied aspects. I must begin by reiterating the caveat from the previous chapter that, although the reasons for expecting affectionate communication to be risky and problematic at times are more than adequate, the empirical research on this characteristic of affectionate behavior is very much in its infancy. In places, therefore, this chapter may seem to be longer on speculation than on actual evidence. In one sense, this is precisely what one might expect; given that affectionate behavior is *typically* associated with positive outcomes, rather than negative, it is understandable that more scientists have not yet turned their attention to its potential risks and pitfalls. There is much to be learned about affectionate communication by examining its dark side, however, and this will be an important topic for future inquiry.

This chapter is divided into two sections. The first examines some of the salient risks associated with expressing affectionate messages to others, whereas the second focuses on the potential problems that can accompany affectionate expressions for recipients. Certainly, not all of these risks and potential problems are salient in every relationship or in every affection exchange. To the extent that they are, however, they can raise the possibility that affectionate behavior may produce relational outcomes that are more aversive than not.

Risks for Senders of Affectionate Messages

Floyd (e.g., Floyd & Morman, 1997; Floyd & Burgoon, 1999), has suggested that senders of affectionate messages must negotiate, to varying degrees, at least three types of risks: the risk of non-reciprocity, the risk of misinterpretation, and the risk of social censure. To this list can be added a fourth, less common risk associated with physical affection: the risk of disease transmission. This section addresses each of these risks, offering speculation as to when each might be salient and how each might be managed by senders. The discussion will pose a number of predictions and research questions in this section because, although research has focused empirical attention on the negative outcomes of affectionate behavior, nearly all of it has addressed this topic from the vantage of receivers rather than senders. Of course, some of the risks and potential problems are similar for senders and receivers; thus, the research on receivers' responses aids in illuminating understanding of the senders' risks. This will be a particularly fruitful area for additional research, however.

Risk of Nonreciprocity

Perhaps the most evident risk to senders of affectionate messages is the risk that receivers will fail to reciprocate them. This is actually two separate risks masquerading as one: first, there is the risk that the *expression* won't be reciprocated, and second, there is the risk that, even if the expression is reciprocated, the actual *sentiment* will not be. Both involve potential threats to senders' positive face, which is their need for approval, acceptance, and affiliation (see Brown & Levinson, 1987; Lim & Bowers, 1991).

One might speculate that this risk is at its most intense during early stages of relationship development. As noted in previous chapters, the initial expression of affection – whether it be an embrace, a kiss, or a verbal declaration of love – is often a critical turning point for a new relationship (Owen, 1987). **When is the initial expression of affection a negative turning point, as opposed to a positive one?** One obvious candidate is when the expression is not reciprocated. In the example from the first chapter, Lisa's failure to reciprocate Jason's verbal expression of love was a principal cause of the problems that ensued. In newly forming relationships, a declaration of affection (whether verbal or nonverbal) is, in part, a sender's invitation for the receiver to make his or her own feelings known. As such, it could operate as a type of "secret test" for gaining information about how one's partner feels about a new relationship (see Baxter & Wilmot, 1984). If the receiver fails to reciprocate the expression, senders may interpret that as an indication that the sentiment is not shared.

Adding insult to injury in cases of nonreciprocity is the strong social expectation that expressions of affection *will* be reciprocated. Gouldner's (1960) moral norm of reciprocity, which is discussed in greater detail below, provides that one beneficial behavior ought to elicit another in response; or, in this case, that one expression of affection ought to elicit another. Indeed, social psychological research indicates that people have overwhelming tendencies to reciprocate positive feelings and evaluations that are directed to them by others (Jones & Wortman, 1973; Kenny & Nasby, 1980). Under typical circumstances, one would expect both senders and receivers to share this expectation. Therefore, if a receiver fails to reciprocate an affectionate message, *even despite the social expectation to do so*, then the offense to the sender may be particularly poignant.

Is the risk of nonreciprocity a salient risk even in established, long-term relationships? Even if it is, one might surmise that the risk is much less salient than in newly forming relationships, for two reasons. First, established relationships usually entail greater behavioral predictability than do new relationships (see, e.g., Parks & Floyd, 1996). That is, people are typically better able to predict the behaviors of their partners in established relationships than in new ones. Thus, **if one expresses affection in an established relationship as opposed to a newly developing relationship, one ought to be less likely to *worry* about whether it will be reciprocated or not because one will be better able to *predict* whether it will be.**

A second reason to expect the risk of nonreciprocity to be less salient in established relationships is that, in such relationships, the partners have usually communicated and reinforced their level of love and affection for each other multiple times over the course of the relationship. Therefore, *if* **an affectionate expression is not reciprocated, for some reason, partners in an established relationship ought to be less concerned that the corresponding sentiment is unshared**. Instead, one might expect that partners in established relationships should be more likely than those in new relationships to attribute the lack of reciprocity to unstable, situational factors (e.g., "he probably just had a lot on his mind at the time") rather than to stable, internal ones (e.g., "this proves she doesn't really love me").

Risk of Misinterpretation

A second risk for senders of affectionate messages, which has been mentioned several times in this book already, is the risk that receivers will misinterpret them. The specific threat is that a receiver may interpret an affectionate behavior as a romantic gesture when it was intended to convey platonic affection, or vice versa. This a salient risk, for two reasons. First, with many types of affectionate behavior, there is ample opportunity for such misinterpretation to occur. As noted in Chapter 4, even a straightforward verbal statement such as "I love you" can be decoded in multiple ways (e.g., "I love you in a romantic way," "I love you as a platonic friend," "I love you like a family member," "I am in love with you"). This risk is magnified as the ambiguity of the gesture increases. For instance, the phrase "I love you" might be more ambiguous when written than when spoken, because vocal and facial cues in the latter situation can aid in clarifying its meaning (see, e.g., Floyd & Morman, 2000b). Likewise, the risk of misinterpretation may be greater for nonverbal expressions of affection than for verbal, as discussed in Chapter 3 (see Floyd, 1999, 2000a).

The second reason that misinterpretation is such a salient risk is that it entails face threats for both the sender and receiver of the expression. By way of example, let us suppose that Marco tells his friend Jean that he loves her and, although he intends to convey platonic love, Jean interprets the expression as a romantic overture. One of two types of face threats might ensue. First, if Jean has romantic interest in Marco, she may reciprocate his expression with a romantic gesture of her own. Since Marco's feelings for her are merely platonic, however, this imposes on him the task of explaining to Jean that she misinterpreted his expression (a form of negative face threat), and it likewise causes embarrassment for Jean and threatens her positive face (via the acknowledgment that Marco does not care for her in a romantic way). Jean's embarrassment and positive face threat could also eventually cause a threat to Marco's positive face, if she feels angry with him for having "led her on."

Let us suppose, instead, that Jean misinterprets Marco's expression as romantic but that she does *not* have a romantic interest in him. In such a situation, it is primarily Jean's face needs that are threatened. Specifically, she inherits the obligation to convey to Marco that her feelings for him are platonic, which entails a form of negative face threat similar to the one Marco faced in the previous scenario. Of course, in this situation, Jean is not actually threatening Marco's positive face, given that his feelings for her were platonic from the beginning, but she would *believe* she is causing a positive face threat nonetheless.

Importantly, the embarrassment and face threats that may accompany the misinterpretation of an affectionate behavior are not limited to verbal expressions. Instead, one would expect the risk of misinterpretation to be inversely related to the amount and quality of contextual information available to the receiver, which is why such a risk may be higher for written than spoken expressions, or for nonverbal than for verbal behaviors.

Risk of Social Censure

A third risk for senders of affectionate expressions is related to variation in receivers' and observers' perceptions of appropriateness, expectancies, and decorum. As discussed in detail in Chapter 4, characteristics of the sender, his or her relationship to the receiver, and the social and environmental context in which they interact can influence people's evaluations of affectionate behaviors. If senders engage in affectionate behaviors that receivers and/or observers judge as inappropriate for the type of relationship or the type of context, they risk censure from others in the form of disapproval or, in extreme cases, retaliatory action. An example of the latter consequence would be an instance of sexual harassment in the professional workplace. Let us suppose that Stephen is a bank manager and Chris is a teller who reports to him. Stephen and Chris are good friends; one afternoon at work, Stephen decides to express his affection by hugging Chris in the lobby of the bank. Given the social context in which the gesture occurs – a professional work environment, with clients and other employees present – most who witness this display, including Chris, deem it inappropriate. Whereas clients and other employees might convey their disapproval mildly (e.g., via facial expressions of concern), Chris may decide to convey it through formalized means, such as by filing a grievance with the bank or accusing Stephen of sexual harassment.

Importantly, Stephen and Chris (because of their friendship) may have been used to embracing each other in more private, nonprofessional contexts. Thus, in this example, it was not the behavior itself that elicited censure from others but, rather, the context in which it was enacted. In other situations, it may be the case that the behavior itself is deemed inappropriate for a given relationship, regardless of the social environment. For instance, a man attempting to convey affection for his sister by kissing her intimately would, in all typical circumstances, incur the disapproval of others no matter what the social situation were. No such censure would typically be expected if he attempted to show affection in a similar manner to his wife, however, provided that he were enacting the behavior in a social context in which it were appropriate.

What influences the perceived appropriateness of affectionate behaviors? Preliminary research, such as that conducted by Floyd and Morman (1997), has already identified some of the aspects of communicators, their relationships, and social contexts that are influential, including the sexes of the sender and receiver, the fundamental nature of their relationship (whether romantic, platonic, or familial), and the privacy and emotional intensity of the environment. Additional research on this topic will contribute to increased understanding about these influences and may also illuminate the manner in which receivers' perceptions of appropriateness differ from those of third-party observers.

These risks – nonreciprocation, misinterpretation, and social censure – are likely not the only risks for senders of affectionate messages, but they appear to be among the most prevalent. A fourth, and comparatively less common, risk, associated only with physical affection, is related to hygienic concerns regarding disease.

Risk of Disease Transmission

For those suffering from communicable disease – or even diseases that one merely believes are communicable through casual contact – affectionate expressions involving physical contact or proximity carry a fourth risk, that of disease transmission. It is probably common for those with acute disorders, such as a cold or flu, to curtail physically affectionate behaviors such as kissing while their condition is contagious. Recent research suggests that some with chronic disorders, even if they cannot be transmitted through casual contact, may similarly curtail physical affection out of fear that the disease will be transmitted to the receiver.

Specifically, Schuster, Beckett, Corona, and Zhou (2005) interviewed 344 American parents drawn from a nationally representative probability sample of HIV-infected adults regarding their beliefs about HIV and their affectionate behavior with their children. Although the authors asked about only three affectionate behaviors – hugging, kissing on the lips, and kissing on the cheek – they found that more than a third (36.1%) of the parents reported avoiding at least one of those affectionate behaviors with their children out of fear of transmitting HIV to the children via that behavior. Avoidance was more common for kissing on the lips than for hugging or kissing on the cheek. The authors also found that the fear of transmitting HIV to a child through affectionate behavior was substantially more common for Hispanic parents than for African American or Caucasian parents and moderately more common for fathers than for mothers. Self-reported knowledge about HIV was also inversely associated with the fear of transmitting it to children. Notably, 42% of the sample reported avoiding at least one of the affectionate behaviors with children, not out of fear of transmitting HIV to the child but out of fear of catching an opportunistic infection *from* the child that would be prove problematic for an HIV-infected adult to handle.

Although this is a risk of greater gravity than nonreciprocity, misinterpretation, or social censure (at least, theoretically), it is also one that is relatively isolated by circumstance, affecting only those who believe themselves to be at risk for transmitting or contracting illness via physical contact. The risks of nonreciprocity, misinterpretation, and social censure should be comparatively more prevalent in their effects on senders of affectionate messages. As noted earlier, however, it is not only senders of affectionate behaviors, but receivers as well, who are susceptible to their potential pitfalls. The remainder of this chapter discusses some of the potential problems facing receivers of affectionate messages. These are referred to as *potential problems* rather than as *risks* because the latter term implies a level of foresight that is more likely to characterize a sender (who can deliberately craft a message and plan the contingencies of its delivery) than a receiver. The shift in terms should not, however, be taken to imply that the potential hazards of affectionate communication are any less salient for receivers than they are for senders.

Potential Problems for Receivers of Affectionate Expressions

As discussed in the previous chapter, humans typically enjoy receiving expressions of affection. Such expressions elicit feelings of being valued, protected, and appreciated, and they may very well be associated with a number of physiological responses that reinforce their reward value. However, as described earlier, affectionate communication entails risks for senders, and, as detailed in this section, it entails potential problems for receivers, as well. This discussion will focus on three potential problems that accompany the receipt of affectionate behaviors: the expectation of reciprocity, relational boundary ambiguity, and perceived manipulation. These problems are referred to as *potential* to highlight the fact that they do not accompany every affectionate exchange, or probably even most. They are, however, possibilities that receivers do encounter and which have the likelihood of influencing the relationships in which they are experienced; as such, they merit scholarly attention.

Expectations for Reciprocity

One potential problem for receivers is that they may immediately feel obligated to reciprocate the expression, whether they would elect to or not. According to Gouldner (1960), humans have an implicit social contract, or moral imperative, that creates a feeling of obligation to reciprocate resources, favors, or acts of kindness received from others. Evolutionary psychologists have concurred; Trivers (1971) suggested that humans practice *reciprocal altruism* by expecting that their good deeds will be reciprocated in kind and by feeling wronged when they are not. Specifically, Cosmides and Tooby (1992) have argued that humans are so attuned to principles of equity and reciprocity of positive behaviors as to have evolved cognitive "detection mechanisms" to draw their attention to instances of cheating. If one does a favor for a friend, for instance, then Goulder, Trivers, Cosmides, and Tooby would all argue that both oneself and one's friend would expect that favor to be repaid at some future point when one is in need of help. If such a time comes when one needs the friend's help and he or she refuses it, the reciprocity principle suggests that one should feel cheated and that the friend should feel guilty. Cosmides and Tooby argue that these emotions are adaptive in that they make "cheating" (by not reciprocating favors) aversive, particularly for the cheater.

As noted above, when one person receives, for instance, a verbal expression of affection (e.g., "I love you"), both the receiver and the sender will, under normal circumstances, expect the expression to be reciprocated in kind. The possibility that it may not be reciprocated is one of the risks assumed by the sender. However, the expectation of reciprocity can place the receiver in the undesirable position of feeling obligated to reciprocate the expression – and to reciprocate it in kind, with an expression of similar intensity – whether or not he or she actually possesses feelings of affection for the sender.

Certainly, one could surmise that this is a larger problem when the affectionate feelings are *not* shared than when they *are*. Such a situation can be examined with reference to politeness theory and face needs (see Brown & Levinson, 1987; Goffman, 1959); specifically, one can consider the potential threats to positive face (the need for approval) and negative face (the need for autonomy). Let us suppose that Craig says "I love you" to his friend Sue and that Sue does not share the sentiment. As articulated above, both will feel (under normal circumstances) that Sue should reciprocate the expression, and that would certainly be one option for her. Aside from the discomfort of lying to Craig about her feelings, however, this option exposes Sue to a potential negative face threat. Specifically, by affirming Craig's feelings, Sue may feel obligated to behave toward him in a manner consistent with his feelings, rather than behaving toward him in the manner she would otherwise elect. For instance, she may feel obliged to spend more time with Craig than she would choose, or to act more interested in him than she would wish to.

A second option would be to reciprocate the expression with one of lesser intensity (e.g., "I like you, too"), and a third option would be not to respond at all. As noted, both of these are likely to threaten Craig's positive face, but they may also threaten Sue's positive *and* negative face. By failing to reciprocate the expression, or by reciprocating with a less intense expression, Sue will most likely communicate to Craig that she does not share his feelings of love. Because this is not likely to be the response Craig wishes, Sue runs the risk of incurring negative feelings from him that are borne out of his disappointment or hurt. This type of response would certainly be expected to threaten Sue's need for approval.

Indeed, Erbert and Floyd (2004) predicted that a receiver's positive face need would predict his or her intention to reciprocate an affectionate expression in kind. After controlling for the sex of the participant and the sex composition of the dyad (same-sex vs. opposite-sex), they found that positive face need was a significant predictor of one's intention to respond in kind to an affectionate expression from a platonic friend.

There are two potential negative face threats to Sue in this situation. First, her negative face may be threatened by her obligation to respond to Craig's expression in the first place, especially if she elects to be honest about her feelings, since she will most likely be aware that she will disappoint Craig. This is similar in nature to the discomfort that people experience when they have to bear bad news to others. Second, Sue may feel that, to mitigate the positive face threat to Craig, she should be especially nice to him, spend more time with him, or otherwise reaffirm her positive (but not loving) feelings for him. To the extent that she feels obliged to do these things when she may have elected not to, this can also constitute a threat to her negative face.

Research on unrequited love has supported the notion that receiving an expression of affectionate feelings that one does not share is a psychologically distressing experience (see, e.g., Baumeister & Wotman, 1992). In a study that examined the experience from the standpoints of both "would-be lovers" (those who conveyed feelings of romantic love to another) and "rejectors" (those who failed to reciprocate the emotions), Baumeister, Wotman, and Stillwell (1993) found that rejectors actually described the experience as being more aversive than did would-be lovers. Baumeister and colleagues offered several observations by way of explanation. For one, they noted that rejecting love may go against basic, innately prepared motives for attachment (Bowlby, 1969, 1973; Hazan & Shaver, 1987; Shaver, Hazan, & Bradshaw, 1988) and the need to belong (Baumeister & Leary, 1995), causing psychological turmoil and internal conflict for rejectors. Second, rejectors commonly reported feeling guilt as a result of their failure to reciprocate the would-be lovers' affections. Indeed, in the Baumeister et al. study, rejectors' guilt was significantly more likely to be reported in their own accounts than in the would-be lovers' accounts, suggesting that rejectors felt guilty more often than the rejected believed.

Importantly, as Baumeister and his colleagues noted, rejectors have the option of reciprocating (or at least, failing to reject overtly) a would-be lover's expression of affection even if they don't share the emotion. As with Sue in the earlier example, this option may temporarily relieve the rejector of guilt or other negative emotions, but it runs the long-term risks of obligating the rejector to spend time unwillingly with the would-be lover and of encouraging the would-be lover's affectionate overtures. Over time, this can encourage the would-be lover in his or her feelings for the rejector. Paradoxically, then, this short-term solution to the rejector's problem can have the long-term effect of making the eventual overt rejection far more traumatic for both parties than it would have been initially.

Might the obligation to reciprocate Craig's expression threaten Sue's face even if she did share his feelings? One might argue that it could, albeit to a lesser degree than if she didn't share his feelings, if Sue were uncomfortable expressing her affection for some reason (perhaps because of the context, or perhaps because she is not an especially affectionate person). In either case, the receipt of an affectionate expression *has the potential* to be problematic because of the strong expectation for reciprocity that is likely to accompany it.

Relational Boundary Ambiguity

As discussed previously, expressions of affection often serve as markers by which relational development is gauged. Owen (1987) reported that people in romantic pairs frequently can recall their first kiss or the first time they said "I love you" to each other, because these expressions often coincide with, or even precipitate, critical turning points in the nature of the relationship (e.g., "it was when she first said she loved me that I knew I wanted her to be my girlfriend").

This aspect of affectionate communication is instrumental for people who are endeavoring to initiate a new relationship or to transform an existing relationship from a platonic to a romantic one. The fact that affectionate behavior is often used for these purposes, however, raises the possibility that expressions of affection could cause relational boundary ambiguity for receivers. For instance, let us suppose that Peter and Gail are platonic friends who frequently spend time together, enjoy each other's company, and often joke that they really should be dating each other. If, in the context of joking about their fit as romantic partners, Gail tells Peter that she loves him, it is possible (and perhaps even likely) that Peter will wonder whether Gail meant her expression as a gesture of platonic love or, instead, as an invitation to explore a romantic relationship. The potential ambiguity of the statement can be problematic for Peter because he must attend to the implications of its various meanings. If he believes it possible that Gail loves him romantically, he must determine whether he shares those feelings, and if he does not, he must ascertain a means of communicating that to Gail, presumably in a manner that will best protect the feelings of both.

Besides requiring Peter to process these relational implications cognitively, the ambiguity of Gail's statement also makes his behavioral response tenuous. If Peter does not feel romantically toward Gail, or if he is uncertain about whether she feels romantically toward him, he may be hesitant to respond to her statement in a manner that Gail could interpret as a romantic gesture. That is, his motivation in such a situation would likely be to respond in such a way that the platonic nature of his sentiment is as unequivocal as possible without causing Gail emotional harm. If, instead, Peter does feel romantic love for Gail, he may be motivated to respond to her statement in a manner that is equally ambiguous, so that he can "test the waters" and see if Gail really does have romantic feelings for him. If she does not, and he has misinterpreted her initial statement, then the ambiguity of Peter's response would allow him to save face by denying that he meant anything but platonic love in return.

There is some evidence to suggest that this type of relational boundary ambiguity is of greater concern in relationships that are not especially close to begin with. Erbert and Floyd (2004) asked participants in their study to think of a particular platonic friend and to imagine receiving one of three different affectionate messages from that friend.[1] The messages were constructed to correspond to three politeness strategies identified by Brown and Levinson (1987). These were: (1) *bald-on-record*, in which the expression is very straightforward and unqualified (e.g., "I really care about you; you're very important to me"); (2) *negative politeness*, in which the expression is qualified in order to mitigate potential negative face threats (e.g., "I don't mean this in a romantic way, but I really care about you"); and (3) *off-the-record*, in which the expression is crafted in such a way that the sentiment is implied rather than directly stated (e.g., "You're pretty cool"). The researchers asked participants to report on the extent to which receiving these affectionate expressions from their specified platonic friends would cause them to wonder whether their friend were making a romantic overture.[2] In other words, the study examined whether these types of affectionate behaviors, enacted in platonic relationships, might cause ambiguity in participants' conceptions of their friendships.

---

[1] Participants were instructed to select one platonic friend whom they considered a *close friend* but not their *best friend*, and who was neither a relative nor a current or former romantic partner.

[2] Relational boundary ambiguity items were: "I would wonder if my friend was trying to 'come on' to me," "I would think that my friend might be wanting something different from our friendship than I want," and "I would wonder whether my friend meant this in a romantic way."

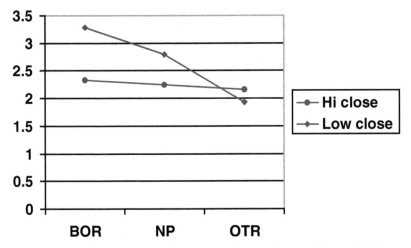

Figure 6.1. Interaction of Affectionate Message Type and Relationship Closeness on Receivers' Reports of Relational Boundary Ambiguity, from Erbert and Floyd (2004)
Note: "BOR" = bald-on-record affection message; "NP" = negative politeness affection message; "OTR" = off-the-record affection message.

Erbert and Floyd found that the type of affectionate expression (bald-on-record, negative politeness, off-the-record) was influential in predicting receivers' likelihood of experiencing relational boundary ambiguity. Importantly, however, this effect was moderated by the closeness of the friendship (as measured by the inclusion of other in the self scale, developed by Aron, Aron, & Smollan, 1992). Specifically, participants reporting on friendships that were not highly close indicated that they would experience the greatest relational boundary ambiguity if they received the bald-on-record message, less if they received the negative politeness message, and the least if they received the off-the-record message. By contrast, participants reporting on friendships characterized by a higher degree of closeness reported no difference among the three messages in terms of the likelihood that they would experience relational boundary ambiguity. As Figure 6.1 demonstrates, those in closer friendships tended to report that relational boundary ambiguity would be less of a concern than did those in less close friendships, except when it came to the off-the-record message. (For those who imagined receiving the off-the-record message, relational boundary ambiguity was more of a concern for participants in closer friendships, although this difference was so small as to be negligible.)

On one hand, it may be evident why the closeness of the friendship influences the likelihood that affectionate messages elicit relational boundary ambiguity. Relationship closeness typically entails, among other things, shared knowledge about the relational partners. That is, people typically feel that they know more about their close relational partners than they do about people to whom they are less close. As a result, one might expect that **people in close relationships are better equipped than people in less close relationships to interpret each other's statements accurately and to sidestep problems of ambiguity** such as those discussed above. On the other hand, however, one might expect that **close friendships, because of their very closeness, are more likely to evolve into romantic relationships than are friendships that are less close.** With respect to the effects of relational closeness on the likelihood of relational boundary ambiguity, these are competing hypotheses, and the data from the Erbert and Floyd experiment support the former prediction. Future research on the potential negative outcomes of affectionate communication could add to understanding of how relationship closeness moderates those outcomes, however.

Affectionate Expressions as Manipulation Attempts

A third potential problem facing receivers of affectionate expressions concerns the possibility that the expression may not be genuine, but may instead have an ulterior motive. By way of example, let us suppose that Patrick and Kristi have been dating for a few months and Patrick wants to initiate sexual interaction but perceives that Kristi is hesitant. To overcome her hesitation, Patrick might employ a strategy whereby he tells Kristi that he loves her and uses phrases like "it's okay for us to have sex if we love each other," or "you would do it if you loved me." Patrick's motivation is to manipulate Kristi into having sex with him; he does not bear genuine feelings of love for her. The risk for Kristi, however, is that she will believe that he does genuinely love her and will therefore acquiesce to his advances, even though she would not have done so if she believed his affectionate expressions were not genuine.

This possibility derives from one of the most fundamental problems inherent in emotional communication: the nature of the link between experience and expression. As discussed in the first chapter, the internal experience of an emotion does not *necessarily* covary with the behaviors through which such an emotion is communicated. For instance, people can elect not to express emotions that they are experiencing, and there are several reasons why they may choose to do so. People may conceal their emotions to maintain decorum; in a somber environment such as a funeral it is generally not proper to display signs of joy or excitement, even though one may be feeling them. Likewise, people might conceal their emotions because they are embarrassed about having them in the first place; if one feels envious about another's good fortune, for instance, one may choose not to express it out of embarrassment at feeling that way. Moreover, people conceal their emotions for the purpose of manipulating others' beliefs; this is the principle behind having a "poker face." Humans continually gather information about each other by attending to emotional cues, particularly facial expressions of emotion. Therefore, the more skilled one is at masking one's emotions, the less information he or she volunteers to others (and the stronger his or her own strategic position may become as a result).

The potential problem for receivers of affectionate behavior arises from the obverse truism, which is that people have the ability to express emotions that they aren't actually experiencing. Humans do this routinely in the service of politeness and common courtesy; they may say "nice to see you" to someone they aren't happy to see or express joy and appreciation about a birthday present they don't actually like. Indeed, researchers use the term *emotion labor* in reference to the types of work that require people to display emotions that they aren't necessarily experiencing. For instance, people in service and entertainment industries are often required to smile and appear happy, whereas law enforcement and correctional officers must sometimes present a dominant, aggressive front, whether their actual emotions warrant it or not. Ploog (1986) reviewed evidence from a number of sources to establish that people can express emotions (particularly through facial and vocal expressions) that are disconnected from their actual emotional experiences.

This aspect of emotional expression, in general, and affectionate expression, in particular, fuels the possibility that one could use affectionate behavior as a manipulation attempt. As an example, let us suppose that Beth and Mike have been dating for a few weeks and that Mike wants Beth to let him use her family's beach house for a weekend with his fraternity brothers. As a persuasion strategy, Mike may tell Beth that he loves her and engage in nonverbal gestures of affection, such as hugging, kissing, or caressing her, even if he does not, in fact, have feelings of love for Beth. If Beth believes, on the basis of these communicative behaviors, that Mike actually does love her, then that may influence her to allow Mike access to the beach house, in which case his strategy will have been successful. There is a risk inherent in this strategy, however; if Beth believes that Mike does not love her but is using these behaviors as a way to manipulate her, she may feel used, belittled, angry, and resentful, and one could easily imagine such a response precipitating the termination of their relationship.

How likely are people to interpret affectionate expressions as manipulation attempts? Initial research on the topic was conducted by Erbert and Floyd (2004). In their study, which is described earlier, participants indicated the extent to which receiving one of three types of affectionate messages (bald-on-record, negative politeness, off-the-record) from a specific platonic friend would make them feel as though their friend were trying to manipulate them.[3] The researchers had predicted, on the basis of politeness theory, that receivers would feel manipulated the most by the bald-on-record message, less by the negative politeness message, and the least by the off-the-record message. This hypothesis reflected the descending degree of directness in these messages; because the bald-on-record message was the most direct and unequivocal, they expected that it would be the most likely to make a receiver feel as though the sender were trying to manipulate him or her. They further anticipated, however, that the effect of the message type on receivers' reports of manipulation would be moderated by two things: the closeness of the friendship and the receivers' trait negative face need. Specifically, they expected that participants would be less likely to feel manipulated by the affection messages if they were reporting on relationships that were close and if they, themselves, had a low negative face need.

Erbert and Floyd tested these predictions using hierarchical regression analyses that controlled for the participants' sex and the sex composition of the friendship (whether same-sex or opposite-sex). Only one of the three predicted effects emerged: participants' trait negative face need significantly predicted their likelihood of feeling manipulated by the affectionate messages. The closeness of the friendship was not influential, and there was no effect of the message type on perceptions of manipulation, once participant sex, relationship sex composition, closeness, and negative face need were controlled for.

The results, therefore, indicated that people are more likely to feel manipulated by affectionate messages if they have a strong need for

---

[3] Perceived manipulation items were: "I would think my friend was just trying to get something from me," "I would think to myself, 'I wonder what he/she wants now,'" and "I would feel like my friend might be trying to manipulate me."

protecting their autonomy (i.e., for *not* being manipulated) than if that need is less strong. This, in itself, is relatively uninformative; in fact, one would expect that people with high negative face needs would be more likely than people with low negative face needs to feel manipulated by any number of communicative events. One reason the other predictions may not have received support is that being manipulated – particularly if it is by a close friend – is likely to elicit feelings of discomfort, which may dissuade research participants from discussing such a situation. Therefore, as a type of social desirability bias, respondents may have been reluctant to report that their friends' expressions of affection might make them feel manipulated, even if they actually did. Erbert and Floyd surmised that the same concern for social desirability might not have influenced participants' willingness to report that they felt relational boundary ambiguity, because having a friend express romantic interest in oneself is likely to make one feel less stigmatized than having a friend try to manipulate oneself through the use of affection.

A more detailed understanding of the use of affectionate communication as a manipulation strategy was the goal in a subsequent study conducted by Floyd, Erbert, Davis, and Haynes (2005). Given the likelihood that receivers might be reluctant to admit that people had tried to manipulate them through affectionate behavior, the researchers asked respondents about their experiences of having done so to others. The sample (which is the same sample from which the analyses reported in Floyd, Hess et al., 2005, were drawn) consisted of 1,032 undergraduate students from several universities and community colleges located throughout the United States. Participants completed an online questionnaire that asked, among other things, whether they had ever expressed affection to someone when they didn't really feel it, but when they were, instead, using the affectionate expression for some other motive. Those who responded affirmatively were instructed to describe the situation, including the relationship they had with the target, what their actual motive was, and the behavior(s) they used to express affection as a means of fulfilling that motive. Importantly, the descriptions were of times when participants had expressed affection that they *did not actually feel*, as opposed to situations when they simply reaffirmed genuine affection for a manipulative purpose.

Preliminary results indicated that 86% of the respondents (or 888 out of 1,032 people) indicated that they had conveyed nongenuine affection for a manipulative purpose on at least one occasion. More than half of these participants indicated that they had done so at least once within the previous month, suggesting that the use of nongenuine affection is not an uncommon manipulative strategy.

There was no sex difference in the tendency to use non-genuine affection manipulatively; women and men were equally likely to have done so. There was also no effect of ethnicity, nor of marital status. However, other demographic and personality trait variables predicted the tendency to have used affectionate communication to manipulate. Specifically, compared to those who had not done so, participants who had used affectionate communication manipulatively were younger, more extroverted, more neurotic, more psychotic, more socially active, more fearful of intimacy, and more affectionate overall.

More interesting were the findings concerning participants' motives and the targets of their manipulation attempts. The three most common targets that participants identified in association with their manipulative use of affection were a platonic friend (34.2%), a current boyfriend/girlfriend (24.4%), or a former boyfriend/girlfriend (11.5%). Together, these three relationships accounted for just over 70% of the instances described.

Participants described a number of different motives for their manipulative use of affectionate communication. Some were *relationship-focused motives*, such as sustaining a relationship or avoiding interpersonal conflict. Others were *target-centered motives*, in which the goal was to do something for the target of the affectionate behavior. These included making the other person feel cared for, providing emotional comfort, indicating sympathy, or avoiding hurting the other person's feelings.

Still other motives were *self-centered motives*, in which the goal was to obtain something from the target of the affectionate message. These included the goals of eliciting instrumental help (such as assistance with a project or task), eliciting material help (such as money), eliciting forgiveness for a past indiscretion in order to appease one's own guilt, and eliciting sexual interaction.

Do receivers ascribe varying amounts of damage to different types of motives for using affectionate behavior manipulatively? That is, would receivers of these various kinds of manipulation attempts evaluate them differently in terms of how problematic they would be? Although this remains to be tested, one might predict that receivers who feel they are being manipulated (through affectionate behavior) to engage in feelings or behaviors that they would not otherwise engage in would feel a greater sense of violation, resentment, and anger toward senders than would those who feel they are being manipulated to think or do things they would elect to do anyway. One might also expect that the use of such a manipulation strategy would be perceived more positively if it ultimately benefited the receiver than if it did not. For example, one might evaluate more negatively a sender who uses affectionate behavior to elicit sex or money than a sender who uses affectionate behavior to comfort someone, even if the sender *feels* no actual affection in either case. This will be among the many interesting issues for future affection research to address.

Although affectionate communication is accompanied by a number of benefits, as illustrated in the previous chapter, it is also subject to several risks and potential problems, both for senders and receivers. The juxtaposition of these two characteristics is, in large part, what makes the study of affectionate communication so intriguing and so worthwhile.

7

A New Theoretic Approach

Don't be afraid of showing affection. Be warm and tender, thoughtful and affectionate. Men are more helped by sympathy than by service.

– Jean Baptiste Lacordaire

There is no shortage of psychological and communicological theories on which to base studies about affectionate behavior. However, even a cursory analysis of the current body of research findings from the perspective of existing theories suggests some consequential holes in the breadth of our theoretic understanding. Perhaps the biggest reason for these deficits is that none of the theories detailed in Chapter 2 provides a comprehensive framework for understanding affectionate communication. Indeed, none of these theories was designed to do so, although some (e.g., somatosensory affectional deprivation theory) are obviously more closely focused on affection than others (e.g., politeness theory). A comprehensive framework is needed, however, both to account for myriad findings in the affectionate communication literature and to provide the level of theoretic sophistication necessary to advance the study of affectionate communication in realms where it will have direct applied benefit, such as in health or persuasion.

Several fundamental questions about affectionate communication were identified in the introductory chapter; these are among those that have received empirical attention thus far. Existing theories have been well suited to answering some of these fundamental questions but they have largely fallen short on others. This chapter begins with a short analysis of how extant theories fare, theoretically or empirically, in their abilities to explain and predict affectionate communication behavior. Next, it provides more extensive introduction to Darwinian principles of

140

adaptation and natural selection, particularly as they are applied to psychological characteristics and behavioral tendencies. Finally, it explicates one candidate for a comprehensive theory of affectionate communication, referred to in previous publications as *affection exchange theory* (see, e.g., Floyd, 2001, 2003; Floyd, Hess et al., 2005; Floyd & Morman, 2002, 2003; Floyd & Morr, 2003; Floyd & Ray, 2003; Floyd, Sargent, & DiCorcia, 2004; Punyanunt-Carter, 2004). The theory is grounded in neo-Darwinian principles and some of the arguments contained within the theory can be found in other venues within the field of evolutionary psychology.

On the Sufficiency of Existing Theories Related to Affectionate Communication

Chapter 2 described the principles of those psychological and communicological theories and paradigms that have framed the study of affectionate communication thus far, as well as some theories and paradigms offering relevant, but as yet untested, predictions about affectionate behavior. This section takes up the question of how well these theories fare in explaining and predicting affectionate communication in human relationships. It is important to reiterate the observation that few of these theories or paradigms were designed with the explicit goal of explaining affectionate behavior, and so the assessment offered here is not one of their general utility but, rather, of their utility at explaining affectionate communication in particular.

Rather than considering each theory separately – which is problematic, given the diversity in their foci and levels of abstraction – this critique focuses on the fundamental questions about affectionate communication that were offered in the first chapter. Existing theories have been profitable for answering some of these questions, so I will discuss those first. Other questions have been less profitably addressed by existing theories – and importantly, *no single theory has been able to address all of these issues under one explanatory framework*. Indeed, this is the goal of the theory to be explicated in this chapter.

Areas in Which Existing Theories Have Been Profitable

This section addresses those areas of the affectionate communication literature in which existing theories have either provided logically sound explanations for behavior, or have produced empirically supported hypotheses, or both. By identifying these as areas where existing theories have been profitable, I do not imply that existing theories are necessarily sufficient, particularly when considering the task of explaining *all* of these areas. Rather, I acknowledge here that several current theories have substantially advanced knowledge in these areas, despite the fact that affectionate communication is not their explicit focus. This section is divided into three general topic areas, which include encoding and decoding, interpretation, and reciprocity.

Questions of Encoding and Decoding. Among the questions posed in the first chapter are those asking what verbal and nonverbal behaviors people use to express affection; how these behaviors are influenced by individual, relational, and contextual factors; and what behaviors people decode as affectionate gestures. These questions are all fundamental to the understanding of affectionate communication, given that they focus on the very elements of the communicative process (encoding and decoding).

Although some of the research on these topics has been inductive, the existing theory perhaps best suited to addressing these issues is the social meaning model. This theoretic model provides that interactants within a given speech community will converge on their meanings for communicative behaviors (particularly nonverbal behaviors), so within-community agreement should be high relative to between-community agreement. This has been a profitable framework for understanding issues such as encoder–decoder agreement on affectionate behavior (Ray & Floyd, 2000), and also more basic questions like how individuals express affection within given relationships. Several studies, for instance, have shown that the means of conveying affection within personal relationships are often strongly influenced by the nature of the relationship (whether romantic, platonic, or familial; e.g., Floyd, 1999; Floyd & Morman, 1997, 2002; Floyd & Morr, 2003). Within the framework of the social meaning model, a relationship type could be considered a type of speech community, suggesting that common ways of encoding or decoding affection in one form of relationship may be substantially less common in others.

With respect to the individual, relational, or contextual factors that most strongly influence how affection is encoded and decoded, expectancy violations theory has also been extremely profitable. This theory provides that individuals have expectations for appropriate ways of communicating that are derived from their assessments of other communicators, the nature of their relationship with the communicators, and the context in which the communication occurs. Deviations from expected behavior are cognitively arousing, according to the theory, and prompt either positive or negative assessments that are based primarily on the characteristics of the actor. Research has shown, for instance, that people expect romantic partners to express affection in more intimate ways than relatives, who, in turn, should express affection more intimately than platonic friends, and that these relational distinctions are particularly salient for male–male interaction (e.g., Floyd, 1997b; Floyd & Morman, 1997). Thus, a given behavior (e.g., bear hug) that represents an expectancy confirmation in one type of relationship (e.g., between brothers) may qualify as an expectancy violation in a different relationship type (e.g., between male friends; see Morman & Floyd, 1998).

Aspects of the social context have also been shown to influence expectations for how affection should be conveyed. Floyd and Morman (1997) showed, for instance, that people saw intimate affectionate behavior (e.g., kissing or hugging) as less appropriate in emotionally neutral situations than in contexts that are emotionally charged, such as a funeral, a wedding, or a graduation ceremony. Invoking the logic behind expectancy violations theory, they surmised that the emotional intensity of some social contexts broadens the range of what is considered normative behavior. Indeed, the consistent findings that women are more affectionate than men (Floyd & Morman, 1998; Shuntich & Shapiro, 1991), that they perceive themselves to be (Floyd, 1997b; D. H. Wallace, 1981), and that both men and women consider it more expected for women to be affectionate than men (Floyd, 1997b) might all be accounted for by the explanation that sex-based expectancies call for women to be substantially more nurturant than men. Therefore, according to expectancy violations theory, men are more likely to violate expectancies by being highly affectionate than nonaffectionate, whereas the opposite is true for women. This explanation would suggest, in other words, that behavioral differences based on sex, or social context, or relationship type, or other individual or relational differences could be at least partially accounted for by differential expectancies.

Both tend and befriend theory and somatosensory affectional deprivation theory can also explain the consistent sex difference in affectionate behavior without reference to socially constructed norms, although their explanations differ from each other and neither has as yet been empirically tested in a manner that would rule out alternative explanations. Specifically, tend and befriend theory would predict that women are more affectionate than men, overall, because women's evolved mechanisms for managing stress (tending and befriending) confer hormonal benefits from affectionate behavior, such as oxytocin reward, that men do not share to the same degree. By contrast, somatosensory affectional deprivation theory provides that the capacity for sensory pleasure is a sexually dimorphic trait, such that females have a higher capacity for integrative physical pleasure (i.e., the congruence of physical, mental, and emotional pleasure) than do males. To the extent that engaging in somatosensory stimulation results in physical pleasure, this theory would predict that women would behave more affectionately than men. Importantly, neither of these explanations precludes the additional influence of socially or culturally bound expectations as sources of variance in affectionate behavior. Rather, these theories would provide that in the absence of powerful sociocultural counter-influences, women would be more affectionate than men irrespective of the social or cultural context.

Another approach, as yet untested, for predicting *how affectionate* a communicator will be (as opposed to the behaviors he or she would use to convey affection) may derive from attachment theory (Bowlby, 1969, 1973). As I discuss in greater detail later, attachment theory would support hypotheses concerning the influence of individual attachment styles on trait levels of affectionate behavior (i.e., how affectionate a given person is, in general). At a minimum, one could derive from attachment theory the hypothesis that those whose attachment styles involve a positive concept of others (secure and preoccupied styles in Bartholomew's (1990) typology) have higher trait levels of affectionate behavior than do those with attachment styles involving a negative concept of others (dismissive and avoidant styles). Such predictions have yet to be tested empirically.

Questions of Interpretation. Closely related to issues of encoding and decoding are those of interpretation, which include making evaluations and attributions for behaviors observed between others. The first chapter asked how people evaluate and explain expressions of affection when they observe them, and several studies have addressed this question. Again, expectancy violations theory and the social meaning model have both provided useful frameworks for understanding and predicting evaluative and attributional responses from observers. One prediction derivable from expectancy violations theory is that unexpected behavior is more likely than expected behavior to provoke evaluations and attributions, and Floyd and Voloudakis (1999b) demonstrated that this was the case with nonverbal affection behavior. Another prediction that is directly derivable from expectancy violations theory, and which would also be supported by the social meaning model, is that observers should evaluate affectionate behavior positively, and make favorable attributions for it, in the absence of a reason not to. That is, positive evaluations and attributions should be the "default," given the generally positive nature of affectionate behavior. Such a prediction could also be derived from Baumeister and Leary's (1995) need to belong, given the role of affectionate behavior in establishing and maintaining social bonds.

Several studies have demonstrated this general pattern, including those by Rane and Draper (1995), Harrison-Speake and Willis (1995), Floyd (1999), and Floyd and Morman (2000b). Each of these studies demonstrated variance in the valence of evaluations or attributions as a function of behavioral, relational, or contextual information; however, research on interpretation of affectionate behavior has found it to be largely characterized as positive, like these theories would suggest.

Of course, communicators do not make evaluations and interpretations only for behaviors they witness among others, but also for behaviors directed at them. Whereas expectancy violations theory would predict that some unexpected affectionate behaviors will be interpreted negatively (Floyd & Burgoon, 1999), while others will be interpreted as pleasant surprises (Floyd & Voloudakis, 1999a), more recent research has used the framework of politeness theory to consider the face-supporting or face-threatening nature of some affectionate behaviors. Recognizing that some affectionate behaviors are unwelcome even if they are not considered inappropriate for a given relationship or social context, Erbert and Floyd (2004) surmised that the behaviors may be interpreted negatively because they carry implicit threats to the receiver's positive or negative face needs. Indeed, their study illustrated that receivers do appreciate face threats in some affectionate behaviors that would seem, on their surface, to be both appropriate and largely positive. This is a relatively novel application of politeness theory; however, it is promising in its demonstration that some affectionate behaviors can be evaluated negatively by receivers because they impose perceived obligations, for example, or imply the speaker's desire for potentially unwanted changes in the nature of the relationship.

Questions of Reciprocity. Finally, several studies have focused on the questions of when people are the most likely to reciprocate affectionate expressions and what consequences ensue when they do not. Indeed, as delineated in the sixth chapter, the risk that one's affectionate gesture will be unreciprocated is among the most potent risks of conveying affection in the first place, so this is an issue with clear theoretic import. As a general principle, social exchange theory would provide that if affectionate communication within a given relationship is perceived as a resource, then relational partners should perceive pressure to maintain a reasonably equitable distribution of affectionate behavior. This suggests, for instance, that relationships in which one partner feels underbenefited with respect to affection (i.e., feels that he or she gives more affection than is received in return) should be less stable than those in which greater equity is maintained. Although it was not conducted explicitly to test social exchange theory, research by Lawson (1988) reports that married women's most commonly cited reason for engaging in extramarital affairs was their husbands' failure to meet their affection needs, making the women feel underbenefited with respect to affection.

The reciprocity conceived of by social exchange theory is relatively broad, however, occurring over the duration of a relationship. What predicts reciprocity of a given behavior *at the time it is enacted* is a more specific issue, and the existing theory that has proven the most useful in addressing this question is interaction adaptation theory. This theory provides that communicators enter interactions with their desires, expectations, and desires operational. Communicators are theorized to evaluate behavior they receive from others against the sum of what they need, expect, and want; behaviors that conform or exceed these are predicted to be reciprocated, whereas behaviors that fall short of these are predicted to be compensated for. Thus, if a student needs, expects, and/or wants moderate attention from his professor and he finds that she is either moderately or highly attentive, he will reciprocate that behavior pattern by being highly attentive himself. If she is relatively non-attentive, he will compensate by being highly attentive, so as to elicit more attentiveness from her in return (see, e.g., Miczo, Allspach, & Burgoon, 1999). Interaction adaptation theory has informed investigations of reciprocity and compensation of affectionate behavior, including those by Floyd and Burgoon (1999) and Floyd and Ray (in press).

Each of these fundamental issues – encoding, decoding, interpretation, and reciprocity – is important to address for a complete understanding of affectionate communication, and these existing theories have proven valuable in at least one of three ways. First, they offer testable hypotheses that await empirical verification, such as the prediction that attachment styles influence trait affection levels. Second, they offer hypotheses that have actually garnered empirical support, such as the prediction that unexpectedly high levels of affectionate behavior from a valued source are evaluated more positively than expected levels. Finally, they can provide explanations for findings not identified under their purview, such as the explanation of social exchange theory for why being underbenefited in marital affection is a principal predictor of extramarital affairs.

On these issues, then, existing theories have been able to contribute in meaningful ways to the understanding of affectionate communication. Two important limitations are troublesome, however, the first being that no single existing theory is able to account for all of these issues (encoding, decoding, interpretation, and reciprocity). That is, none of these theories offers an explanatory framework broad enough to encompass all of these questions. Indeed, none of these theories was designed with that purpose in mind, so this is not a limitation of these theories, *per se.* However, the lack of a broad explanatory framework essentially requires a theoretically piecemeal approach to studying affectionate communication, such that each theory is able to explain only particular elements of the phenomenon (although it may explain them well). A more unified theoretic approach would aid efforts to integrate findings from one realm with those of another, resulting in a clearer omnibus view of affectionate communication.

Second, existing theories have been less profitable in addressing other, often conceptually broader, issues. Of course, theories vary with respect to their levels of abstraction, so it is untenable to expect them to be equally adept at addressing questions that are conceptually broad (e.g., why are people affectionate?) and conceptually narrow (e.g., what are the immunological correlates of nonverbal affection among newlyweds?). Existing theories, and particularly those whose predictions about affectionate behavior have been tested empirically (which primarily represent the sociocultural paradigm), have proven more proficient at answering precise, focused questions than at explaining broader issues relevant to the importance and utility of affectionate communication. Some of these conceptually broader questions are delineated next.

Areas in Which Existing Theories Are Limited

At least three theoretic issues regarding affectionate communication have been insufficiently addressed by existing theories. These relate to the dually social and physiological nature of affectionate behavior, the benefits of giving affection as opposed to receiving it, and the fact that affectionate communication sometimes precedes negative, rather than positive, outcomes. Although some current theories partially address one or two of these issues, none partially addresses all three issues or completely addresses any one. These are offered here only as examples of relevant questions that are insufficiently addressed by the body of existing theory; the implication is not that existing theories are wholly inadequate to address these issues, but that they are sufficiently impaired to warrant the development of a new theoretic framework.

Questions of Dual Physiological and Social Influence. Theories in the bioevolutionary and sociocultural paradigms differ from each other primarily in the relative emphases they place on evolutionary/physiological and social/cultural explanatory mechanisms. If one considers the question, "Why do people hug?," for instance, one can easily formulate sociocultural explanations on the basis of extant theory (e.g., hugging is culturally interpreted as conveying love or respect; hugging symbolizes the socially constructed role of women as caregivers and thus reflects social patriarchy). Bioevolutionary explanations also are easily derived (e.g., hugging evolved from adaptive parental protective instincts; hugging provides somatosensory stimulation necessary for neurological development).

For a question such as this, there is little difficulty in formulating theoretically grounded answers within each paradigm; deriving an explanation that considers *both* sociocultural *and* bioevolutionary influences is considerably more challenging, however. Although few theories in either paradigm explicitly exclude the explanatory mechanisms offered in the other paradigm, some theories do implicitly preclude alternative mechanisms through their assumptions or higher-order propositions. If a theory in the sociocultural paradigm assumes (either explicitly or implicitly) that all social behavior is fundamentally motivated by, for example, the quest for power or status, then although that theory's propositions may not explicitly preclude the possibility of hormonal influences on behavior, that possibility is effectively excluded by the theory's underlying assumptions. Conversely, if a theory in the bioevolutionary paradigm assumes that individual behavior reflects only genetic predispositions, then there is likewise little room to account for variance on the basis of cultural norms.

Certainly, few theories make such exclusionary assumptions explicitly, yet their implicit assumptions can nonetheless strongly preclude the alternative explanations offered by a different theoretic paradigm. This has two deleterious effects, the more obvious of which is that, because almost no social phenomenon (including affectionate communication) can reasonably be said to be influenced only by *either* sociocultural *or* bioevolutionary mechanisms, many theoretic accounts are necessarily incomplete. Indeed, as the preceding chapters have illustrated, affectionate behavior varies both as a function of social or cultural norms (e.g., more intimate affectionate behavior is sanctioned in emotionally charged social contexts than in emotionally neutral ones) and as a function of physiological traits (e.g., people with differentiated diurnal cortisol rhythms are more affectionate than people with undifferentiated rhythms). The point that social behavior is influenced by both sociocultural and bioevolutionary forces may seem so self-evident that it fails to warrant explicit mention, yet communicological theories often strongly favor one form of explanation to the relative exclusion of the other, leading to programs of research that may be severely narrow in their focus.

A second, and perhaps less evident, problem brought on by this type of theoretic myopia is that empirical tests of the theories may not be designed in such a way that the relative influences of "competing" explanations can be parceled out. For instance, the prediction that *fathers show more affection to biological sons than to stepsons* is derivable from at least two competing explanations: (1) in North American cultures, biological nuclear family relationships are privileged over non-biological ones; therefore, men feel closer to their biological sons than to their stepsons and they communicate their affection accordingly; and (2) affectionate communication is a resource with implications for health and survival, and it is evolutionarily adaptive to prefer genetic relatives over others in the provision of resources; therefore, men are more affectionate with biological sons than with stepsons.

In principle, one need only compare affectionate behavior in biological and step relationships to test this prediction, and if one's theory even implicitly precludes the possibility of competing influences, then the motivation to attend to that possibility would be low. The problem with such an approach is that, if the hypothesis is supported (i.e., if men show more affection to their biological sons), both explanations are, by implication, *equally* supported unless the design of the study allows one explanation to be tested while the other is controlled. In the present example, for instance, Floyd and Morman (2002) showed that fathers were more affectionate with biological sons than stepsons even when the emotional closeness of the father–son relationships was controlled for. Importantly, the point of such an approach was not to *rule out* closeness as an influence on paternal affection behavior (indeed, closeness was significantly correlated with men's affectionate communication with their sons), but to test the potential influence of the genetic relationship (biological vs. nonbiological) that was independent of the influence of closeness. Absent such a step, Floyd and Morman would not truly have *tested* their bioevolutionary explanation, but would merely have *demonstrated* it.

Questions of Giving versus Receiving Affection. Particularly with respect to the benefits of affectionate behavior, a substantial majority of existing research has focused on the receipt of affectionate communication as opposed to its provision. Most, if not all, of the sociocultural theories reviewed in the second chapter would adopt such a focus; for example, expectancy violations theory, interaction adaptation theory, and cognitive valence theory would all focus on reacting to received affection, whereas the social meaning model would focus on assigning meaning to affectionate behavior one has received or observed. Some theories in the bioevolutionary paradigm likewise adopt a receiver focus; somatosensory affectional deprivation theory focuses on the benefits of receiving affectionate behavior and the detrimental effects of not receiving it, whereas the need to belong would lead one (at least, implicitly) to focus on behaviors that indicate social inclusion, such as the receipt of affection. Of the bioevolutionary theories described in the second chapter, only tend and befriend theory focuses on the effects of *conveying* affection, and then only for women who are experiencing stress (Darwin's theory of emotion expression addresses only the behavioral means by which affectionate messages are encoded).

Aside from the fact that receiving and expressing affection are strongly reciprocal, there is merit in considering the effects of conveying affection, apart from those of receiving it, for which no existing theory provides an adequate account. Chief among the reasons for studying expressed affection is that it covaries with a host of mental and physical health benefits that are independent of those associated with received affection, as Chapter 5 detailed. Importantly, most of these benefits do not appear to be confined to women – or even to be more characteristic of women than men – as tend and befriend theory implies, nor do they appear to be operative only when people are in distress.[1] Rather, the benefits are diverse and robust for both sexes, yet no existing theory mentioned in the preceding chapters provides a sufficient account for why. Baumeister and Leary's (1995) need to belong could, in principle, be used to explain the mental health benefits of providing affection – to the extent that providing affection to others helps to reinforce one's social inclusion – yet the theory would provide no adequate account for the physical health benefits. Conversely, somatosensory affectional deprivation theory could account for the physical health benefits of expressing affection, but only as a function of the affectionate behavior received in return (i.e., one benefits from being affectionate because one receives affection in return, which is beneficial). Given the empirical evidence that expressed affection covaries with benefits that are independent of those associated with received affection, a more adequate theoretic account is needed.

Questions of Positive versus Negative Outcomes. Perhaps the most counterintuitive aspect of affectionate communication is its potential to elicit negative, rather than positive, outcomes. As detailed in Chapter 6, affectionate behavior conveyed in particular ways or in particular contexts can cause cognitive or emotional distress on the part of the recipient that has the potential to lead not only to compensatory behavior but also to confusion over the status of the relationship and perhaps even to relational deescalation. Whereas only bioevolutionary theories offered partial explanations for the benefits of conveying (as opposed to receiving) affection, only sociocultural theories currently provide any measure of explanation for why affectionate behavior can produce either positive or negative outcomes.

Specifically, expectancy violations theory, cognitive valence theory, and interaction adaptation theory all provide for the possibility that even a behavior as inherently positive as an affectionate expression could be reacted to negatively. (Social exchange theory would certainly provide that if one's affection is not reciprocated, the resulting inequity would be aversive; however, it does not provide the explanatory means for

[1] This assertion is implicit, not explicit, in tend and befriend theory. That is, the theory does not explicitly provide that only women under stress benefit from tending and befriending behaviors; rather, the theory's focus on the uniquely adaptive nature of tending and befriending as women's strategies for managing stress implies, at the very least, that such behaviors (of which affectionate behaviors would be a part) are more beneficial to women than to men.

predicting when nonreciprocity is likely to occur in the first place.) The causal element in all three theories' explanations is a *violation*: the affectionate expression violated the receiver's expectations, cultural norms, desires, individual schemata, perceived needs, or some other property. These three theories vary in which properties are deemed most influential when violated, as well as in the effects of violations. Whereas cognitive valence theory deems any violation of its properties as aversive, the other two allow that some violations can be positive (functioning as, for instance, a pleasant surprise) while many other violations are negative.

To the extent that one's affectionate expression is met with negative emotion or behavior, therefore, these theories would explain such an outcome as following from a violation of the receiver's expectations, values, needs, or other characteristics. Indeed, it is not difficult to conceive of affectionate behaviors that would negatively violate, for instance, one's expectations or social norms; an intimate hug or kiss from a stranger would, in a wide range of circumstances, be considered abnormal and cause a measure of distress for the recipient. The fundamental question here is not why the gesture would be unexpected, but why it would be aversive. Although EVT and IAT do provide that the valence of a violation depends on a receiver's assessment of the sender (whether the sender is rewarding or not) and of the behavior itself (whether it is inherently positive or negative), both theories are broad in their explication of which aspects of the sender or behavior exert the most influence on the valence.

This breadth is probably a necessary feature of these theories, given the range of interpersonal behaviors each is intended to explain, and so this is not a criticism of these theories so much as it is a limitation of their application to affectionate communication. The consequence of this limitation is the lack of a singular explanatory mechanism to account for the sometimes negative effects of affectionate behaviors. The preference for a singular mechanism does not imply that individual, social, cultural, or contextual variation should be (or even can be) disregarded. Rather, it reflects the advantage, in terms of accounting for variance, of referencing behavioral motivations that are not socially or contextually variant, as the theory proposed herein will attempt to offer.

As detailed here, existing theories have been fruitful in guiding exploration of several aspects of affectionate communication, and it is a strength of several of these theories that they have done so despite not having been constructed for that specific purpose. Other aspects of affectionate communication remain insufficiently explained, however, limiting the ability of researchers to explicate and understand these issues. In an attempt to provide a more comprehensive account of human affectionate behavior, this chapter details a new theory that is grounded in the Darwinian concept of natural selection yet takes account of variance in social and contextual norms. Several important prefaces to the theory are provided subsequently.

Prefaces to a Neo-Darwinian Theory of Affectionate Communication

Proposed in this chapter is a new theoretic treatment of affectionate communication that is designed to address the shortcomings of existing theories, particularly with respect to two fundamental questions: why is affectionate communicate communication important, and why can it produce either positive or negative outcomes? I refer to the theory as *neo-Darwinian* to specify that its assumptions are grounded in contemporary thinking regarding the theory of natural selection and its application to human psychology. Importantly, the theory proposed here is not a direct application of the theory of natural selection to the issue of affectionate communication; rather, it builds upon axioms that have their roots in contemporary Darwinian thought.

As a preface, this section provides a rudimentary review of the principles of natural selection and their application to human psychology. Following that is a delineation of five principles that are essential to an appreciation of my theory's assumptions. In no way is this section intended to represent a complete overview of natural selection, evolutionary psychology, or the controversies surrounding either. For such a treatment, readers are referred to sources such as Buss (1999) or Workman and Reader (2004).

A Primer on the Theory of Natural Selection

Phylogeny is the history and development of a species or higher-order grouping of organisms – that is, an account of its change over time. Scientists have long acknowledged that various species possess physical characteristics that appear to serve some functional purpose with regard to survival or procreation, and that some such characteristics change, over long spans of time, within those species. For example, long necks and long muscular tongues allow giraffes to feed on food supplies (leaves) that are inaccessible to other species. The long, colorful plumage of the peacock can help it to attract peahens for mating. The quills and expandable "skin" of the blowfish help it to ward off would-be predators. Changes over time in average neck length, plumage hue, or quill density within each of these species are examples of phylogenetic development, a process better known in contemporary discourse as evolution.

Early evolutionary scientists offered various theoretic accounts for *how* phylogenesis occurs, the most revolutionary of which was Darwin's (1859) theory of evolution by means of natural selection, or TNS (a theory that was simultaneously, and independently, proposed by Alfred Russel Wallace, 1858). TNS espouses four main principles: superfecundity, variation, heritability, and selection. The first principle, *superfecundity*, acknowledges that, in any given generation, many more members of a species are born than can possibly survive and reproduce, creating what Darwin referred to as a "struggle for existence." The second principle, *variation*, indicates that all members of a species have diverse combinations of traits.[2] Humans, for instance, vary one from another in multiple physical traits, including height, body shape, hair and eye color, bone density, sensory ability, and weight. According to the third principle, *heritability*, a proportion of this variation is inherited, or transferred from parents to their biological offspring through the parents' genetic material. For example, two parents with brown eyes will tend to produce offspring with brown eyes, because eye color is a heritable trait.

The fourth, and most innovative, principle in TNS is *selection*, which provides that heritable characteristics that advantage an organism with respect to survival or procreation will be transferred to succeeding generations with a greater frequency than characteristics that do not provide these advantages. That is, genetic traits that prove advantageous to an organism (because they help to meet an environmental challenge to viability or fertility) are *selected for*, or retained from one generation to the next, whereas characteristics that do not prove advantageous are *selected against*, or not retained.

For example, a long neck is advantageous to giraffes because it provides them access to food, which is necessary for survival. Giraffes with the longest necks, therefore, have access to more food than other giraffes, and thus are more likely to survive to sexual maturity. Because they are more likely to survive to sexual maturity, they are more likely to procreate, and because neck length is heritable, succeeding generations of giraffes will have longer average necks than previous generations had.

---

[2] This is true, at least, for sexually reproducing species; see Bjorklund and Pellegrini (2002).

Thus, an environmental challenge (access to food) caused a heritable trait (neck length) to be advantageous in terms of survival and procreation. This example illustrates the principle of *survival of the fittest* (a phrase coined by Herbert Spencer): those organisms best adapted to the demands of their environment are the most likely to survive and reproduce themselves, allowing that advantageous heritable characteristics are passed on to their progeny at a greater frequency than disadvantageous ones.[3] The importance of the environment in this principle is clear, because traits that would prove adaptive in one environment may be maladaptive in another. For example, the physical properties that make many water mammals fast swimmers make them slow movers on land, causing these properties to be adaptive for evading predators in the water but maladaptive for evading predators on land.

Inherent in TNS is the premise that all organisms must continually attend to their needs for survival and procreation. These are not completely orthogonal motivations: procreation is impossible without survival, and survival without procreation does not necessarily contribute one's genetic material to succeeding generations. As Hamilton (1964) acknowledged, however, it need not be one's own reproduction that contributes one's genetic materials to subsequent generations; such a task can be accomplished by other individuals who carry one's genes, such as a sibling, cousin, or niece. Anything one does that furthers the reproductive success of these relatives also furthers one's own reproductive success, by a factor equal to the degree of genetic relatedness with that relative (which is higher for siblings than for nieces and higher for nieces than for cousins). This principle is fundamental to inclusive fitness theory (see also Trivers, 1971).

The application of principles of natural selection to human psychology is founded on recognition that the brain is as much subject to selection pressures as any other physical property and that, consequently, propensities for cognition, emotion, and social behavior can be understood as being adaptive in the same manner that propensities for height, strength, or a long neck can be (see, e.g., Buss, 1999). According to such a perspective, for instance, preferences for physical beauty that are linked to health and fertility, such as body symmetry or a low waist-to-hip ratio, are adaptive because they promote the development of reproductive pair bonds. Emotions such as fear or jealousy are adaptive insofar as they promote vigilance about threats to safety or relational stability. These are simply

---

[3] Importantly, traits need only be partially heritable to be influenced by selective pressures.

two examples; the evolutionary psychological approach would argue that *any* psychological characteristic or propensity that advantages an organism with respect to survival or reproduction, and that is at least partially heritable, is subject to selection pressures in the same manner that physical characteristics are.

These principles underlie the theoretic approach to affectionate communication explicated in this chapter. At least five important prefaces regarding the nature of evolutionary adaptations are important to address before offering such a theory, however, as they will help mitigate potential misunderstandings and premature dismissals of counterintuitive ideas. These prefaces are offered subsequently. Importantly, the ideas represented in these prefaces are neither mine nor those of the affection theory explicated later in this chapter; rather, these are principles of Darwinian thought reflected in TNS and related theories.

Adaptations Deal with Proximal and Ultimate Levels of Causation

The question of why a particular behavior occurs can be answered on at least two levels of abstraction. A *proximal cause* is the condition or set of conditions that appears to have given rise to the behavior in the specific time, place, and manner in which it occurred. For instance, a woman eats dinner because she feels hungry; a man marries his wife because he falls in love with her. By contrast, an *ultimate cause* is the condition or set of conditions that represents the original or higher-order cause of a behavior (and often dictates the connection between the behavior and its proximal causes). Thus, a woman eats dinner because she feels hungry, but she feels hungry because she must eat in order to survive; thus, she experiences the sensation of hunger as a way of motivating her to eat on a regular basis. Likewise, a man marries his wife because he fells in love with her, but he falls in love with her because procreation is a superordinate goal; thus, he experiences the emotion of love and the sensation of attraction as a way of motivating him to seek a mate. These examples illustrate how specific behaviors (eating or marrying) can be considered to be caused both by proximal agents (hunger or love) and by ultimate agent (need for nutrients or motivation to procreate). It is unproductive to debate whether, for instance, hunger or the need for nutrients is the *true* cause of eating because these are not competing explanations. Rather, they simply represent different levels of abstraction, and one of the advantages of the Darwinian approach is that it focuses attention on the ultimate causes for specific emotions, cognitions, or social behaviors that, while they may be unapparent in the immediate situation, may be motivating both the resulting emotion, cognition, or behavior and its proximal causes.

Adaptations Need Not Operate at a Conscious Level

When asked to account for their own behaviors, it is not uncommon for individuals to identify proximal causes with little or no regard for ultimate, higher-order causes. This is often because humans are simply unaware of what the ultimate causes might be or how they might be operating through more proximal causes. Darwinian theories acknowledge that many ultimate causes operate outside of an individual's conscious awareness of them, and they further contend that this is not problematic. For example, if people are asked to explain why they got married, they may be inclined to report that it is because they fell in love with each other, couldn't imagine their lives without each other, and wanted to spend the rest of their lives together; few are likely to indicate that they got married in order to pass their genetic materials on to future generations. However, evolutionary psychology posits that this is, indeed, the ultimate cause of pair bonding, irrespective of people's conscious awareness. Consequently, this theoretic approach to the study of human behavior does not require individuals to be aware of the ultimate causes of their behaviors in order for those ultimate causes to be operative.

Adaptations Need Not Be Adaptive for Present-Day Life

Consideration of modern environments can easily make it difficult to understand how particular adaptations are beneficial. An illustrative example is the human preference for sweet, fatty, and salty foods; one could easily question how such a preference could possibly be adaptive, when overindulgence in these types of foods can lead to obesity, high cholesterol, heart disease, and even death. The answer is that Darwinian theories do not attempt to explain human adaptive behavior with reference to present-day life; rather, they focus on physical and psychological traits that would have been adaptive in the hunter-gatherer societies of our ancestors, or what is commonly referred to as the *environment of evolutionary adaptedness* (Tooby & Cosmides, 1992). The reason is that phylogenetic changes develop slowly, across millennia rather than decades or centuries, and because modern civilization is remarkably young when considered on such a timescale. Agriculture appeared only 10,000 years ago, and civilization is an even more recent phenomenon. Humankind has spent more than 99% of its history living in hunter-gatherer societies, and as Morris (2001) pointed out, it is unlikely that selection pressures have resulted in substantial neural modifications in the short period of time represented by modernity. As a result, some traits that were adaptive in hunter-gatherer environments may be useless or even maladaptive now. For instance, humans must ingest a certain amount of sugar, fat, and salt to survive, so a preference for these types of foods would have helped to ensure that hunter-gatherers consumed these necessary nutrients. In a modern environment where sugar, fat, and salt are more readily available, where general nutrition (at least in the industrialized world) is increasingly improving, and where mechanization often prevents the expenditure of considerable physical energy, such a preference can easily be maladaptive. However, phylogenesis is, in most instances, an exceedingly slow process, making it unlikely that selection pressures would yet have curtailed the preference for such foods.

Adaptations Need Not Be Adaptive for Every Person,
or in Every Instance

This point refers to the specificity at which adaptations operate. It can be difficult for an individual to appreciate how particular traits might be adaptive if, for whatever reason, those traits fail to produce the adaptive outcomes for that individual. The human sex drive is illustrative; the fact that sex is physically pleasurable for humans can be considered to be adaptive in the sense that it motivates the act of intercourse, which is necessary for reproduction of the species.[4] To be adaptive, a trait must prove advantageous in solving an environmental challenge to survival or procreation; this does not imply, however, that the trait must produce its adaptive result for every individual. That is, the human sex drive is not maladaptive for people who are sterile, or people who are celibate, or for women who are postmenopausal; it is adaptive because the challenge of reproduction is met more effectively *with it* than *without it.* Moreover, an adaptation need not produce its adaptive result in every instance. Even though few instances of sexual intercourse result in pregnancy,

---

[4] Advances in reproductive technology, such as *in vitro* fertilization, have, of course, eliminated intercourse as a necessary precursor to reproduction. Because such technologies are products of modern civilization, however, they were not available to those in hunter-gatherer societies, for whom the adaptive nature of the human sex drive would have been selected.

relative to the number of times humans engage in intercourse overall, this does not make the sex drive maladaptive; adaptations need only provide advantages relative to their alternatives.

Adaptations Operate at the Individual Level, Not the Group or Species Level

Humans belong to a number of important groups, including families, social networks, and professional networks that, in various ways, help to ensure their survival. In many cases, therefore, what is beneficial to the group is beneficial to the individual member, and vice versa. Often, however, individual and group priorities are in conflict. An example concerns a communal living situation in which each person's money and possessions are considered to be the collective property of all group members, and all group members are equally cared for. In such a situation, anything that benefits the group as a whole also benefits each member individually, because there is a communal sharing of resources. If, however, a group member were to find a large sum of money about which the other group members were unaware, it would benefit this member to contribute the money to the group, because an economic benefit to the group would benefit all members. However, it would benefit this individual *more* to keep the money and not to disclose it to the group, because this member would then be overbenefited in relation to his or her fellow members. In a grave financial crisis, this member may even be able to survive while others in the group – or the group as a whole – perished. Adaptations work in much the same manner, to advantage the individual rather than any group to which he or she belongs. Therefore, in circumstances when an individual's priorities conflict with a group's, adaptations tend to privilege the success of the individual over that of the group.

To the extent that Darwinian thought is not necessarily intuitive, these prefaces aid in understanding its application to human social behavior. Given these prefaces, I now offer formal explication of my theory. The focus in the subsequent section is on the arguments and logical structure of the theory.

A Theory on Human Affectionate Communication

The theory offered here advances the argument that human affectionate behavior is, in large part, adaptive; that it contributes directly to human survival and procreation; and that affectionate communication therefore produces evolutionary advantages, making affectionate individuals better adapted than nonaffectionate individuals. Working from this premise regarding the ultimate or higher-order function of affectionate behavior, I propose below a set of postulates that specify the variables governing affectionate communication at a more proximal, lower-order level. These postulates constitute my theory of human affectionate communication, which I have tentatively named Affection Exchange Theory.

Preview of Affection Exchange Theory

Affection exchange theory treats affectionate communication as an adaptive behavior that both directly and indirectly contributes to human survival and reproductive success. Darwin (1859) posited that the development and adaptation of all life forms, including those of humans, follow a pattern of natural selection whereby those organisms who are most adaptive to the demands of their environments are the most likely to survive and reproduce. Over time, therefore, the heritable characteristics of those best adapted to their environments are transferred to succeeding generations with greater frequency than are those of less adaptive organisms. In this process, the ability to survive and the ability to procreate successfully are paramount, since success is defined as the transference of one's genes into future generations, a feat that is impossible without both of these abilities.

Affection exchange theory (AET) is not intended to be an extension or modification of the theory of natural selection or any other associated theory. Rather, it treats affectionate communication as a class of behaviors that serves both superordinate evolutionary goals (survival and procreation) and that is, as such, influenced by human motivations to meet these goals. The purpose of AET is therefore to cast affectionate communication in adaptive terms and to begin to specify the biological and environmental factors through which it serves humans' most pressing evolutionary needs.

Assumptions

Three principles fundamental to Darwinian thought serve as the axiomatic foundation for affection exchange theory. The first is that survival and procreation are the two superordinate human motivations. This assumption focuses theoretic attention on the advantages that a prospective adaptation has for survival, reproduction, or both.

Importantly, the goal of procreation encompasses not only the immediate goal to produce offspring, but also the longer-range goal of having one's offspring reproduce themselves so that one's own genes are passed on to future generations (see Fisher, 1930). This point will be important to some of the arguments advanced in this theory. The remaining assumptions, both of which I have addressed above, are that behaviors need not serve a superordinate evolutionary goal in a proximal sense in order to serve it in an ultimate sense, and that individuals need not be consciously aware of the evolutionary goals being served by their behaviors.

Postulates

Affection exchange theory is comprised of the five postulates detailed below. Following some are subpostulates that provide empirical generalizations and applications. These should be understood to be part of the explanatory framework of the theory, rather than hypotheses that are derived from the theory but are not a part of it. Where applicable, sample hypotheses that can be logically deduced from the theory are suggested below.

Postulate 1. The need and capacity for affection are inborn.

As a higher-order postulate, AET offers that humans have both a fundamental need and a fundamental ability to love and receive love from others. This proposition refers to the internal experience of affection rather than to its behavioral manifestations, and it positions the need and capacity for affection among humans' innate experiences. In this regard, AET is consistent with Baumeister and Leary's (1995) explication of the need to belong as a fundamental human motivation for attachment. As innate, the need and capacity for affection should be more stable than inconsistent across historical periods, cultural and geographic boundaries, and socially constructed divisions such as class. Perhaps more important, however, they should be manifested not only in social behavior but also in neural structures and physiological regulation, such that fulfilling the need to love and be loved is beneficial to mental and physical well-being whereas failing to meet it is aversive.

The latter proposition partly characterizes Miller and colleagues' articulation of an *ontogenetic bonding system,* a neurally grounded structure that operates to promote social interaction toward the development or maintenance of dyadic relationships (Miller, Pasta, MacMurray, Chiu, Wu, & Comings, 1999; Miller, Pasta, MacMurray, Muhleman, & Comings,

2000; Miller & Rodgers, 2001). Miller et al. propose that the ontogenetic bonding system motivates humans toward social interaction by characterizing such interaction with feelings of safety and warmth. These authors have implicated activity in neurotransmitter systems, such as those involving oxytocin, vasopressin, prolactin, dopamine, norepinephrine, serotonin, opioids, and cannabinoids, as a proximal agent for inducing the warm and safe feelings that make bonding behaviors rewarding.

As discussed in greater detail later, individual differences are undoubtedly manifested in the ability to convey and receive expressions of affection. Some variation is developmental. As children acquire linguistic and paralinguistic abilities, for instance, they consequently expand their behavioral repertoires for giving and reciprocating affectionate expressions; later development of empathic accuracy (Ickes, 1993), perspective-taking ability (Batson, Early, & Salvarani, 1997), self-monitoring (Snyder & Gangestad, 1986), and interpersonal sensitivity (Montepare, 2004) should similarly aid in decoding affectionate behavior. Nondevelopmental individual variation is also observed, as in the cases of those suffering from alexithymia (Taylor & Bagby, 2000) or Asperger's disorder (Campbell, 2005). The former condition is characterized by difficulty in identifying emotions and in distinguishing between emotional and physical feelings. Thus, hormonal or cardiovascular changes induced by receiving an affectionate expression may not be recognized by an alexithymic individual as corresponding to feelings of love for the sender. The latter condition involves difficulty interpreting the nonverbal behaviors of others (such as nonverbal emotion displays) and a corresponding failure to develop meaningful peer relationships or engage in social or emotional reciprocity. Those with Asperger's disorder would likely find it difficult to decode nonverbal affection displays and would, therefore, be unlikely to reciprocate them in the service of relationship development or maintenance. Moreover, they would likely find it profoundly difficult to distinguish affection displays (whether verbal or nonverbal) that are sincere from those that are not.

Importantly, to call the need and capacity for affection *inborn* is not to deny that they are also subject to environmental conditioning. Indeed, patterns of affection exchange replicate inter-generationally within families, whether the familial relationships are genetic or not (Floyd & Morman, 2000a), and it is not difficult to conceive that positive modeling and reinforcement within one's social environment would encourage at least the capacity for affection whereas punishment would inhibit it.

This postulate proposes only that humans are endowed with the need and ability to love and be loved, although the magnitude and effects of these needs and capacities can differ across groups, across individuals, and even within individuals over time.

Postulate 2. Affectionate feelings and affectionate expressions are distinct experiences that often, but need not, covary.

This point was discussed clearly in the introductory chapter and it is an important higher-order postulate in AET. The same idea could be proposed for all but perhaps the most intense of emotional experiences; assuming communicative competence, individuals can, in most instances, control the external manifestations of their emotional experiences and they do so according to "display rules" evident at cultural, familial, or situational levels (see Ekman, 1997; Halberstadt, 1986). Although people can express feelings (including affectionate feelings) with no attempt to censor their emotion displays, they also can elect to modify their displays in at least five different ways, according to Ekman and Friesen (1975). First, they can *inhibit,* or fail to express the emotion they are experiencing (e.g., feeling love for someone but choosing not to communicate that feeling). Second, they can *simulate,* which means expressing an emotion when no emotion is actually felt (e.g., saying "I love you" only to reciprocate that expression from another who is not actually loved). The third and fourth options are to *intensify* or *deintensify,* which involve portraying the emotional experience as either more intense or less intense than it actually is (e.g., saying "I love you" when only liking is felt, or saying "I like you" when love is actually felt). Finally, communicators can *mask,* which involves conveying one emotion even though a different emotion is actually being experienced (e.g., expressing affection to someone for whom anger or resentment is actually being felt). As noted, the ability to modify emotion displays in these ways should vary with the competence of the communicator and may be weaker when the intensity of the emotion is stronger, leading the emotion to "leak" behaviorally in unintended ways (see Ekman, 1982; Gallois, 1993).

Several studies have suggested that "display rules" at the social or contextual levels can lead people to modify their expressions of affection in perhaps all of the ways Ekman and Friesen (1975) described. For instance, Floyd and Morman (1997) found that both the privacy and the emotional tenor of a social context influence the perceived appropriateness of verbal and nonverbal affection displays. Felt affection between intimates may, for example, be deintensified or even inhibited in public settings but not in private ones; or, as Floyd and Morman found for non-romantic pairs, it may be deintensified or inhibited in private but not in public. Likewise, in emotionally charged situations such as a funeral or a wedding, people consider a broader range of affectionate behaviors to be appropriate than in an emotionally neutral context. It is easy to imagine, therefore, that communicators may intensify or even simulate displays of affection at a wedding or funeral in order to comply with the social demands of the situation, and may even mask socially proscribed emotions (e.g., envy at a wedding or joy at a funeral) with insincere affection displays. Simulation of affectionate communication, in particular, can even be used strategically to serve ulterior motives, such as gaining favor or compliance. In their survey of over a thousand adults from all geographic regions of the U.S., Floyd, Erbert et al. (2005) reported that the strategic use of affection simulation was remarkably common; 86% of the sample indicated having simulated affection displays for strategic purposes, and more than half of those (55.8%) reported having done so *within the previous month.*

That the experience and expression of affection can be conceived of as distinct constructs is important because it raises a number of provocative research questions, such as why communicators would elect to hide affectionate feelings when they have them or when they are likely to express affection that is not being felt. Both instances have implications for the development and maintenance of personal relationships: the former, because it can leave relational partners' needs for affectionate behavior unfulfilled, and the latter, because it can initiate or accelerate relational development under false pretenses. (For more extended discussion on the dissociation of emotional experience and emotional expression, consult Gross, John, & Richards, 2000.)

Postulate 3. Affectionate communication is adaptive with respect to human viability and fertility.

The third, and perhaps most important, higher-order postulate offers that the exchange of affectionate behavior benefits both senders and receivers by serving their superordinate motivations for survival and procreation and is, in this sense, an evolutionarily adaptive behavior.

The links between affectionate communication, viability, and fertility can be appreciated at both ultimate and proximal levels of causality. Links at the ultimate level focus on the contribution of affectionate communication to the formation of significant pair bonds and their protective and resource-sharing characteristics, as well as to the representation of parenting potential. Focus at the proximal level is on the physical pathways via which giving and receiving affection manifest their benefits. Importantly, these are not competing explanations for the same outcome, but instead represent explanations cast at differing levels of abstraction. Ultimate links are examined in the first two subpostulates.

SUBPOSTULATE 3A. Affectionate communication serves the superordinate motivation for viability by promoting the establishment and maintenance of significant human pair bonds.[5]

Unlike many other mammals, humans routinely form pair bonds, or significant and long-term relationships with each other that may be monogamous, polygamous, or polyandrous in form (Daly & Wilson, 1983; Kenrick & Trost, 1987). MacDonald (1992) argued that pair bonding and its associated affection in intimate relationships are human adaptations evolved for the purpose of protecting the young. In an evolutionary sense, effort and resources expended in the service of producing offspring are wasted, with respect to reproductive success, if the offspring fail to survive to maturity; thus, providing for and protecting the young are critical for reproductive success. Such provisioning and protection are more efficiently disbursed when a child's parents compose a bonded, cooperative pair, because they each have an evolutionary stake in that child's well being that is not shared by guardians who have no biological bond with the child (see Lamb, Pleck, Charnov, & Levine, 1987).

This reasoning can be extended to apply not only to the young but to those of all ages. Human pair bonding, whether sexual or platonic in nature, invariably entails the sharing of resources that contribute to long-term viability.[6] These can include material resources such as food or money, protection from physical or psychological threats, and emotional

---

[5] I acknowledge here that the term *pair bonding* is normally used only in reference to long-term romantic relationships. My use of the term in this discussion is intentionally broader, encompassing both romantic and platonic dyadic relationships that involve a significant affectional bond, because resources important to long-term viability are garnered from both.

[6] Such an approach should be distinguished from the theoretic paradigm known as communibiology (Beatty & McCroskey, 1997, 1998, 2000a, b; Beatty, McCroskey, & Heisel, 1998; Beatty, McCroskey, & Valencic, 2001). Although communibiology acknowledges the adaptive function of physical characteristics and posits a link between such characteristics and observed social behavior, it focuses specifically on the ways in which the brain's structures, often manifested through temperament, influence communicative processes. Thus, although AET and communibiology share conceptual space, they differ somewhat in their focus and in their levels of specificity.

resources such as social support and empathy. These types of resources contribute to human viability throughout the life course, not just during the developmentally dependent period. Consequently, to the extent that affectionate communication contributes to the establishment and maintenance of significant pair bonds (which a host of empirical studies has demonstrated; see Bell & Healey, 1992; Owen, 1987), it therefore contributes to long-term viability through these associated resources.

With respect to AET, perhaps the most important characteristic distinguishing between romantic and platonic pair bonds, however, is the probability of producing genetic offspring. Although Hamilton (1964) articulated that individual reproduction is not *necessary* for reproductive success (given that one also achieves such success via the reproduction of genetic relatives), it is certainly *sufficient* for reproductive success if offspring survive to sexual maturity. Therefore, to the extent that affectionate behavior increases the likelihood of individual reproductive potential, it consequently contributes to reproductive success. AET proposes that expressing affection increases reproductive opportunity by portraying the communicator as having high parental fitness, as the next subpostulate details.

SUBPOSTULATE 3B. Affectionate communication serves the superordinate motivation for fertility by representing to potential mating partners that the communicator is a viable partner and a fit potential parent.

Darwin used the term *sexual selection* to refer to the process by which traits evolve due to their benefits for reproduction rather than survival. Reproductive success is never guaranteed when humans interact sexually, partly because not all individuals are willing or able to undertake the long-term responsibility of rearing offspring. Therefore, included among the traits that contribute to reproductive success must be the ability to discriminate between fit and unfit partners, or what is referred to here as *potential parental fitness*.

According to this subpostulate, affectionate communication contributes to reproductive success specifically because it portrays, whether accurately or not, a high degree of potential parental fitness to recipients who are potential reproductive partners. Specifically proposed is that, relative to low degrees of affectionate behavior, highly affectionate behavior implies the emotional capacity and drive necessary to be a committed romantic partner and a capable parent. In the former case, overt expressions of affection such as saying "I love you" convey an intent to pair bond (or remain pair bonded), because it is often through the use of such expressions that significant relationships are initiated (Owen, 1987).

Reiteration of the third axiom is warranted here, given that AET would not propose that recipients of affectionate behavior engage in a conscious mental calculus aimed at evaluating the potential parental fitness of the communicator. From the perspective of AET, and of much of evolutionary psychology, conscious processing of this nature is unnecessary; if affectionate communication does portray potential parental fitness, then AET would propose that even subconscious attendance to affectionate behavior when choosing a mating partner would be selected for through the process of sexual selection. Consequently, this subpostulate would not necessarily lead to the hypothesis that highly affectionate communicators are consciously perceived by others as having high potential parental fitness. It would, however, logically suggest that highly affectionate individuals are more likely than less affectionate counterparts to be in long-term romantic relationships (which maximize the potential for successful rearing of offspring through maturity; see above), and indeed, Floyd (2003) demonstrated that this was the case.

A compelling example of affectionate communication signaling potential parental fitness concerns the use of the affectionate voice. Several studies have documented that in affectionate interactions with romantic partners, humans have a tendency to adopt a vocalic pattern known as *babytalk* or *parentese* (Ferguson, 1977; Garnica, 1977; Zebrowitz, Brownlow, & Olson, 1992), a form of speaking that mimics verbal interaction with infants. Babytalk has been observed in multiple cultures in North America, Asia, Europe, and Africa and is practiced both men and women (irrespective of whether they are parents) and by children (Ferguson, 1964; Fernald & Simon, 1984; Shute & Wheldall, 1989; Toda, Fogal, & Kawai, 1990). Apart from its linguistic features – which include the use of idioms and "pet" names, simplified sentence structure, and word repetition – babytalk is also characterized by increased vocal pitch and pitch variance, exaggerated intonation, and a decrease in amplitude (Fernald & Simon, 1984; Zebrowitz et al., 1992). Importantly, several studies have indicated that it is the acoustic properties of babytalk, rather than its linguistic features, that most strongly elicit positive affect from the receiver (Fernald, 1989; 1993; Werker & McLeod, 1989).

That adults often speak to their romantic partners using the same vocalic and linguistic patterns that are regularly employed with infants (Bombar & Littig, 1996) is significant from the vantage of AET because, in so doing, individuals implicitly convey to their partners a capacity for nurturance and a capability of caring for offspring. To avoid wasting reproductive effort, AET proposes that humans are inclined to attend to such cues when selecting potential mating partners, in much the same way that research indicates they attend to physical cues to phenotypic quality, such as facial attractiveness (Johnston & Franklin, 1993), fluctuating asymmetry (Thornhill, Gangestad, & Comer, 1995), or waist-to-hip ratio (Singh, 1993).

Trivers (1972) observed that the assessment of fitness (in its various forms) for a potential reproductive partner is not equally consequential for women and men (nor for females and males of many species); rather, he noted that a poor mating choice is far more detrimental to women, in terms of resource depletion, than to men. Trivers proposed that this was due to *differential parental investment*, or the minimum investment of resources required to rear a healthy child. For females of many species, the minimum required investment is substantial; it includes, among other things, the time, physical stress, and emotional strain involved in gestation, the loss of further reproductive opportunity (and, perhaps, social or economic opportunity) during gestation, and the health risks associated with delivery. By sharp contrast, males' minimum required investment is the time and energy expended during insemination. Notably, these represent in Trivers's theory the *minimum* required investments, not the socially or politically desirable investments of women's and men's resources. Trivers predicted that, in any species, whichever sex has the greater minimum parental investment will exercise greater selectivity in choosing sexual partners of the opposite sex. Consequently, for humans and many other species, Trivers's theory would indicate that males compete for sexual access to females, rather than the other way around, because females have substantially more resources at stake when selecting reproductive partners.

The implication of Trivers's theory for affectionate communication is that, compared to men, women should be more motivated to attend (at least subconsciously) to their reproductive partners' potential to be fit parents and good providers for themselves and their children. Several studies have demonstrated just such a propensity in patterns of human mate selection (e.g., Buss, 1989; Feingold, 1992; Kenrick, Groth, Trost, & Sadalla, 1993; Kenrick, Sadalla, Broth, & Trost, 1990). Therefore, if affectionate communication connotes a tendency to be a committed partner and a fit parent, this should be more consequential to women's mate choices than to men's. This idea is formalized in the third subpostulate.

SUBPOSTULATE 3C. The relationship between affectionate communication and reproductive opportunity is stronger for women's mate selections than for men's.

Several testable hypotheses can be deduced from this third subpostulate. Most notably, (1) men more than women use affectionate communication strategically for the purpose of initiating sexual opportunity; (2) the use of affectionate communication is a relatively successful strategy for inducing sexual opportunity; and (3) the influence of affectionate communication on the creation of sexual opportunity is stronger for women than for men. It may even be the case that affectionate behavior can be used strategically to induce reproductive opportunity even without being perceived by the target as manipulative, and that this may enhance the success of the strategy. These hypotheses have potentially important implications not only for sexual behaviors in established, consensual relationships but also for issues such as sexual coercion and date rape (which are often instigated verbally, in the absence of any physical force; see Caraway, 1998). For instance, men may be more inclined than women to use affectionate communication strategically to induce sexual interaction with a partner who might otherwise be unwilling (for a discussion on sex differences in experiences of sexual coercion, see O'Sullivan, Byers, & Finkelman, 1998).

Accompanying these ultimate explanations for the influence of affectionate communication on well-being is the proximal explanation that giving and receiving expressions of affection covary with important regulatory physiological functions in such a way that the benefits and liabilities of affection exchange are manifested psychosomatically. Rather than being a competing explanation for why affectionate communication contributes to viability and fertility, the focus on proximal psychophysiological processes explains the manners in which affectionate behavior can serve relational maintenance and convey parental fitness at a localized level. Importantly, this proximal explanation also suggests more specific avenues of inquiry for understanding the relationships between affectionate behavior and physical and mental health.

SUBPOSTULATE 3D. The experiences of feeling, communicating, and receiving affection covary with immunocompetence and regulatory physiological pathways for stress and reward.

Consistent with the proposition that the capacity for affection is inborn, this subpostulate suggests that when humans feel, convey, or receive affection from others, these are accompanied by activity in the physiological systems that regulate immunity, stress management, and reward sensations. This subpostulate is intentionally broad in two respects: it specifies only covariation rather than directional causality, and it references pathways for stress and reward without articulating the specific physiological mechanisms involved. There are two reasons for this breadth, the first of which stems from the observation, articulated throughout this book, that affection exchange can be accompanied by either joy or distress. To refer unqualifiedly to affection experiences as having only positive physiological consequences would therefore be unwarranted. The second reason reflects the specificity of empirical work on the physiological correlates of affection, specifically, and of social relationships, in general. Although this research (much of which is detailed in Chapters 5 and 6) has specified numerous aspects of immunocompetence, stress reactivity, and hormonal reward that covary with relational interactions such as affection exchange, many potential "markers" of these regulatory systems may as yet be unexamined. As empirical research on these proximal pathways for affectionate communication and well-being becomes further developed and articulated, increased specificity in this subpostulate will be facilitated.

Despite its current breadth, however, this subpostulate suggests numerous avenues for studying and understanding how the experience and expression of affection can covary with humans' disease immunity, stress management, and physiological reward sensations, all of which are potentially relevant for the more ultimate pathways of relationship development and parental fitness discussed earlier. Examples discussed in earlier chapters include Floyd, Mikkelson et al.'s (in press) demonstration that engaging in affectionate expression during acute stress accelerated the return of cortisol to baseline values, even relative to thinking about a loved one but not expressing one's feelings, and Grewen et al.'s (2005) finding that engaging in nonverbal affectionate behavior with a heterosexual romantic partner reduced cortisol levels for both men and women, and increased serum oxytocin for women. These and other findings indicate that, under the right circumstances, affectionate interaction (accompanied, in both of these examples, by affectionate feelings) is manifested in physiological processes that induce calm, ameliorate pain, and diminish stress. Less understood are the conditions under which the same behaviors may *initiate* physiological stress responses and *reduce* immunocompetence, although behavioral measures, such as those reported by Floyd and Burgoon (1999), have indicated that unwanted affection prompts compensatory behavior (which may suggest a correspondingly aversive physiological reaction).

An important challenge for research on these proximal pathways will be to distinguish the relative contributions of affectionate behavior and affectionate emotion to psychosomatic well-being. As Floyd, Erbert et al. (2005) suggested, receiving verbal expressions of affection that the recipient deems to be insincere or manipulative can be distressing. This would suggest that the eventual effects of an affectionate expression on physiological health are dependent (at least to a substantial degree) on the receiver's assessment of the emotional validity of the expression. Other research provides reason to question this proposition, however. For instance, Turner et al. (1999) reported that affectionate touch was accompanied by increases in oxytocin even though the touch was performed by the researchers themselves, not by relational partners of the participants. Similarly, Grewen et al. (2005) reported that the reduction in cortisol observed after romantic partners engaged in nonverbal affectionate behavior was unaffected by the partners' reports of how supportive their relationship was; cortisol levels were equally decreased after affectionate interaction for those in more supportive and less supportive relationships. Indeed, partner support similarly did not qualify responses to affectionate behavior for oxytocin, heart rate, norepinephrine, or diastolic blood pressure. Grewen and colleagues observed that partner support influenced reactivity to affectionate behavior only in systolic blood pressure, and then only for women. Other research has found that cardioprotective effects of touch can be induced even by strangers (e.g., Drescher, Whitehead, Morrill-Corbin, & Cataldo, 1985).

As a partial explanatory mechanism not only for diversity in the valence of responses to affectionate behavior but also for discrepancies in the relative effects of affectionate behavior and its underlying emotion, AET acknowledges individual variation in the inborn need and capacity for affection by formalizing the earlier discussion on individual variation in the form of a fourth postulate.

Postulate 4. Humans vary in their optimal tolerances for affection and affectionate behavior.

This chapter earlier discussed some developmental and nondevelopmental sources of individual variation in the ability to convey and receive expressions of affection. Proposed here is that, irrespective of differences in developmental stage and absent physical or mental constraints on the ability to encode or decode affectionate messages, individuals vary in their needs and abilities to experience affectionate emotions and in their traitlike tendencies to communicate affection or receive affectionate expressions. Initial research on traitlike tendencies for expressing and receiving expressions of affection was done by Floyd (2003), who compared highly affectionate and nonaffectionate individuals on a battery of psychosocial assessments. With a sample size of only 109, Floyd found considerable variation in scores on both trait affection given and trait affection received: On seven-point scales, both measures produced scores ranging from a low of 2.00 to a high of 7.00, indicating substantial individual variation in traitlike tendencies to express and receive affectionate behaviors. Later research by Floyd, Hess et al. (2005) found similar individual variation.

Attachment styles appear to account for some of the individual variation in tendencies to convey or receive affectionate expressions. Bartholomew's four-category model of adult attachment styles represents the combination of positive and negative concepts of self with positive and negative concepts of others (Bartholomew, 1990; Bartholomew & Horowitz, 1991). With respect to affectionate communication, one could reason on the basis of Bartholomew's model that *secures* (who manifest positive concepts of self and others) would give and receive more affection than *dismissives* and *fearful-avoidants* (both of whom manifest negative concepts of others). Relative to dismissives and fearful-avoidants, that is, secures should have greater desire to convey affection to others (given that their concept of others is positive rather than negative), and should therefore receive more affectionate communication in return. The placement of *preoccupieds* (who manifest negative concepts of self but positive concepts of others) in this hierarchy is less straightforward. Their positive concept of others may encourage preoccupieds to be particularly demonstrative of affection, in order that the affection received from others in return might assuage their negative concept of self; contrariwise, their negative self concept may make preoccupieds feel so unworthy of others' affection that they convey and receive little affection from others, implicitly validating their negative view of themselves.

Data from Floyd's (2003) study of highly affectionate communicators indicate that adults with different attachment styles do differ in their traitlike affectionate communication tendencies.[7] Secures in that study reported significantly higher trait expressed affection (5.49 on a 7-point scale) than did dismissives (4.60), preoccupieds (4.44), and

---

[7] I report the statistical results here as they do not appear in this form in Floyd (2003).

fearful-avoidants (4.36). Similarly, with respect to trait affection received, secures (5.44) scored significantly higher than dismissives (4.81) and fearful-avoidants (4.79), who in turn scored significantly higher than pre-occupieds (4.24). Although effect sizes for attachment style were modest (partial $\eta^2 = .18$ for affection given and .13 for affection received), these results do indicate that attachment style is one significant source of individual variation, at least in affectionate behavior. (Whether it similarly influences the experience of affectionate emotion is unknown, but attachment theory would provide a sound basis for predicting as much.)

Early family experiences also appear to account for individual variation in adult affectionate behavior. A growing literature attests to the effects of early family environment – particularly parental affection, caregiving, and conflict – on adults' physical health, mental health, and relationship success (see, e.g., Luecken & Lemery, 2004; Nemeroff, 2004). The communicative environment in the family of origin also appears to influence experiences and tendencies toward affectionate behavior in adulthood. For instance, Wallace (1981) demonstrated that the affectional climate in the family of origin affects the expression of affection, particularly romantic or sexual affection, during adulthood. For both women and men in his study, the extent to which interaction in the family of origin was characterized by the open expression of affection among parents, children, and other relatives was directly predictive of their expression of sexual affection in adulthood.

Similarly, Floyd and Morman (2000a) studied the effects of affectionate communication received from fathers in men's families of origin on the men's subsequent affectionate behavior with their own sons. On the basis of modeling and compensation hypotheses, Floyd and Morman hypothesized a U-shaped quadratic relationship wherein men who were raised either with highly affectionate or highly distant fathers would be the most affectionate with their own sons, whereas men raised with fathers who communicated moderate affection would be the least affectionate with their own sons. This curvilinear association was predicted by combining the proposal of the modeling hypothesis – that children replicate positive behaviors from adults with whom they identify – with that of the compensation hypothesis – that children compensate for negative behaviors, particularly when identification is weak. As hypothesized, Floyd and Morman found that men who were the most affectionate with their own sons were those raised in households with either very affectionate fathers or fathers who were distant and nonaffectionate. This finding further demonstrates the association between early family communicative environment and communicative tendencies in adulthood.

Certainly, attachment style and early family conditioning are not the only sources of individual variation. Others might include physical attractiveness, health status, temperament, intelligence, or various dimensions of personality, any of which could conceivably influence the strength of one's need for affection and capacity and tendency for conveying it. Importantly, however, AET does not simply recognize variation in the need, capacity, and tendency toward affection and affectionate behavior, but posits that individuals have a range of optimal tolerance for affection and affectionate behavior. The range of optimal tolerance is bounded on the lower end by *need*, or how much affectionate emotion or behavior is required; it is bounded on the upper end by *desire*, or how much affectionate emotion or behavior is wanted.

One woman, for example, may have a relatively high need to be loved, whereas another is content without much affection from others. These two women would differ in the lower limits, or minimum thresholds, of their optimal tolerances for affectionate emotion. Similarly, if one man's ideal is to be strongly loved, appreciated, and sought out by others, whereas another man prefers a more moderate level of love, appreciation, and attention, these two would differ in the upper limits, or maximum thresholds, of their optimal tolerances for affection. As further explicated below, the minimum threshold represents the point *below which* the amount of affection one receives fails to meet the person's basic affection need, whereas the maximum threshold represents the point *above which* the amount of affection one receives exceeds what he or she is comfortable with. Either situation can be problematic, but they are problematic in different ways, as AET will detail.

With respect to the fourth postulate, then, the optimal tolerance for affection and affectionate behavior represents a range spanning the lowest sufficient amount to the highest desired amount. According to the postulate, both the width of the range and the absolute values for the minimum and maximum thresholds will vary somewhat from person to person. Figure 7.1 provides three graphic representations of the range of optimal tolerance for affectionate emotion as individual examples.

The concept of the range of optimal tolerance has two direct implications for the third postulate, which provides that affection and affectionate communication are adaptive. The first implication qualifies subpostulate 3d, in particular, and is presented here as a new subpostulate:

Sarah has a relatively low need for affection, meaning that she can function just fine without a great deal of love or appreciation from others. However, she has a fairly high desire, which means that even though she can get by without a great deal of affection, she really prefers to be loved, well liked, and appreciated, and for others to desire her company and attention.

Very low - Very high

           Need (min. threshold)   Desire (max. threshold)

Nicholas has a similarly low need for affection; like Sarah, he can get by without having lots of love or appreciation from others. Unlike Sarah, however, he does not particularly desire a great deal of affection. Consequently, his range of optimal tolerance is much narrower than Sarah's, even though their minimum thresholds are the same. By comparison, then, a high degree of affection from others would be perceived by Sarah as positive, but by Nicholas as negative.

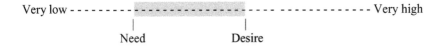

Very low - Very high

          Need   Desire

Eve has a very high need for affection. She requires love and approval from others, and cannot seem to function when she feels that others don't care deeply about her. Her range of optimal tolerance is very narrow, however; as long as her need for affection is met, Eve does not particularly desire a much higher degree of affection. It should be noted here that the higher one's need (or minimum threshold) is, the more narrow the range of optimal tolerance necessarily will be.

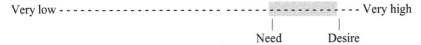

Very low - Very high

                           Need   Desire

Figure 7.1. Examples of Optimal Tolerance for Affectionate Emotion for Three Hypothetical Individuals

SUBPOSTULATE 4A. The experience, expression, and receipt of affection contribute to immunocompetence and regulatory pathways for reward and stress management when they occur within an individual's range of optimal tolerance.

This qualifies subpostulate 3d by specifying that when the experience or expression of affection occurs within the range of optimal tolerance, it does not merely covary with immunocompetence or regulatory functions, but it enhances them. According to this idea, for example, receiving an expression of affection whose magnitude or level of intimacy exceeds what one needs but does not exceed what one is comfortable with should initiate hormonal reward (e.g., the release of dopamine, oxytocin, or endogenous opioids), fortify immunity, and ameliorate the physiological stress response and/or buffer the individual against the effects of subsequent stressors. Each of these pathways suggests verifiable associations between affectionate communication and physiological reactivity. This subpostulate is supported, for instance, by evidence that oxytocin is secreted (at least for women) in response to nonverbal affectionate behavior (Grewen et al., 2005) and that cortisol secretion is inhibited during the expression of verbal (Floyd, Mikkelson et al., in press) or nonverbal (Grewen et al., 2005) affection. Because these studies examined affectionate behaviors within established relationships and because participants in both studies had sufficient control over the prescribed affectionate behaviors to dictate their level of intimacy, the presumption that the observed behaviors were within the communicators' range of optimal tolerance is warranted. Future research can greatly extend this line of inquiry by examining the effects of affectionate behavior that is within one's optimal tolerance range on such biomarkers as β-endorphins, dopamine, or Epstein-Barr virus antibodies.

The second implication is that, if receiving affectionate behavior that falls within one's range of optimal tolerance makes positive contributions to physiological well-being, then parents can fortify their children's health by communicating affection to them, thereby indirectly contributing to the parents' own reproductive success. Formalized as a second subpostulate:

SUBPOSTULATE 4B. Affectionate communication to one's biological offspring enhances reproductive success by contributing to the health and viability of the offspring, so long as the affectionate behavior falls within the receivers' range of optimal tolerance.

This subpostulate rests on the logical assumption that healthier individuals have more opportunity than unhealthy individuals to reproduce successfully, ceteris paribus. Indeed, research has shown that bodily symmetry, a marker of genetic health and the robustness of the immune system, is positively associated with the lifetime number of sexual partners and inversely associated with age at first intercourse for men (Thornhill & Gangestad, 1994). Furthermore, men's body symmetry positively predicts their female sexual partners' probability of achieving orgasm, which significantly increases the likelihood of impregnation (see Gangestad & Simpson, 2000). Because facial and body symmetry, which are products of genetic health and immunocompetence, strongly predict ratings of physical attractiveness (Mealy, Bridgestock, & Townsend, 1999; Gangestad, Thornhill, & Yeo, 1994), it is easy to understand why more symmetrical individuals have greater reproductive opportunity and therefore to appreciate a positive relationship between health and procreative success. Indeed, research indicates that more attractive men have higher semen quality (ascertained by motility, morphology, and concentration) than their less attractive counterparts (Soler, Núñez, Gutiérrez, Núñez, Medina, Sancho, Álvarez, & Núñez, 2003).

If receiving expressions of affection (provided they do not violate the recipient's optimal tolerance) fortifies health, and if health correlates with productive opportunity, then it is logical to deduce that those who receive high degrees of affectionate communication from others will have more procreative success than those who do not, other things being equal. This has a direct implication for parents, therefore, in that they can further their own procreative success by expressing affection to their biological children, given that their children's reproductive success covaries, by extension, with their own.

Importantly, this subpostulate applies only to affection communicated to one's *biological* children. Affection, or any resource, given to nonbiological children (such as stepchildren or adopted children) does not directly contribute to one's own procreation goal at all, because nonbiological children do not carry one's genetic material. In conjunction with subpostulate 4b, this observation suggests at least two testable hypotheses, the first being that parents communicate more affection to biological than nonbiological children (a principle theoretically supported, if affection is counted as a resource, by Daly & Wilson's theory of discriminative parental solicitude; see Daly & Wilson, 1983, 1985, 1988, 1995, 1996). In partial support of this hypothesis, Floyd and Morman (2002) found, in two studies, that men were significantly more affectionate with biological sons than with stepsons, and that this difference could not be accounted for by differences in the closeness of those relationships (i.e., fathers were not more affectionate with biological sons simply because they felt closer to them). However, Floyd and Morman did not identify a significant difference in the amount of affection men reported communicating to biological sons and adopted sons. A relatively small cell size for the adoptive relationships may have assuaged the statistical power necessary to identify a significant difference; contrariwise, fathers may psychologically orient toward adoptive sons in a manner more similar to biological sons than stepsons. Additional tests of this hypothesis will undoubtedly contribute to a more complete understanding of communication in nonbiological parental relationships.

A second hypothesis suggested by this subpostulate is that children's probability of reproducing is a predictor of the quantity of resources (including affectionate behavior) that they receive from their biological parents. That is, if biological children are unlikely to reproduce, for some reason, then it is logical to predict that parents will expend fewer resources on them than they do on biological children who are more likely to procreate. In fact, it may be the case that biological children who are unlikely to reproduce approximate nonbiological children in their receipt of resources, including affectionate communication. For example, some research has suggested that developmentally disabled children, who may be less likely than normally developing children to pair bond, receive less affection from their parents, on average (Compton & Niemeyer, 1994; see also Schmidt & SeiffgeKrenke, 1996). It bears reiterating that few parents probably make such discriminations consciously. Implicit in these hypotheses, and in much discussion on evolutionary psychology, is the idea that because individuals are motivated to maximize their survival and procreative success, they act in ways that serve these goals, but conscious awareness of the link between one's behaviors and these superordinate goals is neither presumed nor probably required.

What, then, of affectionate behaviors that violate the range of optimal tolerance? As noted earlier, AET predicts that they will engender unfavorable consequences, but that those consequences will differ depending on whether the behavior is below the minimum threshold or above the maximum threshold. To make this prediction more explicit, it is necessary first to acknowledge that senders and receivers of affectionate behavior are subject to their own optimal tolerances, such that a given behavior may not violate the sender's range but may violate the receiver's. AET makes no discrimination between the effects of tolerance-violating behaviors for senders versus receivers; rather, this distinction is acknowledged here to indicate that the physiological effects of affectionate behaviors are not predominantly resident in the behaviors themselves, but in their relation to the optimal tolerances of those giving and receiving them. (AET does not preclude the possibility that some physiological effects – even physiological benefits – of affectionate behaviors are resident in the behaviors themselves, but instead proposes that they are predominantly resident in the optimal tolerances of the senders and receivers.)

By proposing a range of behaviors and discussing the effects of behaviors that violate that range, AET shares conceptual space with theories such as expectancy violations theory (EVT: Burgoon, 1978). EVT postulates a range of expected behavior, outside of which a behavior is considered to be an expectancy violation. Like EVT, AET proposes that violating behaviors are noticed, and that they initiate cognitive appraisals on the part of the recipient. However, AET further proposes that violating behaviors initiate sympathetic nervous system (SNS) arousal that becomes the primary focus of the recipient's cognitive appraisals (wherein the violating behavior and the characteristics of the sender are the primary foci of cognitive appraisals in EVT). Stated as a formal postulate:

Postulate 5. Conveying or receiving affectionate behaviors that violate one's range of optimal tolerance initiates noticeable sympathetic nervous system arousal and further initiates a cognitive appraisal of the same.

That individuals would notice when they are sending or (more often) receiving affectionate behaviors that are less intense than what they need or more intense than what they want may seem so self-evident that it needn't be formally articulated. Two aspects of this postulate are less intuitive, however, the first being that the violating behavior evokes SNS arousal, not simply cognitive attention. SNS arousal is comprised of physiological changes, such as increases in heart rate, blood pressure, blood sugar, respiratory rate, and pupil dilation, which have the effects of increasing available muscle energy and mental acuity (see, e.g., Floyd, Haynes, & Mikkelson, 2005; Marieb, 2003). Although the SNS is aroused during exercise, excitement, and the experience of positive emotional states such as joy or interest, it is also activated in response to perceived threat as an adaptive way to prepare the body to assess the threat and to fight or flee from it (Floyd, 2004; Ganong, 2001). As articulated in further detail below, it is this latter function of SNS arousal that AET posits here.

The second less intuitive aspect of this postulate is that the cognitive appraisal generated by out-of-tolerance affectionate behavior is posited to be *initially* of the SNS arousal, not of the behavior, sender, or context itself. In other words, AET provides that when communicators send or receive affectionate behavior that violates their range of optimal tolerance, they will cognitively assess the valence and meaning of their physiological arousal before assessing that of the behavior itself. This proposal is founded on the adaptive nature of SNS arousal in the face of perceived threat; when an environmental challenge is perceived, the SNS is aroused automatically and a decision as to whether to fight or flee from the challenge is required (often immediately). Although individuals can cognitively assess complex attributions, evaluations, and relational message interpretations for affectionate behaviors (as Chapter 4 detailed), AET proposes that they must first attend to the meaning of their SNS arousal. This proposal can account, for example, for a situation in which a receiver is made uncomfortable by the intimacy level of an affectionate gesture received from another, even though the receiver can articulate no specific reason for the discomfort. Here, the receiver has cognitively assessed the SNS arousal initiated by the gesture and has experienced discomfort even though he or she has yet to articulate the aspects of the behavior, sender, or context that would have caused such a reaction.

Another important difference between AET and EVT is that the latter theory provides for both positive and negative violations from a range of expected behavior. By contrast, AET provides that all violations of the range of optimal tolerance for affection produce negative outcomes. As mentioned earlier, however, violations of the minimum and maximum thresholds are posited to be negative in different ways. Further articulation of this idea begins with the following subpostulate, which articulates the type of threat produced by a violation of the minimum threshold:

SUBPOSTULATE 5A. A violation of the minimum threshold in the range of optimal tolerance constitutes a threat to viability.

In the range of optimal tolerance, the minimum threshold represents the minimum amount of affection that a given person needs to give or receive. As explained earlier in this chapter (and in more detail in Chapter 5), the need for affectionate communication is not simply a psychological or emotional need; it is, in many ways, a genuine physical need as well. Research has shown not only that giving and receiving affection are associated with physical benefits, but also that deprivation of affectionate interaction is associated with pronounced physical detriments, such as compromised immune function, reduced ability to heal after trauma, or delayed development in newborns. All of these detriments constitute threats, in varying degrees, to a person's viability. Anecdotal accounts notwithstanding of people dying of a broken heart or perishing for lack of love, reductions in immunocompetence or the ability to heal can threaten viability and long- and short-term well being. As clearly suggested by the pioneering research of Harlow (1958) with monkeys, and Prescott (1971, 1975, 1980) with humans, a threshold exists for the minimum amount of affection an organism must receive in order to sustain normal development, and substantial physical and mental deficits often accompany the failure to receive the necessary amount of affectionate behavior. AET extends this research by positing a corollary minimum threshold for the *expression* of affection, such that humans need not only to receive a minimum amount of affection from others, but also to give a minimum amount to others.

Darwinian principles dictate that humans and other organisms have evolved mechanisms to counter threats to viability. These undoubtedly include compensatory physiological systems that respond to the physical effects of a detrimental social experience (such as failing to receive the minimum amount of affection) by fortifying other physical systems to compensate for the threat (e.g., increasing secretion of oxytocin to counter the hypothalamic-pituitary-adrenal stress response that may be activated by the failure to receive needed affection). Consistent with other theoretic treatments, such as Baumeister and Leary's (1995) need to belong and Miller and Rodgers's (2001) ontogenetic bonding system, AET provides that the motivation to give and receive affectionate communication is, in and of itself, adaptive for the prevention of the physical and mental deficiencies that accompany the failure to give or receive adequate affection.

Giving or receiving affectionate communication that violates the maximum threshold in the range of optimal tolerance is a qualitatively different experience. Whereas the minimum threshold represents the minimal amount of affectionate behavior that a person can give or receive before experiencing the detrimental physical and mental effects of deprivation, the maximum threshold reflects the greatest amount of affectionate communication that an individual desires to give or receive. Giving or receiving affectionate behavior that violates the maximum threshold does not necessarily lead to the physical and mental problems that go along with violations of the minimum threshold, according to AET. Rather, this theory proposes that it initiates an immediate stress response due to the possibility that it may represent interference with an individual's ability to successfully achieve his or her procreation goals. Stated as a second subpostulate:

SUBPOSTULATE 5B. A violation of the maximum threshold in the range of optimal tolerance initially initiates a physiological stress response that covaries in intensity with the probability that the violating behavior represents a threat to one's procreation success.

Whether genuine or not, affectionate behaviors that are more intense or intimate than one desires convey, at least potentially, a relational interest that is more intense or intimate than one desires (see Floyd, 2000b). In other words, a person who receives an affectionate expression that violates his or her maximum threshold is forced to confront the possibility that such an expression signals a desire for more relational intimacy, emotional closeness, and/or sexual involvement than he or she is comfortable with. This inference is unwarranted in some instances, such as when the affectionate behavior does not convey genuine emotion but is expressed in the service of an ulterior motive. In many other instances, even when the emotion is genuine, the gesture represents a desire on the part of the sender to accelerate relational development in a purely platonic, nonsexual fashion.

In some cases, however, the desire for increased emotional or relational intimacy implied by a threshold-violating affectionate gesture constitutes a legitimate threat to an individual's successful procreation. By *successful*, I refer not only to the production of children but also to the production of children in concert with a healthy and wisely chosen partner. As articulated in this chapter and elsewhere in this book, the choice of a mate is consequential to procreative success – and many times more so for women than for men – because potential mates widely vary in their ability to contribute to healthy offspring who will survive to sexual maturity. To maximize procreative success, therefore, requires individuals not only to identify mates with the desired physical and emotional characteristics, but also to attract them while simultaneously managing intra-sexual competition for access to those mates. This requires, among other things, that those seeking mates be vigilant in assessing the quality of potential partners, be willing to make relational commitment to a partner who represents a good "fit," and, importantly, be unwilling to make relational commitments to prospective partners who do not (lest they reduce their availability to higher quality partners).

Expressions of undesired levels of affection from others can potentially thwart these goals, particularly the goal of remaining relationally uncommitted before one has identified a quality viable partner. In Figure 7.1, Sarah had a fairly high maximum threshold, meaning that she enjoys giving and receiving highly affectionate expressions. If her platonic friend James expressed affection to her in a manner that confirmed to her range of optimal tolerance (e.g., a brief hug), AET predicts that Sarah would react positively. If James were to give Sarah a longer, more intense hug, however, this could well violate her maximum threshold, being a more intimate expression of affection than Sarah is comfortable with. According to AET, Sarah's initial reaction to the event will be a physiological stress response, because there is a potential for the hug to represent a desire for greater relational involvement than Sarah wants, which may threaten (however briefly) her ability to attract a quality mate (or to remain committed to the mate she may already have). Acknowledgment of her stress response may cause Sarah to evaluate the interaction negatively, and/or to compensate for it behaviorally (see Floyd & Burgoon, 1999); contrariwise, the social demands of the situation may require her to reciprocate the undesired behavior, in which case she violates her optimal tolerance as a sender instead of a receiver.

The subpostulate also provides that the stress response will covary in intensity with the probability that the event threatens procreative success. Thus, in this example, the same threshold-violating hug from Sarah's female friend Jill would not be expected to produce as intense a stress response, given the lesser general probability that Jill is romantically interested in Sarah than that James is. Likewise, the same hug from Sarah's brother Sam also would be expected to produce a less intense stress response, given that family members, or even quasi-family members (those raised together as relatives but without any genetic ties), tend not to develop sexual attraction for each other (cf. Westermarck effect; Westermarck, 1921).

As with other subpostulates, it is important to reiterate the disclaimer that AET does not propose that maximum threshold-violating behaviors are stress-inducing because people *consciously* perceive threats to their procreative success. Indeed, as I noted earlier under the fifth postulate, the principle that threshold-violating behaviors induce SNS arousal, which becomes the immediate target of people's cognitive assessments, accounts for a number of situations in which individuals react negatively to affectionate expressions even when they cannot articulate why. In the example above, Sarah needn't have mentally calculated the probability that James's hug represented a threat to her ability to procreate successfully before she realized that the hug made her uncomfortable. AET proposes that the SNS has evolved to be vigilant to such threats and initially to react accordingly, while awaiting the person's conscious attribution or interpretation for the behavior.

Collectively, the fifth postulate and its two subpostulates can account for a range of situations in which giving or receiving affectionate communication is, counterintuitively, distressing. As in the example of Sarah and James, people sometimes receive expressions of affection from others that are more intense than they are comfortable with. Politeness norms may even dictate that they must reciprocate those expressions in kind, further compounding their discomfort. At the other end of the continuum, relational partners (perhaps especially those in newly developing relationships) may come to their relationship with different affection needs, and if one partner has a particularly high need for affection, he or she may experience fairly frequent distress if that need is not fulfilled.

This chapter has reviewed the strengths and liabilities of existing sociocultural and bioevolutionary theories for explaining patterns of human affection exchange and has explicated a new theory designed to provide a more focused and more comprehensive account of affectionate behavior than has been offered before. Several empirical investigations have already provided support for various hypotheses derived from AET, and as additional tests are conducted, they will help to ascertain how well AET can account for the diversity of behaviors through which affection is conveyed, motivations for which it is expressed, and cognitive or behavioral outcomes it produces. As such research occurs, it will necessarily lead to modifications of the theory to increase its precision and focus. This process can lead only to a more complete understanding of the substantial role that affectionate communication plays in the human social agenda.

8

Affectionate Communication in Human Interaction

We can live without religion and meditation, but we cannot survive without human affection.

– Dalai Lama

The preceding chapters have examined multiple aspects of the expression and exchange of affectionate communication in human interaction. Several theoretic treatments of affectionate behavior have been described and critiqued, and a large body of empirical findings has been synthesized around several fundamental questions concerning why, how, to whom, and with what effects people convey affection to each other. The body of research on affectionate communication is indeed eclectic in terms of its focus, its methodology, and its theoretic underpinnings. Although eclecticism serves the purposes of ensuring that diverse ideas are considered and that observed patterns are not conceptually or operationally bound, it can have the additional effect of making the literature appear not to support any general conclusions.

Such is not the case with affectionate communication, however. To bring this volume to a close, I have elected to identify and discuss what I believe are the most important observations about affectionate communication that have found support in the empirical literature. Although some of these conclusions are relatively intuitive, others are not; the fact that the body of research supports both types of conclusion is, I believe, testament to the provocative and often paradoxical nature of human affectionate communication.

Some Qualified Conclusions about Affectionate Communication

As noted, research on affectionate communication supports a diverse range of conclusions, some of the most important of which are discussed here. Where appropriate, qualifiers are identified and discussed so that each conclusion can be appreciated with proper evaluation of the research that generated it. Concluding remarks follow this section.

Affectionate Communication Is Ubiquitous in Human Relationships

The exchange of affectionate communication characterizes a wide range of intimate, personal, and social relationships. In developing relationships, people use affectionate behavior to signal their desires for relational escalation, and the enactment of significant affectionate gestures – such as the first kiss or the first exchange of the words "I love you" – is often considered a turning point in relationship development. Contrariwise, shifts toward less frequent or less intense forms of affection display may coincide with, and serve as evidence of, relational deterioration, even prompting the occurrence of extrarelational affairs.

In established relationships, including those among romantic partners, friends, family members, and even social acquaintances, affectionate communication is linearly and strongly related to a number of positive relational qualities. Relationships characterized by frequent affectionate behavior tend to be closer, more satisfying, and more engaging than those that are not. People who frequently communicate affection to a relational partner (whether a romantic, platonic, or familial partner) also tend to like, love, and be socially attracted to that partner more than those who do not. Highly affectionate relationships are more stable over time, and involve more intimacy and self-disclosure, than less affectionate relationships. In short, affectionate human relationships tend to be *good* human relationships.

Despite its associations with positive relational characteristics, affectionate communication varies across relationships in some systematic ways. As one might well intuit, it is more frequent and more intimate in romantic than nonromantic relationships. In nonromantic relationships, however, men tend to exchange affection more with relatives than with friends – even if they are emotionally closer to their friends than their relatives – whereas women tend not to manifest the same difference. Within families, affectionate behavior is more common in biological relationships than in some nonbiological ones (such as steprelation-ships) but not others (such as adoptive relationships). Moreover, relation-ships vary not only in the frequency of affectionate behaviors but also in their form. Male–male platonic and familial relationships, for instance, convey affection more through indirect, instrumental means (e.g., doing favors for each other) than through more direct verbal or nonverbal expressions, whereas female–female and opposite-sex relationships are less frequently characterized by such a distinction. Unsurprisingly, instru-mental means of conveying affection are more strongly associated with closeness and satisfaction in male–male relationships than in other rela-tional configurations.

If the ubiquity and positivity of affectionate communication are intui-tive, they are nonetheless consequential because of the importance of personal relationships themselves. It is difficult, if not impossible, to exag-gerate the importance of human interpersonal relationships; like many species, humans are inherently social beings, and their satisfaction with their relationships is among the strongest predictors of their satisfaction with life (see, e.g., Glenn & Weaver, 1981). By implication, then, under-standing better those communicative behaviors that demonstrate reliable and substantial associations with relationship success holds much promise for improving the human condition, and it is clear that affectionate communication is among these.

Affectionate Communication Overlaps Only Partially with Affectionate Emotion

Researchers have recognized for some time that although the internal experience and the external expression of emotion frequently coincide, they are somewhat independent. Indeed, Ekman and Friesen's (1975) dis-play rules acknowledge that communicators can fail to express emotions they are feeling and can express emotions that they are failing to feel. The imperfect connection between emotion and expression is particu-larly important for affection, given that affection is an externally oriented emotion (i.e., one feels affection *for* someone or something else). It may be relatively inconsequential to one individual whether a conversational partner is accurately displaying his or her happiness, fear, or surprise. If that partner is feeling or displaying affection for the individual, however, that has direct implications for the nature of the relationship between the individual and the partner. Therefore, to the extent that the partner is hiding the affection he or she is feeling, or is communicating affection that he or she is not feeling, these have consequences for the individual that other emotions or emotion displays may not.

Indeed, as discussed in earlier chapters, there are several reasons why individuals may elect not to convey (or at least, to downplay the intensity of) affection they are experiencing. For instance, they may fear putting the receiver "on that spot," making him or her feel obligated to reciprocate, or they may worry that the receiver will fail to reciprocate the expression. Likewise, they may be concerned that a recipient would misinterpret the affectionate gesture as more or less intense than intended, or that the recipient would believe the expression to be insincere. They may also fail to express felt affection if doing so would violate the norms of the relationship or the social context.

Similarly, research indicates that people can and do express affection in the absence of the emotion (or at least, express affection more intensely than they are feeling it). Several motives can be served by such a move. For instance, communicators may falsely convey affection in order to garner favor or elicit instrumental support from another. By the same token, they may do so in the service of politeness (e.g., reciprocating another's affectionate expression) or as a means of comforting or consoling another. People also may express false affection as a means of initiating sexual interaction, a strategy with an evident potential to succeed, given the extent to which people need and desire affection.

The somewhat orthogonal relationship between affection and affectionate behavior suggests, among other things, that the ability to discriminate accurately between affectionate expressions that are genuine and those that are not would be a characteristic of socially skilled communicators.

Affectionate Communication Is Strongly Influenced by Social and Cultural Norms

That affectionate behavior should be affected by social or cultural norms may seem entirely self evident. Indeed, the communication of a range of emotions is encouraged, constrained, or proscribed by the normative demands of the social context and the gender roles of the participants, the nature and developmental stage of their relationship, and the cultural prescriptions for when and how emotion is to be displayed, to name only a few influences (see, e.g., Metts & Planalp, 2002). As detailed in earlier chapters, the expression of affection is likewise influenced by norms of propriety associated with the type of relationship in which it is occurring (e.g., intimate affection is considered more appropriate in romantic than in platonic relationships), the sex composition of the relationship (e.g., direct affectionate expressions are more expected in female–female than in male–male pairs), and aspects of the social context, such as privacy or emotional intensity. Direct expressions of affection, particularly nonverbal ones, are also observed more frequently among those from high-contact cultures, such as Latin Americans, than among those from medium- or low-contact cultures. Importantly, those in the latter types of cultures may not necessarily convey less affection than their high-contact counterparts; rather, they may simply be more inclined to communicate their affection via more indirect means.

One of the social institutions that clearly exerts influence not only on how affectionate people are but also on how they convey their affection, is the family (Floyd & Morman, 2000a; Wallace, 1981). Research on the effects of early family environment appears to show that people learn a repertoire for affectionate behavior from the behaviors they observed their parents using with them and with each other. As Floyd and Morman (2000a) showed, people sometimes replicate these patterns with their own children, and sometimes compensate for them. It is important to note, however, that the designs of many studies of early family environment have not allowed for the parceling out of variance associated with heritable personality traits. That is, children may communicate the way their parents do because they learned those communicative behaviors through observation and reinforcement; they also may replicate their parents' communication because they have genetically inherited the same predispositions as their parents. In other words, parents who are prone to act aggressively may pass that predisposition on to their offspring genetically *and* they may teach their children aggressive behaviors by enacting their own behavioral predispositions. Importantly, neither explanation precludes the other, but studies that fail to account for heritability may easily overestimate the proportion of variance accounted for by learning and reinforcement. This is not an issue with other social or cultural institutions (e.g., school, media, government) but it is an important methodological consideration when studying families.

Affectionate Communication Is Strongly Linked to Mental and Physical Health

A substantial body of literature attests to the health benefits of various forms of affectionate behavior, particularly touch. As this research has reported, not only does affectionate communication correlate with a host of mental and physical health benefits (often substantially so), but increasing affectionate behavior in the wake of compromised health often accelerates recovery or leads to more complete recovery (relative to control groups). One implication of these findings is that affectionate behavior may comprise a component of clinically significant nonpharmacological interventions for various acute and chronic conditions. As noted in Chapter 2, such interventions are already in common use with affectionate therapeutic touch, and there is evidence that affectionate writing may be used in similarly effective ways (see Floyd, Mikkelson et al., in press).

One important limitation of this research, as yet undiscussed, is its inability to rule out the placebo effect as a possible explanation for observed benefits. *Placebo effects* are observable or perceived improvements in health that are not attributable to the treatment; in pharmacological trials, for instance, control group participants are unknowingly given a substance (in the same regimen as those in the experimental group) that looks and tastes identical to the treatment but is biologically inert. Despite not receiving the treatment, however, those in the placebo group routinely see clinically significant improvements in their conditions. Indeed, a meta-analysis of the placebo effect in 19 double-blind clinical trials of antidepressant medication found that the effect sizes produced by experimental and placebo groups were substantially correlated ($r = .90$; Kirsch & Sapirstein, 1998).[1] Although various explanations for the placebo effect have been offered, most focus on the possibility that it is the patients' expectation of improvement that leads their condition to improve, despite not being treated medically. A critical aspect of the placebo effect, however, is that patients must not know whether they are taking the biologically active treatment or the placebo (i.e., they must be blind to the condition), and this is nearly impossible with many nonpharmacological interventions. That is, it would be difficult, if not impossible, to design a study of the health benefits of affectionate behavior that included a placebo condition, as there are few if any conditions in which people would be unaware of whether they were receiving affectionate expressions from others (indeed, unlike with pharmacological treatments, one could argue that knowledge of the affectionate gesture

---

[1] It should be noted that not all scientists agree that the placebo effect exists; some have suggested that it becomes clinically nonsignificant when compared to no-treatment control groups (see, e.g., Hróbjartsson & Götzsche, 2001).

is absolutely necessary to its effects). This feature of affectionate communication (and of other nonpharmacological treatments, such as Pennebaker's therapeutic writing interventions; see Pennebaker, 1997) effectively prevents research from ruling out the alternative explanation that it is people's belief in the power of affectionate behavior, and not the affectionate behavior itself, that leads to their observed improvements. To the extent that people can efficiently manage the risks of affectionate communication, however, the question of whether its benefits derive from the behaviors themselves or from people's attitudes about the behaviors may be substantially less compelling than it would be for a pharmacological treatment.

Although most research on affection and health has focused on how affectionate communication influences health, a smaller number of studies has shown that some health conditions influence affectionate behavior. As noted in Chapter 6, for instance, Schuster et al. (2005) reported that parents infected with human immunodeficiency virus curtailed their physical affection for their children (relative to noninfected controls) out of concern for infecting the children. It is certainly reasonable to predict that physical affection is similarly curtailed by adults with contagious acute conditions (e.g., flu virus); whether the same pattern characterizes those with other chronic conditions – even if they are only believed to be communicable through casual contact – remains to be seen.

Affectionate Communication Benefits Those Who Give It as Well as Those Who Receive It

Much of the research focused on the health benefits of affectionate behavior has focused on recipients, rather than providers, of affectionate expressions. A resource orientation to affectionate communication would certainly suggest this focus; to the extent that affectionate behavior is conceived of as a resource (similar to money or time), it is logical to focus on the benefits of receiving it. One of the innovative aspects of much recent affection research, however – particularly in the health arena – has been its demonstration that affectionate communication is beneficial not only when it is received but also when it is given.

This is often a moot distinction in routine relational interaction, given the strongly reciprocal nature of expressed and received affection. (This is true both in established relationships, in which affectionate expressions are often reciprocated because the underlying emotion is shared, and in less intimate social relationships, in which expressions of affection may be reciprocated out of politeness.) However, theories such as tend and befriend theory, and affection exchange theory, provide that people elicit benefits not only by receiving affectionate gestures but also by providing them, at least during periods of acute distress. Indeed, empirical research on people's traitlike tendencies to give and receive affection has demonstrated that although expressed and received affection overlap in their abilities to account for variance in individual and relational benefits, expressed affection accounts for significant variance above and beyond that accounted for by received affection.

One way in which this observation can potentially be applied is in the development of therapeutic interventions, like those discussed above. For instance, to the extent that befriending others can help to attenuate the effects of acute or chronic stress (as tend and befriend theory suggests), behavioral interventions involving increased expressions of affection to loved ones could be designed and their stress-attenuation effects tested clinically. Similarly, the affectionate writing exercise used by Floyd, Mikkelson et al. (in press) to study reductions in cortisol following acute stress could be tested against other forms of writing – including Pennebaker's therapeutic writing treatment and appropriate controls – for its efficacy in generating short-term and long-term benefits to physical or mental health. What is particularly noteworthy about writing interventions is that they preclude the possibility that their benefits are caused in any manner by affectionate communication received in return, since in neither Floyd, Mikkelson et al.'s study nor in the typical Pennebaker therapeutic writing experiment are the written products given to anyone other than the researchers. Consequently, one can have greater confidence that observed benefits are those of having *expressed*, rather than of having *received*, the affectionate or traumatic emotions.

Affectionate Communication's Effects Can Be Strongly Negative as Well as Strongly Positive

Finally, a consistent theme through much of the research described in this text is that, although affectionate communication is normally perceived to be positive (or at the very least, innocuous), there are particular situations in which its risks outweigh its benefits and it produces negative relational outcomes. Several of the most evident risks for communicators of affection were described in Chapter 6, including risks of nonreciprocity, misinterpretation, or social censure. Moreover, receivers of affectionate expressions are also exposed to various risks, including discomfort from reciprocity expectations, threats to negative face, and even the risk of being manipulated by an insincere affectionate expression that is decoded as genuine.

Although it is by no means normative that affectionate behavior is detrimental, the relational risks to senders and receivers warrant further investigation, particularly insofar as insincere affectionate expressions can be successfully used as manipulation attempts. Whereas some motives for expressing unfelt affection may be benevolent (e.g., to provide comfort), or at least, innocuous (e.g., to reciprocate an affectionate gesture in the service of politeness), others can be malicious and can expose their victims to other forms of risk, such as expressing insincere affection to elicit money or sexual contact. What is perhaps most important to understand about the expression of insincere affection as a manipulation strategy is not why people adopt this strategy but why it is sometimes successful. Affection exchange theory offers that this strategy is successful because people are motivated to invest in those who love them; therefore, being shown that one is loved initiates such a motivation. More specifically, AET would explain the strategy's success in eliciting sexual access as also involving connotations of the communicator's parental fitness. To the extent that people, particularly adolescents and young adults, are sufficiently vulnerable to the seductions of insincere affection as to agree to sexual contact with the communicator, then this risk of affectionate communication is far from a trivial one.

Afterthoughts

Few communicative behaviors are more consequential to the quality and satisfaction of human relationships than the communication of affection. Indeed, it is little exaggeration to suggest that, without affectionate behavior to initiate and maintain them, many of the most important relationships in the life course would be forsaken. In spite of its centrality – or perhaps, in part, because of it – affectionate communication often seems to occur in a perfunctory manner, without much conscious attention being paid to its intricacies. Even so, it influences so many diverse aspects of individual and relational life that humans would be hard pressed to do without it. In this way, affectionate behavior can truly be considered a fundamental component of human communicative experience.

References

Aboyoun, D. C., & Dabbs, J. M. (1998). The Hess pupil dilation findings: Sex or novelty? *Social Behavior and Personality, 26,* 415–420.

Acker, L. E., Acker, M. A., & Pearson, D. (1973). Generalized imitative affection: Relationship to prior kinds of imitation training. *Journal of Experimental Child Psychology, 16,* 111–125.

Acker, L. E., & Marton, J. (1984). Facilitation of affectionate-like behaviors in the play of young children. *Child Study Journal, 14,* 255–269.

Ågmo, A., & Berenfeld, R. (1990). Reinforcing properties of ejaculation in the male rat: Role of opioids and dopamine. *Behavioral Neuroscience, 104,* 177–182.

Akil, H., Watson, S. J., Young, E., Lewis, M. E., Khachaturian, H., & Walker, J. M. (1984). Endogenous opioids: Biology and function. *Annual Review of Neuroscience, 7,* 223–255.

Altemus, M., Deuster, E. G., Carter, C. S., & Gold, P. (1995). Suppression of hypothalamic-pituitary-adrenal axis responses to stress in lactating women. *Journal of Clinical Endocrinology and Metabolism, 80,* 2954–2959.

Amico, J. A., Johnston, J. M., & Vagnucci, A. H. (1994). Suckling induced attenuation of plasma cortisol concentrations in postpartum lactating women. *Endocrinology Research, 20,* 79–87.

Andersen, P. A. (1983, May). *Nonverbal immediacy in interpersonal communication.* Paper presented to International Communication Association, Dallas, TX.

Andersen, P. A. (1984, April). *An arousal-valence model of nonverbal immediacy exchange.* Paper presented to Central States Speech Association, Chicago, IL.

Andersen, P. A. (1989, May). *A cognitive valence theory of intimate communication.* Paper presented to International Conference on Personal Relationships, Iowa City, IA.

Andersen, P. A. (1992, June). *Excessive intimacy: An account analysis of behaviors, cognitive schema, and relational outcomes.* Paper presented to International Society for the Study of Personal Relationships, Orono, ME.

Andersen, P. A., Guerrero, L. K., Buller, D. B., & Jorgensen, P. F. (1998). An empirical comparison of three theories of nonverbal immediacy exchange. *Human Communication Research, 24,* 501–535.

Andersen, P. A., Todd-Mancillas, W. R., & DiClemente, L. (1980). The effects of pupil dilation in physical, social, and task attraction. *Australian Scan: Journal of Human Communication, 7 & 8*, 89–95.

Anderson, C. M., & Martin, M. M. (1995). The effects of communication motives, interaction involvement, and loneliness on satisfaction: A model of small groups. *Small Group Research, 26*, 118–137.

Andreassi, J. L. (2000). *Psychophysiology: Human behavior and physiological response* (4th ed.). Mahwah, NJ: Lawrence Erlbaum Associates.

Argiolas, A., & Gess, G. L. (1991). Central functions of oxytocin. *Neuroscience Biobehavioural Reviews, 15*, 217–231.

Argyle, M., & Dean, J. (1965). Eye-contact, distance, and affiliation. *Sociometry, 28*, 289–304.

Arletti, R., Benelli, A., & Bertolini, A. (1992). Oxytocin involvement in male and female sexual behavior. *Annals of the New York Academy of Sciences, 652*, 180–193.

Aron, A., & Aron, E. N. (1986). *Love as the expansion of the self: Understanding attraction and satisfaction.* New York: Hemisphere.

Aron, A., Aron, E. N., & Smollan, D. (1992). Inclusion of other in the self scale and the structure of interpersonal closeness. *Journal of Personality and Social Psychology, 63*, 596–612.

Aron, A., Norman, C. C., Aron, E. N., McKenna, C., & Heyman, R. E. (2000). Couples' shared participation in novel and arousing activities and experienced relationship quality. *Journal of Personality and Social Psychology, 78*, 273.

Bandura, A. (1971). *Social learning theory.* Morristown, NJ: General Learning Press.

Barbato, C. A., & Perse, E. M. (1992). Interpersonal communication motives and the life position of elders. *Communication Research, 19*, 516–531.

Barber, B. K., & Thomas, D. L. (1986). Dimensions of fathers' and mothers' supportive behavior: The case for physical affection. *Journal of Marriage and the Family, 48*, 783–794.

Barber, N. (2002). *The science of romance: Secrets of the sexual brain.* Amherst, NY: Prometheus.

Bartholomew, K. (1990). Avoidance of intimacy: An attachment perspective. *Journal of Social and Personal Relationships, 7*, 147–158.

Bartholomew, K., & Horowitz, L. M. (1991). Attachment styles among young adults: A test of a four category model. *Journal of Personality and Social Psychology, 61*, 226–244.

Bateman, A. J. (1948). Intra-sexual selection in *Drosophila. Heredity, 2*, 349–368.

Batson, C. D., Early, S., & Salvarani, G. (1997). Perspective taking: Imagining how another feels versus imagining how you would feel. *Personality and Social Psychology Bulletin, 23*, 751–758.

Bauer, M., Priebe, S., Haering, B., & Adamczak, K. (1993). Long-term mental sequelae of political imprisonment in East Germany. *Journal of Nervous and Mental Disease, 181*, 257–262.

Baum, M. J. (2002). Neuroendocrinology of sexual behavior in the male. In J. B. Becker, S. M. Breedlove, D. Crews, & M. M. McCarthy (Eds.), *Behavioral endocrinology* (2nd ed.) (pp. 153–203). Cambridge, MA: MIT Press.

Baumeister, R. F., & Leary, M. R. (1995). The need to belong: Desire for interpersonal attachments as a fundamental human motivation. *Psychological Bulletin, 117*, 497–529.

Baumeister, R. F., & Wotman, S. R. (1992). *Breaking hearts: The two sides of unrequited love*. New York: Guilford.

Baumeister, R. F., Wotman, S. R., & Stillwell, A. M. (1993). Unrequited love: On heartbreak, anger, guilt, scriptlessness, and humiliation. *Journal of Personality and Social Psychology, 64*, 377–394.

Baxter, L. A., & Wilmot, W. W. (1984). "Secret tests": Social strategies for acquiring information about the state of the relationship. *Human Communication Research, 11*, 171–202.

Beatty, M. J., & McCroskey, J. C. (1997). It's in our nature: Verbal aggressiveness as temperamental expression. *Communication Quarterly, 45*, 446–460.

Beatty, M. J., & McCroskey, J. C. (1998). Interpersonal communication as temperamental expression: A communibiological paradigm. In J. C. McCroskey, J. A. Daly, M. M. Martin, & M. J. Beatty (Eds.), *Communication and personality: Trait perspectives* (pp. 41–67). Cresskill, NJ: Hampton Press.

Beatty, M. J., & McCroskey, J. C. (2000a). A few comments about communibiology and the nature/nurture question. *Communication Education, 49*, 25–28.

Beatty, M. J., & McCroskey, J. C. (2000b). Theory, scientific evidence, and the communibiological paradigm: Reflections of misguided criticism. *Communication Education, 49*, 36–44.

Beatty, M. J., McCroskey, J. C., & Heisel, A. D. (1998). Communication apprehension as temperamental expression: A communibiological paradigm. *Communication Monographs, 64*, 197–219.

Beatty, M. J., McCroskey, J. C., & Valencic, K. M. (2001). *The biology of communication: A communibiological perspective*. Cresskill, NJ: Hampton Press.

Becker, J. B. (2002). Hormonal influences in sensorimotor function. In J. B. Becker, S. M. Breedlove, D. Crews, & M. M. McCarthy (Eds.), *Behavioral endocrinology* (2nd ed.) (pp. 497–525). Cambridge, MA: MIT Press.

Becker, J. B., & Breedlove, S. M. (2002). Introduction to behavioral endocrinology. In J. B. Becker, S. M. Breedlove, D. Crews, & M. M. McCarthy (Eds.), *Behavioral endocrinology* (2nd ed.) (pp. 3–38). Cambridge, MA: MIT Press.

Bell, R. A., Buerkel-Rothfuss, N. L., & Gore, K. E. (1987). "Did you bring the yarmulke for the cabbage patch kid?" The idiomatic communication of young lovers. *Human Communication Research, 14*, 47–67.

Bell, R. A., & Healey, J. G. (1992). Idiomatic communication and interpersonal solidarity in friends' relational cultures. *Human Communication Research, 18*, 307–335.

Bem, S. L. (1974). The measurement of psychological androgyny. *Journal of Consulting and Clinical Psychology, 42*, 155–162.

Berscheid, E., Snyder, M., & Omoto, A. M. (1989). The relationship closeness inventory: Assessing the closeness of interpersonal relationships. *Journal of Personality and Social Psychology, 57*, 792–807.

Bjorklund, D. F., & Pellegrini, A. D. (2002). *The origins of human nature: Evolutionary developmental psychology*. Washington, DC: American Psychological Association.

Bombar, M. L., & Littig, L. W. (1996). Babytalk as a communication of intimate attachment: An initial study in adult romances and friendships. *Personal Relationships, 3*, 137–158.

Bonta, J., & Gendreau, P. (1995). Re-examining the cruel and unusual punishment of prison life. In T. J. Flanagan (Ed.), *Long-term imprisonment: Policy, science,
and correctional practice* (pp. 75–84). Thousand Oaks, CA: Sage.

Booth-Butterfield, M., & Trotta, M. R. (1994). Attributional patterns for expressions of love. *Communication Reports, 7,* 119–129.

Bowlby, J. (1969). *Attachment and loss. Vol. 1: Attachment.* New York: Basic Books.

Bowlby, J. (1973). *Attachment and loss. Vol. 2: Separation anxiety and anger.* New
York: Basic Books.

Bradbury, T. N., & Fincham, F. D. (1990). Attributions in marriage: Review and
critique. *Psychological Bulletin, 107,* 3–33.

Bradbury, T. N., & Fincham, F. D. (1992). Attributions for behavior in marital
interaction. *Journal of Personality and Social Psychology, 63,* 613–628.

Bradley, G. W. (1978). Self-serving biases in the attribution process: A reexami-
nation of the fact or fiction question. *Journal of Personality and Social Psychology,
36,* 56–71.

Brown, P., & Levinson, S. C. (1987). *Politeness: Some universals in language usage.*
Cambridge: Cambridge University Press.

Burgoon, J. K. (1978). A communication model of personal space violations:
Explication and an initial test. *Human Communication Research, 4,* 129–142.

Burgoon, J. K. (1995). Cross-cultural and intercultural applications of expectancy
violations theory. In R. L. Wiseman (Ed.), *International and intercultural communication annual: Vol. 19. Intercultural communication theory* (pp. 194–214).
Thousand Oaks, CA: Sage.

Burgoon, J. K., Allspach, L. E., & Miczo, N. (1997, February). *Needs, expectancies, goals, and initial interaction: A view from interaction adaptation theory.* Paper
Presented to Western States Communication Association, Monterey, CA.

Burgoon, J. K., Coker, D. A., & Coker, R. A. (1986). Communicative effects of
gaze behavior: A test of two contrasting explanations. *Human Communication
Research, 12,* 495–524.

Burgoon, J. K., Dillman, L., & Stern, L. A. (1993). Adaptation in dyadic
interaction: Defining and operationalizing patterns of reciprocity and compensation. *Communication Theory, 4,* 293–316.

Burgoon, J. K., & Hale, J. L. (1984). The fundamental topoi of relational communication. *Communication Monographs, 51,* 193–214.

Burgoon, J. K., & Hale, J. L. (1987). Validation and measurement of the fundamental themes of relational communication. *Communication Monographs, 54,*
19–41.

Burgoon, J. K., & Hale, J. L. (1988). Nonverbal expectancy violations: Model elab-
oration and application to immediacy behaviors. *Communication Monographs,
55,* 58–79.

Burgoon, J. K., & Le Poire, B. A. (1993). Effects of communication expectancies, actual communication, and expectancy disconfirmation on evaluations
of communicators and their communication behavior. *Human Communication
Research, 20,* 67–96.

Burgoon, J. K., & Le Poire, B. A. (1999). Nonverbal cues and interpersonal
judgments: Participant and observer perceptions of intimacy, dominance, composure, and formality. *Communication Monographs, 66,* 105–124.

Burgoon, J. K., Manusov, V., Mineo, P., & Hale, J. L. (1985). Effects of eye gaze on hiring, credibility, attraction, and relational message interpretation. *Journal of Nonverbal Behavior, 9*, 133–146.

Burgoon, J. K., & Newton, D. A. (1991). Applying a social meaning model to relational message interpretations of conversational involvement: Comparing observer and participant perspectives. *Southern Communication Journal, 56*, 96–113.

Burgoon, J. K., Newton, D. A., Walther, J. B., & Baesler, E. J. (1989). Nonverbal expectancy violations and conversational involvement. *Journal of Nonverbal Behavior, 13*, 97–120.

Burgoon, J. K., Stern, L. A., & Dillman, L. (1995). *Interpersonal adaptation: Dyadic interaction patterns.* New York: Cambridge University Press.

Burgoon, J. K., & Walther, J. B. (1990). Nonverbal expectancies and the evaluative consequences of violations. *Human Communication Research, 17*, 232–265.

Burgoon, J. K., Walther, J. B., & Baesler, E. J. (1992). Interpretations, evaluations, and consequences of interpersonal touch. *Human Communication Research, 19*, 237–263.

Buss, D. M. (1989). Sex differences in human mate preferences: Evolutionary hypotheses tested in 37 cultures. *Behavioral and Brain Sciences, 12*, 1–49.

Buss, D. M. (1994). The strategies of human mating. *American Scientist, 82*, 238–249.

Buss, D. M. (1999). *Evolutionary psychology: The new science of the mind.* Boston: Allyn and Bacon.

Buss, D. M., & Schmidt, D. P. (1993). Sexual strategies theory: An evolutionary perspective on human mating. *Psychological Review, 100*, 204–232.

Cacioppo, J. T., Tassinary, L. G., & Berntson, G. G. (Eds.). (2000). *Handbook of psychophysiology* (2nd ed.). Cambridge: Cambridge University Press.

Calzada, E. J., & Eyberg, S. M. (2002). Self-reported parenting practices in Dominican and Puerto Rican mothers of young children. *Journal of Clinical Child and Adolescent Psychology, 31*, 354–363.

Campbell, J. M. (2005). Diagnostic assessment of Asperger's disorder: A review of five third-party rating scales. *Journal of Autism and Developmental Disorders, 35*, 25–35.

Caraway, S. J. (1998). Sexual coercion: Factors associated with women's reported experience of verbal coercion. (Doctoral dissertation, University of North Dakota, 1998). *Dissertation Abstracts International, 58* (9-B), 5109.

Carmichael, M. S., Humbert, R., Dixen, J., Palmiana, G., Greenleaf, W., & Davidson, J. M. (1987). Plasma oxytocin increase in the human sexual response. *Journal of Clinical Endocrinology and Metabolism, 64*, 27–31.

Carmichael, M. S., Warburton, V. L., Dixen, J., & Davidson, J. M. (1994). Relationships among cardiovascular, muscular, and oxytocin responses during human sexual activity. *Archives of Sexual Behavior, 23*, 59–79.

Carter, C. S. (1992). Oxytocin and sexual behavior. *Neuroscience Biobehavioral Reviews, 16*, 131–144.

Carter, C. S. (2002). Hormonal influences in human sexual behavior. In J. B. Becker, S. M. Breedlove, D. Crews, & M. M. McCarthy (Eds.), *Behavioral endocrinology* (2nd ed.) (pp. 205–222). Cambridge, MA: MIT Press.

Carter, C. S., & Altemus, M. (1997). Integrative functions of lactational hormones in social behavior and stress management. In C. S. Carter, I. I. Lederhendler, & B. Kirkpatrick (Eds.), *The integrative neurobiology of affiliation* (pp. 361–372). New York: Annals of the New York Academy of Sciences.

Chiodera, P., Salvarani, C., Bacchi-Modena, A., Spallanzani, R., Cigarini, C., Alboni, A., Gardini, E., & Coiro, V. (1991). Relationship between plasma profiles of oxytocin and adrenocorticotropin hormones during suckling or breast stimulation in women. *Hormone Research, 35,* 119–123.

Christopher, S. E., Bauman, K. E., & Veness-Meehan, K. (1999). Measurement of affectionate behaviors adolescent mothers display toward their infants in neonatal intensive care. *Journal of Comprehensive Pediatric Nursing, 22,* 1–11.

Chrousos, G., & Gold, P. (1992). The concepts of stress and stress system disorders. *Journal of the American Medical Association, 267,* 1244–1252.

Coe, C. L., & Lubach, G. R. (2001). Social context and other psychological influences on the development of immunity. In C. D. Ryff & B. H. Singer (Eds.), *Emotion, social relationships, and health* (pp. 243–261). Oxford: Oxford University Press.

Compton, M. V., & Niemeyer, J. A. (1994). Expressions of affection in young children with sensory impairments: A research agenda. *Education and Treatment of Children, 17,* 68–85.

Cosmides, L. L., & Tooby, J. (1992). Cognitive adaptations for social exchange. In J. Barkow, L. Cosmides, & J. Tooby (Eds.), *The adapted mind* (pp. 163–228). New York: Oxford University Press.

Dabbs, J. M. (1997). Testosterone and pupillary response to auditory sexual stimuli. *Physiology and Behavior, 62,* 909–912.

Dainton, M. (1998). Everyday interaction in marital relationships: Variations in relative importance and event duration. *Communication Reports, 11,* 101–109.

Daly, M., & Wilson, M. (1983). *Sex, evolution, and behavior* (2nd ed.). Belmont, CA: Wadsworth.

Daly, M., & Wilson, M. (1985). Child abuse and other risks of not living with both parents. *Ethology and Sociobiology, 6,* 197–210.

Daly, M., & Wilson, M. (1988). *Homicide.* Hawthorne, NY: Aldine.

Daly, M., & Wilson, M. (1995). Discriminative parental solicitude and the relevance of evolutionary models to the analysis of motivational systems. In M. S. Gazzaniga (Ed.), *The cognitive neurosciences* (pp. 1269–1286). Cambridge, MA: MIT Press.

Daly, M., & Wilson, M. (1996). Violence against stepchildren. *Current Directions in Psychological Science, 5,* 77–81.

Damsma, G., Day, J., & Fibiger, H. C. (1989). Lack of tolerance to nicotine-induced dopamine release in the nucleus accumbens. *European Journal of Pharmacology, 168,* 363–368.

Damsma, G., Pfaus, J. G., Wenkstern, D., Phillips, A. G., & Fibiger, H. C. (1992). Sexual behavior increases dopamine in the nucleus accumbens and striatum of male rats: Comparisons with novelty and locomotion. *Behavioral Neuroscience, 106,* 181–191.

Darwin, C. (1859). *On the origin of species.* London: J. Murray.

Darwin, C. (1872/1965). *The expression of the emotions in man and animals.* Chicago: University of Chicago Press.

Davis, J. (1984). *Endorphins: New waves in brain chemistry.* Garden City, NY: Dial Press.

Diego, M. A., Field, T., Hernandez-Reif, M., Shaw, K., Friedman, L., & Ironson, G. (2001). HIV adolescents show improved immune function following massage therapy. *International Journal of Neuroscience, 106,* 35–45.

Dillard, J. P., Solomon, D. H., & Palmer, M. T. (1999). Structuring the concept of relational communication. *Communication Monographs, 66,* 49–65.

Doherty, W. J. (1991). Beyond reactivity and the deficit model of manhood: A commentary on articles by Napier, Pittman, and Gottman. *Journal of Marital and Family Therapy, 17,* 29–32.

Downs, V. C., & Javidi, M. (1990). Linking communication motives to loneliness in the lives of older adults: An empirical test of interpersonal needs and gratifications. *Journal of Applied Communication Research, 18,* 32–48.

Draper, T. W., & Gordon, T. (1986). Men's perceptions of nurturing behavior in other men. *Psychological Reports, 59,* 11–18.

Drescher, V. M., Whitehead, W. E., Morrill-Corbin, E. D., & Cataldo, M. F. (1985). Physiological and subjective reactions to being touched. *Psychophysiology, 22,* 96–100.

Dutton, D. G., & Aron, A. (1974). Some evidence for heightened sexual attraction under conditions of high anxiety. *Journal of Personality and Social Psychology, 30,* 510–517.

Eberly, M. B., & Montemayor, R. (1999). Adolescent affection and helpfulness toward parents: A 2-year follow-up. *Journal of Early Adolescence, 19,* 226–248.

Eibl-Eibesfeldt, I. (1972). Similarities and differences between cultures in expressive movements. In R. A. Hinde (Ed.), *Non-verbal communication* (pp. 294–314). Cambridge, MA: Harvard University Press.

Ekman, P. (Ed.). (1982). *Emotion in the human face* (2nd ed.). Cambridge: Cambridge University Press.

Ekman, P. (1997). Should we call it expression or communication? *Innovation, 10,* 333–344.

Ekman, P., & Friesen, W. V. (1969). The repertoire of nonverbal behavior: Categories, origins, usual, and coding. *Semiotica, 1,* 49–98.

Ekman, P., & Friesen, W. V. (1975). *Unmasking the face: A guide to recognizing emotions from facial clues.* Englewood Cliffs, NJ: Prentice Hall.

Ekman, P., Friesen, W. V., & Ellsworth, P. (1972). *Emotion in the human face.* New York: Pergamon.

Erbert, L. A., & Floyd, K. (2004). Affectionate expressions as face-threatening acts: Receiver assessments. *Communication Studies, 55,* 230–246.

Escovar, P. L., & Lazarus, P. J. (1982). Cross-cultural child-rearing practices: Implications for school psychologists. *School Psychology International, 3,* 143–148.

Feingold, A. (1992). Gender differences in mate selection preferences: A test of the parental investment model. *Psychological Bulletin, 112,* 125–139.

Ferguson, C. A. (1964). Baby talk in six languages. *American Anthropologist, 66,* 103–114.

Ferguson, C. A. (1977). Baby talk as a simplified register. In C. E. Snow & C. A. Ferguson (Eds.), *Talking to children* (pp. 209–235). Cambridge: Cambridge University Press.

Fernald, A. (1989). Intonation and communicative intent in mothers' speech to infants: Is the melody the message? *Child Development, 60,* 1497–1510.

Fernald, A. (1993). Approval and disapproval: Infant responsiveness to vocal affect in familiar and unfamiliar languages. *Child Development, 64,* 657–674.

Fernald, A., & Simon, T. (1984). Expanded intonation contours in mothers' speech to newborns. *Developmental Psychology, 20,* 104–113.

Field, T., Cullen, C., Diego, M., Hernandez-Reif, M., Sprinz, P., Beebe, K., Kissell, B., & Bango-Sanchez, V. (2001). Leukemia immune changes following massage therapy. *Journal of Bodywork and Movement Therapies, 3,* 1–5.

Field, T., Henteleff, T., Hernandez-Reif, M., Martinez, E., Mavunda, K., Kuhn, C., & Schanberg, S. (1998). Children with asthma have improved pulmonary functions after massage therapy. *Journal of Pediatrics, 132,* 854–858.

Field, T., & Hernandez-Reif, M. (2001). Sleep problems in infants decrease following massage therapy. *Early Child Development and Care, 168,* 95–104.

Field, T., Hernandez-Reif, M., LaGreca A., Shaw, K., Schanberg, S., & Kuhn, C. (1997). Massage therapy lowers blood glucose levels in children with diabetes mellitus. *Diabetes Spectrum, 10,* 237–239.

Fisher, R. A. (1930). *The genetical theory of natural selection.* Oxford: Oxford University Press.

Floyd, K. (1995). Gender and closeness among friends and siblings. *Journal of Psychology, 129,* 193–202.

Floyd, K. (1996). Communicating closeness among siblings: An application of the gendered closeness perspective. *Communication Research Reports, 13,* 27–34.

Floyd, K. (1997a). Brotherly love II: A developmental perspective on liking, love, and closeness in the fraternal dyad. *Journal of Family Psychology, 11,* 196–209.

Floyd, K. (1997b). Communicating affection in dyadic relationships: An assessment of behavior and expectancies. *Communication Quarterly, 45,* 68–80.

Floyd, K. (1997c). Knowing when to say "I love you": An expectancy approach to affectionate communication. *Communication Research Reports, 14,* 321–330.

Floyd, K. (1998). *Evaluative and behavioral reactions to nonverbal liking behavior.* Unpublished doctoral dissertation, Department of Communication, University of Arizona.

Floyd, K. (1999). All touches are not created equal: Effects of form and duration on observers' perceptions of an embrace. *Journal of Nonverbal Behavior, 23,* 283–299.

Floyd, K. (2000a). Affectionate same-sex touch: Understanding influences on observers' perceptions. *Journal of Social Psychology, 140,* 774–788.

Floyd, K. (2000b). Attributions for nonverbal expressions of liking and disliking: The extended self-serving bias. *Western Journal of Communication, 64,* 385–404.

Floyd, K. (2001). Human affection exchange: I. Reproductive probability as a predictor of men's affection with their sons. *Journal of Men's Studies, 10,* 39–50.

Floyd, K. (2003). Human affection exchange: V. Attributes of the highly affectionate. *Communication Quarterly, 50,* 135–152.

Floyd, K. (2004). An introduction to the uses and potential uses of physiological measurement in the study of family communication. *Journal of Family Communication, 4,* 295–318.

Floyd, K. (in press). Human affection exchange: XII. Affectionate communication is related to diurnal variation in salivary free cortisol. *Western Journal of Communication.*

Floyd, K., & Burgoon, J. K. (1999). Reacting to nonverbal expressions of liking: A test of interaction adaptation theory. *Communication Monographs, 66,* 219–239.

Floyd, K., & Erbert, L. A. (2003). Relational message interpretations of nonverbal matching behavior: An application of the social meaning model. *Journal of Social Psychology, 143,* 581–598.

Floyd, K., Erbert, L. A., Davis, K. L., & Haynes, M. T. (2005). *Human affection exchange: XVI. An exploratory study of affectionate expressions as manipulation attempts.* Manuscript submitted for publication.

Floyd, K., Haynes, M. T., & Mikkelson, A. C. (2005). *The biology of human communication.* Florence, KY: Thomson Learning.

Floyd, K., Hess, J. A., Miczo, L. A., Halone, K. K., Mikkelson, A. C., & Tusing, K. J. (2005). Human affection exchange: VIII: Further evidence of the benefits of expressed affection. *Communication Quarterly, 53,* 285–303.

Floyd, K., & Mikkelson, A. C. (2002, November). *Psychometric properties of the affectionate communication index in family communication research.* Paper presented to National Communication Association, New Orleans, LA.

Floyd, K., & Mikkelson, A. C. (2004, May). *Human affection exchange: IX. Neurological hemispheric dominance as a discriminator of behavioral reactions to expressed affection.* Paper presented to International Communication Association, New Orleans, LA.

Floyd, K., Mikkelson, A. C., Tafoya, M. A., Farinelli, L., La Valley, A. G., Judd, J., Haynes, M. T., Davis, K. L., & Wilson, J. (in press). Human affection exchange: XIII. Affectionate communication accelerates neuroendocrine stress recovery. *Health Communication.*

Floyd, K., & Morman, M. T. (1997). Affectionate communication in nonromantic relationships: Influences of communicator, relational, and contextual factors. *Western Journal of Communication, 61,* 279–298.

Floyd, K., & Morman, M. T. (1998). The measurement of affectionate communication. *Communication Quarterly, 46,* 144–162.

Floyd, K., & Morman, M. T. (2000a). Affection received from fathers as a predictor of men's affection with their own sons: Tests of the modeling and compensation hypotheses. *Communication Monographs, 67,* 347–361.

Floyd, K., & Morman, M. T. (2000b). Reacting to the verbal expression of affection in same-sex interaction. *Southern Journal of Communication, 65,* 287–299.

Floyd, K., & Morman, M. T. (2002). Human affection exchange: III. Discriminative parental solicitude in men's affection with their biological and nonbiological sons. *Communication Quarterly, 49,* 310–327.

Floyd, K., & Morman, M. T. (2003). Human affection exchange: II. Affectionate communication in father-son relationships. *Journal of Social Psychology, 143,* 599–612.

Floyd, K., & Morman, M. T. (2005). Fathers' and sons' reports of fathers' affectionate communication: Implications of a naïve theory of affection. *Journal of Social and Personal Relationships, 22*, 99–109.

Floyd, K., & Morr, M. C. (2003). Human affection exchange: VII. Affectionate communication in the sibling/spouse/sibling-in-law triad. *Communication Quarterly, 51*, 247–261.

Floyd, K., & Parks, M. R. (1995). Manifesting closeness in the interactions of peers: A look at siblings and friends. *Communication Reports, 8*, 69–76.

Floyd, K., & Ray, G. B. (in press). Adaptation to expressed liking and disliking in initial interactions: Response patterns for nonverbal involvement and pleasantness. *Southern Journal of Communication*.

Floyd, K., & Ray, G. B. (2003). Human affection exchange: IV. Vocalic predictors of perceived affection in initial interactions. *Western Journal of Communication, 67*, 56–73.

Floyd, K., Sargent, J. E., & Di Corcia, M. (2004). Human affection exchange: VI. Further tests of reproductive probability as a predictor of men's affection with their sons. *Journal of Social Psychology, 144*, 191–206.

Floyd, K., & Tusing, K. J. (2002, July). *"At the mention of your name": Affect shifts induced by relationship-specific cognitions*. Paper presented to International Communication Association, Seoul, South Korea.

Floyd, K., & Voloudakis, M. (1999a). Affectionate behavior in adult platonic friendships: Interpreting and evaluating expectancy violations. *Human Communication Research, 25*, 341–369.

Floyd, K., & Voloudakis, M. (1999b). Attributions for expectancy violating changes in affectionate behavior in platonic friendships. *Journal of Psychology, 133*, 32–48.

Foa, U. G., Megonigal, S., & Greipp, J. R. (1976). Some evidence against the possibility of utopian societies. *Journal of Personality and Social Psychology, 34*, 1043–1048.

Gallois, C. (1993). The language and communication of emotion: Universal, interpersonal, or intergroup? *American Behavioral Scientist, 36*, 309–338.

Gangestad, S. W., & Simpson, J. A. (2000). The evolution of human mating: Trade-offs and strategic pluralism. *Behavioral and Brain Sciences, 23*, 573–644.

Gangestad, S. W., Thornhill, R., & Yeo, R. A. (1994). Facial attractiveness, developmental stability, and fluctuating asymmetry. *Ethology and Sociobiology, 15*, 73–85.

Ganong, W. F. (2001). *Review of medical physiology* (20th ed.). Los Altos, CA: Lange Medical.

Garnica, O. K. (1977). Some prosodic and paralinguistic features of speech to young children. In C. E. Snow & C. A. Ferguson (Eds.), *Talking to children* (pp. 63–88). Cambridge: Cambridge University Press.

Gessa, G. L., Muntoni, F., Collu, M., Vargiu, L., & Mereu, G. (1985). Low doses of ethanol activate dopaminergic neurons in the ventral tegmental area. *Brain Research, 348*, 201–204.

Giese, D. J., Sephton, S. E., Abercrombie, H. C., Duran, R. E. F., & Spiegel, D. (2004). Repression and high anxiety are associated with aberrant diurnal cortisol rhythms in women with metastatic breast cancer. *Health Psychology, 23*, 645–650.

Glenn, N. D., & Weaver, C. N. (1981). The contribution of marital happiness to global happiness. *Journal of Marriage and the Family, 42,* 161–168.

Goffman, E. (1959). *The presentation of self in everyday life.* New York: Doubleday.

Goffman, E. (1967). *Interaction ritual: Essays in face-to-face behavior.* New York: Doubleday.

Gough, H. G. (1957). *Manual for the California Psychological Inventory.* Palo Alto, CA: Consulting Psychologists Press.

Gouldner, A. W. (1960). The norm of reciprocity: A preliminary statement. *American Sociological Review, 25,* 161–178.

Gove, W. R., Hughes, M., & Style, C. B. (1983). Does marriage have positive effects on the psychological well being of the individual? *Journal of Health and Social Behavior, 24,* 122–131.

Grammer, K. (1989). Human courtship behaviour: Biological basis and cognitive processing. In A. E. Rasa, C. Vogel, & E. Voland (Eds.), *The sociobiology of sexual and reproductive strategies* (pp. 147–169). London: Chapman and Hall.

Gray, P. B., Kahlenberg, S. M., Barrett, E. S., Lipson, S. F., & Ellison, P. T. (2002). Marriage and fatherhood are associated with lower testosterone in males. *Evolution and Human Behavior, 23,* 193–201.

Green, V. A., & Wildermuth, N. L. (1993). Self-focus, other-focus, and interpersonal needs as correlates of loneliness. *Psychological Reports, 73,* 843–850.

Greenspan, F. S., & Baxter, J. D. (1994). *Basic and clinical endocrinology.* Norwalk, CT: Appleton & Lange.

Grewen, K. M., Girdler, S. S., Amico, J., & Light, K. C. (2005.). Effects of partner support on resting oxytocin, cortisol, norepinephrine, and blood pressure before and after warm partner contact. *Psychosomatic Medicine, 67,* 531–538.

Gross, J. J., John, O. P., & Richards, J. M. (2000). The dissociation of emotion expression from emotion experience: A personality perspective. *Personality and Social Psychology Bulletin, 26,* 712–726.

Gulledge, A. K., Gulledge, M. H., & Stahmann, R. B. (2003). Romantic physical affection types and relationship satisfaction. *The American Journal of Family Therapy, 31,* 233–242.

Guyton, A. C. (1977). *Basic human physiology: Normal function and mechanisms of disease.* Philadelphia: Saunders.

Halberstadt, A. G. (1985). Race, socioeconomic status, and nonverbal behavior. In A. W. Siegman & S. Feldman (Eds.), *Multichannel integrations of nonverbal behavior* (pp. 227–266). Hillsdale, NJ: Lawrence Erlbaum Associates.

Halberstadt, A. G. (1986). Family socialization of emotional expression and nonverbal communication styles and skills. *Journal of Personality and Social Psychology, 51,* 827–836.

Hale, J. L., & Burgoon, J. K. (1984). Models of reactions to changes in nonverbal immediacy. *Journal of Nonverbal Behavior, 8,* 287–315.

Hall, E. T. (1974). *Handbook for proxemic research.* Washington, DC: Society for the Anthropology of Visual Communication.

Hamilton, W. D. (1964). The genetical evolution of social behavior. I & II. *Journal of Theoretical Biology, 7,* 1–52.

Harlow, H. F. (1958). The nature of love. *American Psychologist, 13,* 573–685.

Harrison-Speake, K., & Willis, F. N. (1995). Ratings of the appropriateness of touch among family members. *Journal of Nonverbal Behavior, 19*, 85–100.

Hart, S., Field, T., Hernandez-Reif, M., Nearing, G., Shaw, S., Schanberg, S., & Kuhn, C. (2001). Anorexia symptoms are reduced by massage therapy. *Eating Disorders, 9*, 289–299.

Hazan, C., & Shaver, P. (1987). Romantic love conceptualized as an attachment process. *Journal of Personality and Social Psychology, 52*, 511–524.

Hedge, G. A., Colby, H. D., & Goodman, R. L. (1987). *Clinical endocrine physiology.* Philadelphia: W. B. Saunders.

Heider, F. (1958). *The psychology of interpersonal relations.* New York: Wiley.

Hernandez-Reif, M., Field, T., & Hart, S. (1999). Smoking cravings are reduced by self-massage. *Preventive Medicine, 28*, 28–32.

Hernandez-Reif, M., Field, T., Krasnegor, J., Theakston, H., Hossain, Z., & Burman, I. (2000). High blood pressure and associated symptoms were reduced by massage therapy. *Journal of Bodywork and Movement Therapies, 4*, 31–38.

Hernandez-Reif, M., Field, T., Largie, S., Cullen, C., Beutler, J., Sanders, C., Weiner, W., Rodriguez-Bateman, D., Zelaya, L., Schanberg, S., & Kuhn, C. (2002). Parkinson's disease symptoms are differentially affected by massage therapy versus progressive muscle relaxation: A pilot study. *Journal of Bodywork and Movement Therapies, 6*, 177–182.

Hess, E. H. (1975). The role of pupil size in communication. *Scientific American, 233*, 110–119.

Hess, J. A. (2003). Measuring distance in personal relationships: The relational distance index. *Personal Relationships, 10*, 197–215.

Hopper, R., Knapp, M. L., & Scott, L. (1981). Couples' personal idioms: Exploring intimate talk. *Journal of Communication, 31*, 23–33.

Hróbjartsson, A., & Götzsche, P. C. (2001). Is the placebo powerless? An analysis of clinical trials comparing placebo with no treatment. *New England Journal of Medicine, 344*(21), 1594–1602.

Hu, Y., & Goldman, N. (1990). Mortality differentials by marital status: An international comparison. *Demography, 27*, 233–250.

Hughes, M., & Gove, W. R. (1981). Living alone, social integration, and mental health. *American Journal of Sociology, 87*, 48–74.

Huston, T. L., Caughlin, J. P., Houts, R. M., Smith, S. E., & George, L. J. (2001). The connubial crucible: Newlywed years as predictors of marital delight, distress, and divorce. *Journal of Personality and Social Psychology, 80*, 237–252.

Huston, T. L., & Chorost, A. F. (1994). Behavioral buffers on the effect of negativity on marital satisfaction: A longitudinal study. *Personal Relationships, 1*, 223–239.

Huston, T. L., & Vangelisti, A. L. (1991). Socioemotional behavior and satisfaction in marital relationships: A longitudinal study. *Journal of Social and Personal Relationships, 61*, 721–733.

Ickes, W. (1993). Empathic accuracy. *Journal of Personality, 61*, 587–610.

Insel, T. R. (1997). A neurobiological basis of social attachment. *American Journal of Psychiatry, 154*, 727–735.

Izard, C. E. (1971). *The face of emotion.* New York: Appleton.

Janov, A. (2000). *The biology of love.* Amherst, NY: Prometheus.

Johnston, V. S., & Franklin, M. (1993). Is beauty in the eye of the beholder? *Ethology and Sociobiology, 14,* 183–199.

Jones, E. E., & Wortman, C. (1973). *Ingratiation: An attributional approach.* Morristown, NJ: General Learning Press.

Jorm, A. F., Dear, K. B. G., Rodgers, B., & Christensen, H. (2003). Interaction between mother's and father's affection as a risk factor for anxiety and depression symptoms. *Social Psychiatry and Psychiatric Epidemiology, 38,* 173–179.

Jourard, S. M. (1966). An exploratory study of body-accessibility. *British Journal of Social and Clinical Psychology, 5,* 221–231.

Karney, B. R., Bradbury, T. N., Fincham, F. D., & Sullivan, K. T. (1994). The role of negative affectivity in the association between attributions and marital satisfaction. *Journal of Personality and Social Psychology, 66,* 413–424.

Kelley, H. H. (1972). Attribution and social interaction. In E. E. Jones et al. (Eds.), *Attributions: Perceiving the causes of behavior* (pp. 1–26). Morristown, NJ: General Learning Press.

Kenny, D. A., & Nasby, W. (1980). Splitting the reciprocity correlation. *Journal of Personality and Social Psychology, 38,* 249–256.

Kenrick, D. T., Groth, G., Trost, M. R., & Sadalla, E. K. (1993). Integrating evolutionary and social exchange perspectives on relationships: Effects of gender, self-appraisal, and involvement level on mate selection. *Journal of Personality and Social Psychology, 64,* 951–969.

Kenrick, D. T., Sadalla, E. K., Groth, G., & Trost, M. R. (1990). Evolution, traits, and the stages of human courtship: Qualifying the parental investment model. *Journal of Personality, 58,* 97–116.

Kenrick, D. T., & Trost, M. R. (1987). A biosocial model of relationship formation. In K. Kelley (Ed.), *Females, males, and sexuality: Theories and research* (pp. 58–100). Albany: SUNY Press.

Kerver, M. J., van Son, M. J. M., & de Groot, P. A. (1992). Predicting symptoms of depression from reports of early parenting: A one-year prospective study in a community sample. *Acta Psychiatrica Scandinavia, 86,* 267–272.

King, C. E., & Christensen, A. (1983). The relationship events scale: A Guttman scaling of progress in courtship. *Journal of Marriage and the Family, 45,* 671–678.

Kirsch, I., & Sapirstein, G. (1998). Listening to Prozac but hearing placebo: A meta-analysis of antidepressant medication. *Prevention & Treatment, 1,* Article 0002a. Available on the World Wide Web: http://www.journals.apa.org/prevention/volume1/pre0010002a.html.

Kirschbaum, C., & Hellhammer, D. H. (1989). Salivary cortisol in psychobiological research: An overview. *Neuropsychobiology, 22,* 150–169.

Kirschbaum, C., & Hellhammer, D. H. (1994). Salivary cortisol in psychoneuroendocrine research: Recent developments and applications. *Psychoneuroendocrinology, 19,* 313–333.

Komisaruk, B. R., & Whipple, B. (1989). Love as sensory stimulation: Physiological consequences of its deprivation and expression. *Psychoneuroendocrinology, 23,* 927–944.

Krieger, D. (1973, August). *The relationship of touch with intent to help or heal to subjects' in-vivo hemoglobin values: A study in personalized interaction.* Paper presented to American Nurses' Association Ninth Nursing Research Conference, San Antonio, TX.

Kurup, R. K., & Kurup, P. A. (2003). Hypothalamic digoxin, hemispheric dominance, and neurobiology of love and affection. *International Journal of Neuroscience, 113*, 721–729.

Lamb, M. E., Pleck, J., Charnov, E., & Levine, J. (1987). A biosocial perspective on paternal behavior and involvement. In J. Lancaster, J. Altmann, A. Rossi, & L. Sherrod (Eds.), *Parenting across the lifespan: Biosocial dimensions* (pp. 111–142). New York: Aldine de Gruyter.

Larsson, K., & Ahlenius, S. (1986). Masculine sexual behavior and brain monoamines. In M. Segal (Ed.), *Psychopharmacology of sexual disorders* (pp. 15–32). London: Libbey.

Lawson, A. (1988). *Adultery: An analysis of love and betrayal.* New York: Basic Books.

Lim, T. S., & Bowers, J. W. (1991). Facework: Solidarity, approbation, and tact. *Human Communication Research, 17*, 415–449.

Luecken, L. J., & Lemery, K. (2004). Early caregiving and adult physiological stress responses. *Clinical Psychology Review, 24*, 171–191.

Luginbuhl, J. E. R., Crowe, D. H., & Kaplan, J. P. (1975). Causal attributions for success and failure. *Journal of Personality and Social Psychology, 31*, 86–93.

MacDonald, K. (1992). Warmth as a developmental construct: An evolutionary analysis. *Child Development, 63*, 753–773.

Mackinnon, A., Henderson, A. S., & Andrews, G. (1993). Parental "affectionless control" as an antecedent to adult depression: A risk factor refined. *Psychological Medicine, 23*, 135–141.

Manusov, V. (1990). An application of attribution principles to nonverbal behavior in romantic dyads. *Communication Monographs, 57*, 104–118.

Manusov, V., Floyd, K., & Kerssen-Griep, J. (1997). Yours, mine, and ours: Mutual attributions for nonverbal behaviors in couples' interactions. *Communication Research, 24*, 234–260.

Marieb, E. N. (2003). *Essentials of human anatomy and physiology* (7th ed.). San Francisco: Benjamin Cummings.

Maslow, A. H. (1970). *Motivation and personality* (2nd ed.). New York: Harper & Row.

McCabe, M. P. (1987). Desired and experienced levels of premarital affection and sexual intercourse during dating. *Journal of Sex Research, 23*, 23–33.

McCarthy, M. M., & Becker, J. B. (2002). Neuroendocrinology of sexual behavior in the female. In J. B. Becker, S. M. Breedlove, D. Crews, & M. M. McCarthy (Eds.), *Behavioral endocrinology* (2nd ed.) (pp. 117–151). Cambridge, MA: MIT Press.

McCroskey, J. C., & McCain, T. A. (1974). The measurement of interpersonal attraction. *Speech Monographs, 41*, 261–266.

McCroskey, J. C., & Young, T. J. (1981). Ethos and credibility: The construct and its measurement after three decades. *Central States Speech Journal, 32*, 24–34.

McDaniel, E., & Andersen, P. A. (1998). International patterns of interpersonal tactile communication: A field study. *Journal of Nonverbal Behavior, 22*, 59–73.

McEwan, B. (1999). Stress and the brain. In R. Conlan (Ed.), *States of mind: New discoveries about how our brains make us who we are* (PP. 81–102). New York: Wiley.

Mealy, L., Bridgestock, R., & Townsend, G. (1999). Symmetry and perceived facial attractiveness: A monozygotic twin comparison. *Journal of Personality and Social Psychology, 76*, 151–158.

Metts, S., & Planalp, S. (2002). Emotional communication. In M. L. Knapp & J. A. Daly (Eds.), *Handbook of interpersonal communication* (3rd ed.) (pp. 339–373). Thousand Oaks, CA: Sage.

Miczo, N., Allspach, L. E., & Burgoon, J. K. (1999). Converging on the phenomenon of interpersonal adaptation: Interaction adaptation theory. In L. K. Guerrero, J. A. DeVito, & M. L. Hecht (Eds.), *The nonverbal communication reader: Classic and contemporary readings* (2nd ed.) (pp. 462–471). Prospect Heights, IL: Waveland Press.

Miller, W. B., Pasta, D. J., MacMurray, J., Chiu, C., Wu, S., & Comings, D. E. (1999). Genetic influences in childbearing motivation: A theoretical framework and some empirical evidence. In L. J. Severy & W. B. Miller (Eds.), *Advances in population: Psychosocial perspectives* (Vol. 3, pp. 53–102). London: Jessica Kingsley.

Miller, W. B., Pasta, D. J., MacMurray, J., Muhleman, D., & Comings, D. E. (2000). Genetic influences on childbearing motivation: Further testing a theoretical framework. In J. L. Rodgers, D. C. Rowe, & W. B. Miller (Eds.), *Genetic influences on human fertility and sexuality: Theoretical and empirical contributions from the biological and behavioral sciences* (pp. 33–66). Boston: Kluwer Academic Publishers.

Miller, W. B., & Rodgers, J. L. (2001). *The ontogeny of human bonding systems: Evolutionary origins, neural bases, and psychological manifestations.* Boston: Kluwer Academic Publishers.

Montagu, A. (1978). *Touching: The human significance of the skin* (2nd ed.). New York: Harper & Row.

Montepare, J. M. (2004). Exploring interpersonal sensitivity: What, who, why, and to what end? *Journal of Nonverbal Behavior, 28,* 143–144.

Morman, M. T., & Floyd, K. (1998). "I love you, man": Overt expressions of affection in male-male interaction. *Sex Roles, 38,* 871–881.

Morman, M. T., & Floyd, K. (1999). Affectionate communication between fathers and young adult sons: Individual- and relational-level correlates. *Communication Studies, 50,* 294–309.

Morman, M. T., & Floyd, K. (2002). A "changing culture of fatherhood": Effects on affectionate communication, closeness, and satisfaction in men's relationships with their fathers and their sons. *Western Journal of Communication, 66,* 395–411.

Morris, R. (2001). *The evolutionists: The struggle for Darwin's soul.* New York: W. H. Freeman.

Murphy, M. R., Checkley, S. A., Seckl, J. R., & Lightman, S. L. (1990). Naloxone inhibits oxytocin release at orgasm in man. *Journal of Clinical Endocrinology and Metabolism, 65,* 1056–1063.

Murphy, M. R., Seckl, J. R., Burton, S., Checkley, S. A., & Lightman, S. L. (1990). Changes in oxytocin and vasopressin secretion during sexual activity in men. *Journal of Clinical Endocrinology and Metabolism, 65,* 738–741.

Murray, H. A. (1943). *Thematic Apperception Test manual.* Cambridge, MA: Harvard University Press.

Nelson, E. E., & Panksepp, J. (1998). Brain substrates of infant-mother attachment: Contributions of opioids, oxytocin, and norepinephrine. *Neuroscience and Biobehavioral Reviews, 22,* 437–452.

Nelson, R. J. (2000). *An introduction to behavioral endocrinology* (2nd ed.). Sunderland, MA: Sinauer Associates.

Nemeroff, C. B. (2004). Neurobiological consequences of childhood trauma. *Journal of Clinical Psychiatry, 65,* 18–28.

Noller, P. (1978). Sex differences in the socialization of affectionate expression. *Developmental Psychology, 14,* 317–319.

Oliver, J. M., Raftery, M., Reeb, A., & Delaney, P. (1993). Perceptions of parent-offspring relationships as functions of depression in offspring: "Affectionless control," "negative bias," and "depressive realism." *Journal of Social Behavior and Personality, 8,* 405–424.

Olson, M., & Sneed, N. (1995). Anxiety and therapeutic touch. *Issues in Mental Health Nursing, 16,* 97–108.

Oring, E. (1984). Dyadic traditions. *Journal of Folklore Research, 21,* 19–28.

O'Sullivan, L. F., Byers, E. S., & Finkelman, L. (1998). A comparison of male and female college students' experiences of sexual coercion. *Psychology of Women Quarterly, 22,* 177–195.

Owen, W. F. (1987). The verbal expression of love by women and men as a critical communication event in personal relationships. *Women's Studies in Communication, 10,* 15–24.

Palmer, M. T., & Simmons, K. B. (1995). Communicating intentions through nonverbal behaviors: Conscious and unconscious encoding of liking. *Human Communication Research, 22,* 128–160.

Panksepp, J. (1992). Oxytocin effects on emotional processes: Separation distress, social bonding, and relationships to psychiatric disorders. In C. A. Pedersen, J. D. Caldwell, G. F. Jirikowski, & T. R. Insel (Eds.), *Oxytocin in maternal, sexual, and social behaviors* (pp. 243–252). New York: New York Academy of Sciences.

Panksepp, J. (1998). *Affective neuroscience: The foundations of human and animal emotions.* New York: Oxford University Press.

Parks, M. R. (1995). Ideology in interpersonal communication: Beyond the couches, talkshows, and bunkers. In B. R. Burleson (Ed.), *Communication yearbook 18* (pp. 480–497). Newbury Park, CA: Sage.

Parks, M. R., & Floyd, K. (1996). Making friends in cyberspace. *Journal of Communication, 46,* 80–97.

Parrott, T. M., & Bengtson, V. L. (1999). The effects of earlier intergenerational affection, normative expectations, and family conflict on contemporary exchanges of help and support. *Research on Aging, 21,* 73–105.

Parsons, R. J., Cox, E. O., & Kimboko, P. J. (1989). Satisfaction, communication and affection in caregiving: A view from the elder's perspective. *Journal of Gerontological Social Work, 13,* 9–20.

Pedersen, C. A., Caldwell, J. D., Walker, C., Ayers, G., & Mason, G. A. (1994). Oxytocin activates the postpartum onset of rat maternal behavior in the ventral tegmental and medial preoptic areas. *Behavioral Neuroscience, 108,* 1163–1171.

Pennebaker, J. W. (1997). Writing about emotional experiences as a therapeutic process. *Psychological Science, 8,* 162–166.

Pfaff, D. W. (1999). *DRIVE: Neurobiological and molecular mechanisms of sexual motivation.* Cambridge, MA: MIT Press.

Pfaus, J. G., Damsma, G., Nomikos, G. G., Wenkstern, D. G., Blaha, C. D., Phillips, A. G., & Fibiger, H. C. (1990). Sexual behavior enhances central dopamine transmission in the male rate. *Brain Research, 530,* 345–348.

Ploog, D. (1986). Biological foundations of the vocal expressions of emotions. In R. Plutchik & H. Kellerman (Eds.), *Emotion: Theory, research, and experience* (Vol. 3, pp. 173–197). New York: Academic Press.

Porges, S. W. (1995). Orienting in a defensive world: Mammalian modification of our evolutionary heritage. A polyvagal theory. *Psychophysiology, 32*, 301–318.

Porges, S. W. (1996). Physiological regulations in high-risk infants: A model for assessment and potential intervention. *Development and Psychopathology, 8*, 43–58.

Porges, S. W. (1997). Emotion: An evolutionary by-product of the neural regulation of the autonomic nervous system. In C. S. Carter, I. I. Lederhendler, & B. Kirkpatrick (Eds.), *The integrative neurobiology of affiliation* (pp. 65–82). New York: Annals of the New York Academy of Sciences.

Porges, S. W. (1998). Love: An emergent property of the mammalian autonomic nervous system. *Psychoneuroendocrinology, 23*, 837–861.

Porterfield, S. P. (2001). *Endocrine physiology* (2nd ed.). St. Louis, MO: Mosby.

Prager, K. J., & Buhrmester, D. (1998). Intimacy and need fulfillment in couple relationships. *Journal of Social and Personal Relationships, 15*, 435–469.

Prescott, J. W. (1970). Early somatosensory deprivation as an ontogenetic process in the abnormal development of the brain and behavior. In I. E. Goldsmith & J. Morr-Jankowski (Eds.), *Medical primatology* (pp. 356–375). New York: S. Karger.

Prescott, J. W. (1971). Early somatosensory deprivation as an ontogenetic process in abnormal development of the brain and behavior. In I. E. Goldsmith & J. Morr-Jankowski (Eds.), *Medical primatology* (pp. 356–375). New York: S. Karger.

Prescott, J. W. (1973). Sexual behavior in the blind. *Medical Aspects of Human Sexuality, 7*, 59–60.

Prescott, J. W. (1975). Body pleasure and the origins of violence. *The Futurist*, April, 64–74.

Prescott, J. W. (1976a). Phylogenetic and ontogenetic aspects of human affectional development. In R. Gemme & C. C. Wheeler (Eds.), *Progress in sexology. Proceedings of the 1976 International Congress of Sexology* (pp. 431–457). New York: Plenum Press.

Prescott, J. W. (1976b). Somatosensory deprivation and its relationship to the blind. In Z. S. Jastrzembska (Ed.), *The effects of blindness and other impairments on early development* (pp. 65–121). New York: American Foundation for the Blind.

Prescott, J. W. (1979). Deprivation of physical affection as a primary process in the development of physical violence: A comparative and cross-cultural perspective. In D. G. Gil (Ed.), *Child abuse and violence* (pp. 66–137). New York: American Orthopsychiatric Association.

Prescott, J. W. (1980). Somatosensory affectional deprivation (SAD) theory of drug and alcohol use. In D. J. Lettieri, M. Sayers, &. H. W. Pearson (Eds.), *Theories on drug abuse: Selected contemporary perspectives* (pp. 286–302). Washington, DC: National Institute of Drug Abuse.

Prescott, J. W., & Wallace, D. (1978). Role of pain and pleasure in the development of destructive behaviors: A psychometric study of parenting, sexuality, substance abuse and criminality. In *Invited papers of the colloquium on the correlates of crime and the determinants of criminal behavior* (pp. 229–279). McLean, VA: Mitre Corporation.

Punyanunt-Carter, N. M. (2004). Reported affectionate communication and satisfaction in marital and dating relationships. *Psychological Reports, 95*, 1154–1160.

Quinn, W. H. (1983). Personal and family adjustment in later life. *Journal of Marriage and the Family, 45*, 57–73.

Rabinowitz, F. E. (1991). The male-to-male embrace: Breaking the touch taboo in a men's therapy group. *Journal of Counseling and Development, 69*, 574–576.

Rane, T. R., & Draper, T. W. (1995). Negative evaluations of men's nurturant touching of young children. *Psychological Reports, 76*, 811–818.

Ray, G. B., & Floyd, K. (2000, May). *Nonverbal expressions of liking and disliking in initial interaction: Encoding and decoding perspectives.* Paper presented to Eastern States Communication Association, Pittsburgh, PA.

Regan, P. C., Jerry, D., Narvaez, M., & Johnson, D. (1999). Public displays of affection among Asian and Latino heterosexual couples. *Psychological Reports, 84*, 1201–1202.

Reid, P. T., Tate, C. S., & Berman, P. W. (1989). Preschool children's self-presentation in situations with infants: Effects of sex and race. *Child Development, 60*, 710–714.

Reissman, C., Aron, A., & Bergen, M. R. (1993). Shared activities and marital satisfaction: Causal direction and self-expansion versus boredom. *Journal of Social and Personal Relationships, 10*, 243–254.

Richard, P., Moos, F., & Freund-Mercier, M. J. (1991). Central effects of oxytocin. *Physiological Review, 71*, 331–370.

Richmond, V. P., & McCroskey, J. C. (1990). Reliability and separation of factors on the assertiveness-responsiveness measure. *Psychological Reports, 67*, 449–450.

Rinck, C. M., Willis, F. N., & Dean, L. M. (1980). Interpersonal touch among residents of homes for the elderly. *Journal of Communication, 30*, 44–47.

Robbins, T. W., & Everitt, B. J. (1996). Neurobehavioral mechanisms of reward and motivation. *Current Opinion in Neurobiology, 6*, 228–268.

Roberts, R. E. L., & Bengtson, V. L. (1996). Affective ties to parents in early adulthood and self-esteem across 20 years. *Social Psychology Quarterly, 59*, 96–106.

Ross, L. (1977). The intuitive psychologist and his shortcomings: Distortions in the attribution process. In L. Berkowitz (Ed.), *Advances in experimental social psychology* (Vol. 10, pp. 173–220). New York: Academic Press.

Rotter, J. B., Chance, J. E., & Phares, E. J. (1972). *Applications of a social learning theory of personality.* New York: Holt, Rinehart & Winston.

Rubin, R. B., & Martin, M. M. (1998). Interpersonal communication motives. In J. C. McCroskey, J. A. Daly, M. M. Martin, & M. J. Beatty (Eds.), *Communication and personality: Trait perspectives* (pp. 287–307). Cresskill, NJ: Hampton Press.

Rubin, R. B., Perse, E. M., & Barbato, C. A. (1988). Conceptualization and measurement of interpersonal communication motives. *Human Communication Research, 14*, 602–628.

Russell, A. (1997). Individual and family factors contributing to mothers' and fathers' positive parenting. *International Journal of Behavioral Development, 21*, 111–132.

Salt, R. E. (1991). Affectionate touch between fathers and preadolescent sons. *Journal of Marriage and the Family, 53*, 545–554.

Samson, H. H., Hodge, C. W., Tolliver, G. A., & Haraguchi, M. (1993). Effect of dopamine agonists and antagonists on ethanol reinforced behavior: The involvement of the nucleus accumbens. *Brain Research Bulletin, 30*, 133–141.

Sanchez-Anguiano, A. (1999). Psychological effects of captivity among United States Navy aviators, Vietnam: A longitudinal study, 1974–1997. (Doctoral dissertation, University of South Florida, 1999). *Dissertation Abstracts International, 60* (3-B), 1046.

Sapolsky, R. M. (2002). Endocrinology of the stress-response. In J. B. Becker, S. M. Breedlove, D. Crews, & M. M. McCarthy (Eds.), *Behavioral endocrinology* (2nd ed., pp. 409–450). Cambridge, MA: MIT Press.

Schachner, L., Field, T., Hernandez-Reif, M., Duarte, A., & Krasnegor, J. (1998). Atopic dermatitis symptoms decrease in children following massage therapy. *Pediatric Dermatology, 15*, 390–395.

Schmidt, C., & SeiffgeKrenke, I. (1996). Perceptions of friendships and family relations in chronically ill and healthy adolescents: Quality of relationships and change over time. *Psychologie in Erziehung und Unterricht, 43*, 155–168.

Schopler, J., & Layton, B. (1972). Determinants of the self-attribution of having influenced another person. *Journal of Personality and Social Psychology, 22*, 326–332.

Schultz, N. C., & Schultz, C. L. (1987). Affection and intimacy as a special strength of couples in blended families. *Australian Journal of Sex, Marriage & Family, 8*, 66–72.

Schutz, W. (1958). *FIRO: A three-dimensional theory of interpersonal behavior.* New York: Rinehart.

Schutz, W. (1966). *The interpersonal underworld.* Palo Alto, CA: Science and Behavior Books.

Schuster, M. A., Beckett, M. K., Corona, R., & Zhou, A. J. (2005). Hugs and kisses: HIV-infected parents' fears about contagion and the effects on parent-child interaction in a nationally representative sample. *Archives of Pediatric and Adolescent Medicine, 159*, 173–179.

Schwartz, G. E., & Russek, L. G. (1998). Family love and lifelong health? A challenge for clinical psychology. In D. K. Routh & R. J. DeRubeis (Eds.), *The science of clinical psychology: Accomplishments and future directions* (pp. 121–146). Washington, DC: American Psychological Association.

Shaver, P., Hazan, C., & Bradshaw, D. (1988). Love as attachment: The integration of three behavioral systems. In R. J. Sternberg & M. L. Barnes (Eds.), *The psychology of love* (pp. 68–99). New Haven, CT: Yale University Press.

Shuntich, R. J., Loh, D., & Katz, D. (1998). Some relationships among affection, aggression, and alcohol abuse in the family setting. *Perceptual and Motor Skills, 86*, 1051–1060.

Shuntich, R. J., & Shapiro, R. M. (1991). Explorations of verbal affection and aggression. *Journal of Social Behavior and Personality, 6*, 283–300.

Shute, B., & Wheldall, K. (1989). Pitch alterations in British motherese: Some preliminary acoustic data. *Journal of Child Language, 16*, 503–512.

Singh, D. (1993). Adaptive significance of waist-to-hip ratio and female physical attractiveness. *Journal of Personality and Social Psychology, 65*, 293–307.

Smith, D. E., Willis, F. N., & Gier, J. A. (1980). Success and interpersonal touch in a competitive setting. *Journal of Nonverbal Behavior, 5*, 26–34.

Snyder, M., & Gangestad, S. (1986). On the nature of self-monitoring: Matters of assessment, matters of validity. *Journal of Personality and Social Psychology, 51*, 125–139.

Sodersten, P., Henning, M., Melin, P., & Ludin, S. (1983). Vasopressin alters female sexual behaviour by acting on the brain independently of alterations in blood pressure. *Nature, 301*, 608–610.

Soler, C., Núñez, M., Gutiérrez, R., Núñez, J., Medina, P., Sancho, M., Álvarez, J., & Núñez, A. (2003). Facial attractiveness in men provides clues to semen quality. *Evolution and Human Behavior, 24*, 199–207.

Spanier, G. (1976). Measuring dyadic adjustment: New scales for measuring the quality of marriage and similar dyads. *Journal of Marriage and the Family, 38*, 15–28.

Spence, J. E., & Olson, M. (1997). Quantitative research on therapeutic touch: An integrative review of the literature 1985–1995. *Scandinavian Journal of Caring Sciences, 11*, 183–190.

Steward, A. L., & Lupfer, M. (1987). Touching as healing: The effect of touch on students' perceptions and performance. *Journal of Applied Social Psychology, 17*, 800–809.

Storey, A. E., Walsh, C. J., Quinton, R. L., & Wynne-Edwards, K. E. (2000). Hormonal correlates of paternal responsiveness in new and expectant fathers. *Evolution and Human Behavior, 21*, 79–95.

Swain, S. (1989). Covert intimacy: Closeness in men's friendships. In B. Risman & P. Schwartz (Eds.), *Gender in intimate relationships: A microstructural approach* (pp. 71–86). Belmont, CA: Wadsworth.

Taylor, G. J., & Bagby, R. M. (2000). An overview of the alexithymia construct. In R. Bar-On & J. D. A. Parker (Eds.), *The handbook of emotional intelligence* (pp. 41–67). San Francisco: Jossey-Bass.

Taylor, S. E. (2002). *The tending instinct: How nurturing is essential to who we are and how we live.* New York: Times Books.

Taylor, S. E., Klein, L. C., Lewis, B. P., Gruenewald, T. L., Guring, R. A. R., & Updegraff, J. A. (2000). Biobehavioral responses to stress in females: Tend-and-befriend, not fight-or-flight. *Psychological Review, 107*, 411–429.

Thibaut, J., & Kelley, H. (1959). *The social psychology of groups.* New York: Wiley.

Thornhill, R., & Gangestad, S. W. (1994). Human fluctuating asymmetry and sexual behavior. *Psychological Science, 5*, 297–302.

Thornhill, R., Gangestad, S. W., & Comer, R. (1995). Human female orgasm and mate fluctuating asymmetry. *Animal Behavior, 50*, 1601–1615.

Toda, S., Fogel, A., & Kawai, M. (1990). Maternal speech to three-month-old infants in the United States and Japan. *Journal of Child Language, 17*, 279–294.

Tolstedt, B. E., & Stokes, J. P. (1983). Relation of verbal, affective, and physical intimacy to marital satisfaction. *Journal of Counseling Psychology, 30*, 573–580.

Tooby, J., & Cosmides, L. (1992). Psychological foundations of culture. In J. Barkow, L. Cosmides, & J. Tooby (Eds.), *The adapted mind* (pp. 19–36). New York: Oxford University Press.

Trivers, R. L. (1971). The evolution of reciprocal altruism. *Quarterly Review of Biology, 46*, 35–57.

Trivers, R. L. (1972). Parental investment and sexual selection. In B. Campbell (Ed.), *Sexual selection and the descent of man 1871–1971* (pp. 136–179). Chicago: Aldine.

Turner, R. A., Altemus, M., Enos, T., Cooper, B., & McGuinness, T. (1999). Preliminary research on plasma oxytocin in normal cycling women: Investigating emotion and interpersonal distress. *Psychiatry, 62*, 97–113.

Twardosz, S., Botkin, D., Cunningham, J. K., Weddle, K., Sollie, D., & Schreve, C. (1987). Expression of affection in day care. *Child Study Journal, 17*, 133–151.

Twardosz, S., Schwartz, S., Fox, J., & Cunningham, J. L. (1979). Development and evaluation of a system to measure affectionate behavior. *Behavioral Assessment, 1*, 177–190.

Uvnäs-Moberg, K. (1998). Oxytocin may mediate the benefits of positive social interaction and emotions. *Psychoneuroendocrinology, 23*, 819–835.

Uvnäs-Moberg, K. (2003). *The oxytocin factor: Tapping the hormone of calm, love, and healing*. Cambridge, MA: Perseus.

Waite, L. J. (1995). Does marriage matter? *Demography, 32*, 483–507.

Wallace, A. R. (1858). On the tendency of varieties to depart indefinitely from the original type. *Journal of the Proceedings of the Linnean Society (Zoology), 3*, 53–62.

Wallace, D. H. (1981). Affectional climate in the family of origin and the experience of subsequent sexual-affectional behaviors. *Journal of Sex and Marital Therapy, 7*, 296–306.

Waring, E. M., McElrath, D., Lefcoe, D., & Weisz, G. (1981). Dimensions of intimacy in marriage. *Psychiatry, 44*, 169–175.

Watzlawick, P., Beavin, J. H., & Jackson, D. D. (1967). *Pragmatics of human communication: A study of interactional patterns, pathologies, and paradoxes*. New York: Norton.

Weiner, B. (1985). "Spontaneous" causal thinking. *Psychological Bulletin, 97*, 74–84.

Werker, J. F., & McLeod, P. J. (1989). Infant preference for both male and female infant-directed talk: A developmental study of attentional and affective responses. *Canadian Journal of Psychology, 43*, 230–246.

Westermarck, E. A. (1921). *The history of human marriage* (5th ed.). London: Macmillan.

Whitcher, S., & Fisher, J. D. (1979). Multidimensional reaction to therapeutic touch in a hospital setting. *Journal of Personality and Social Psychology, 37*, 87–96.

Wilkinson, C. A. (2000). Expressing affection: A vocabulary of loving messages. In K. M. Galvin & P. J. Cooper (Eds.), *Making connections: Readings in relational communication* (2nd ed.) (pp. 160–167). Los Angeles: Roxbury.

Williams, S. J., & Willis, F. N. (1978). Interpersonal touch among preschool children at play. *The Psychological Record, 28*, 501–508.

Willis, F. N., & Hoffman, G. E. (1975). Development of tactile patterns in relation to age, sex, and race. *Developmental Psychology, 11*, 866.

Willis, F. N., & Reeves, D. L. (1976). Touch interactions in junior high students in relation to sex and race. *Developmental Psychology, 12*, 91–92.

Willis, F. N., Reeves, D. L., & Buchanan, D. R. (1976). Interpersonal touch in high school relative to sex and race. *Perceptual and Motor Skills, 43*, 843–847.

Willis, F. N., Rinck, C. M., & Dean, L. M. (1978). Interpersonal touch among adults in cafeteria lines. *Perceptual and Motor Skills, 47*, 1147–1152.

Winslow, J. T., Hastings, N., Carter, C. S., Harbaugh, C. R., & Insel, T. R. (1993). A role for central vasopressin in pair bonding in monogamous prairie voles. *Nature, 365*, 545–548.

Winslow, J. T., & Insel, T. R. (1991). Social status in pairs of male squirrel monkeys determines response to central oxytocin administration. *Journal of Neuroscience, 11*, 2032–2038.

Wise, R. A. (1989). Brain dopamine and reward. *American Review of Psychology, 40*, 191–225.

Wise, R. A. (1996). Neurobiology of addiction. *Current Opinion in Neurobiology, 6*, 243–251.

Witt, D. M., Carter, C. S., & Walton, D. (1990). Central and peripheral effects of oxytocin administration in prairie voles (*Microtus ochrogaster*). *Pharmacological and Biochemical Behavior, 37*, 63–69.

Witt, D. M., & Insel, T. R. (1991). A selective oxytocin antagonist attenuates progesterone facilitation of female sexual behavior. *Endocrinology, 128*, 3269–3276.

Witt, D. M., Winslow, J. T., & Insel, T. R. (1992). Enhanced social interactions in rates following chronic, centrally infused oxytocin. *Pharmacological and Biochemical Behavior, 43*, 855–861.

Wood, J. T., & Inman, C. C. (1993). In a different mode: Masculine styles of communicating closeness. *Journal of Applied Communication Research, 21*, 279–295.

Workman, L., & Reader, W. (2004). *Evolutionary psychology: An introduction.* Cambridge: Cambridge University Press.

Zebrowitz, L. A., Brownlow, S., & Olson, K. (1992). Baby talk to the babyfaced. *Journal of Nonverbal Behavior, 16*, 143–158.

Zinger, I. (1999). The psychological effects of 60 days in administrative segregation. (Doctoral dissertation, Carleton University, 1999). *Dissertation Abstracts International, 60* (6-B), 2932.

Index

9 780521 731744